The Road to
Marston Moor

The Road to Marston Moor

David Cooke

Pen & Sword
MILITARY

First published in Great Britain in 2007 by
Pen & Sword Military
an imprint of
Pen & Sword Books Ltd
47 Church Street
Barnsley
South Yorkshire
S70 2AS

ISBN 978–1–84415–638–2

A CIP catalogue record for this book is
available from the British Library.

Typeset in 11/13 Ehrhardt by Concept, Huddersfield, West Yorkshire
Printed and bound in England by CPI UK

Pen & Sword Books Ltd incorporates the imprints of Pen & Sword Aviation,
Pen & Sword Maritime, Pen & Sword Military, Wharncliffe Local History,
Pen & Sword Select, Pen & Sword Military Classics and Leo Cooper.

For a complete list of Pen & Sword titles please contact
Pen & Sword Books Limited
47 Church Street, Barnsley, South Yorkshire, S70 2AS, England
E-mail: enquiries@pen-and-sword.co.uk
Website: www.pen-and-sword.co.uk

Contents

List of Maps

(all map scales are in miles)

List of Plates

(between pages 120–121; all plates from the author's collection)

Chapter 1

The Road to War

We have no other intention but by our government to honour Him by Whom Kings reign and to procure the good of our people, and for this end to preserve the right and authority wherewith God hath vested us.
Charles I

Just after midnight on 20 January 1644 Colonel Sir Francis Anderson received a message from his scouts patrolling the border at Berwick: the Scots had crossed the border in force. The day before, he had been informed by other scouting parties that a body of Scots had crossed the Tweed at Coldstream and were now encamped in the villages surrounding Wark. The long awaited Scots invasion of Northumberland and the North of England was well and truly under way.

How had this come to pass? Why was a foreign army invading England in support of English rebels who had rebelled against their anointed King? At this period Scotland was a sovereign nation with its own Church and Parliament but ruled by the same monarch, Charles I. This being the case, the Scots were not only supporting a rebellion against the King of England but also rebelling against their own King. This was not the first time that the Scots had risen against King Charles. In both 1639 and 1640 English and Scots armies had manoeuvred along the Tweed in what has become known as the First and Second Bishops' Wars. Why the Bishops' Wars? Simple, the Scots did not wish to have bishops and the Book of Common Prayer foisted on to them by the Church of England and a King who, although born in Scotland, had visited their country rarely.

To find the root of the rebellion by both the King's English and Scottish subjects one must go back a number of years. It is beyond the scope of this work to cover the causes of the Civil Wars in any depth but a brief explanation is necessary.

When Charles came to the throne in 1625 he strongly believed in the divine right of Kings to rule their subjects as they saw fit, as had his predecessors. Parliament was a tool through which this could be achieved. Nowadays, when

Parliament rules the country and is a permanent establishment, it seems strange that the King could call Parliament and then dismiss it as and when he liked. Unfortunately Charles's Parliaments did not agree with this. As a result Charles dismissed them in 1629 and carried on a personal rule for eleven years.

One of the main functions of Parliament had been to vote funds for the King's use in governing the country. Without Parliament Charles had to find other ways to raise revenue. He began to sell titles and monopolies, raise his own taxes and expand existing ones. Inland counties became subject to Ship Money, a tax usually levied in coastal areas to cover the costs of their defence from seaborne attack, which caused much discontent. The King went on to exacerbate the problem when he introduced the Book of Common Prayer first in England and then in Scotland. In England a number of extreme Protestant sects, usually referred to as Puritans, viewed the Church of England as one step removed from Roman Catholicism and the introduction of the new prayer book seems to have reinforced this opinion.

If the King had managed to antagonise many of his English subjects he had made the situation in Scotland much worse. The Scots, staunchly Presbyterian in the main, refused to accept the new prayer book. Matters moved rapidly. The King began to raise forces in the North of England and the Scots, having signed the Solemn League and Covenant, also began to raise an army. Both armies closed along the Tweed. In June 1639 the King decided that he was not ready to fight the Scots and signed an agreement with them. Charles was to show his true colours. While his commissioners were in deep discussion with the Scots he began preparations for a war against them in 1640. With the cost of this war in mind he called Parliament.

On Monday 25 April the first Parliament for eleven years was opened. It proved to be as unruly as his earlier Parliaments and lasted for only three weeks and is, not surprisingly, referred to as the Short Parliament. During this period the first shots of the Second Bishops' War were fired. From the English point of view this war was a disaster. Having failed to agree terms the Scots Army crossed the Tweed and advanced on Newcastle. On 28 August the English Army was defeated at Newburn (Clarendon called it 'that infamous, irreparable rout'). On the 29th the remnants of the English Army abandoned Newcastle and on the 30th the Earl of Leven led his army into the city. For all intents and purposes the Second Bishops' War was over.

The Scots continued to occupy Newcastle until an agreement had been reached, not with the King but with Parliament, at a cost of £850 a day in reparations. On 3 November 1640 the King called the final Parliament of his reign. The Long Parliament, as it has become known, would lead to his downfall. The Scots withdrew their army but retained possession of Berwick.

With the Scots withdrawal the King might have thought things would settle down – he would have been wrong. Parliament continued to oppose the King during 1641. The hated Star Chamber was abolished and the King's staunchest supporter, the Earl of Strafford, was indicted and condemned by the House of Commons. In November 1641 the Grand Remonstrance was passed by eleven votes in the House of Commons and as the year closed Parliament had the upper hand. On 4 January 1642 the King decided that his situation needed a drastic solution. Marching into the House of Commons, backed by a file of musketeers, the King attempted to arrest five of its members and Lord Mandeville, later the Earl of Manchester. The five members, John Pym, John Hampden, Arthur Haselrig, Denzil Holles and William Strode, and Lord Mandeville were not to be found. In the King's own words: 'I see all the birds are flown.'

With the failed attempt to arrest the members of the two Houses the situation deteriorated and the King left his capital and set up his court at York. He would not enter London for seven years and then as a prisoner on trial for his life. Both sides began preparations for a war that must come. In an attempt to stabilise his position in the north and obtain a major port and armoury through which arms and ammunition could be imported the King attempted to seize Hull.

Arriving before its gates on 23 April the King was denied entrance by Sir John Hotham, Parliament's governor. This was the first overtly hostile act by Parliament against the King. In the weeks that followed, forces began to be raised throughout the country and both sides jockeyed for position with skirmishes taking place in several regions. Both sides professed a desire for a peaceful settlement while preparing for war. Parliament raised an army to fight against the Irish rebels but very few of the troops saw action in Ireland. They formed the core of the Earl of Essex's army.

To counteract this growing Parliamentarian army the King issued Commissions of Array to his supporters but the response was disappointing. Charles decided on decisive action. Still not understanding the depth of feeling against him, and particularly against his supporters, he decided to declare war on his rebel Parliament. Once he had done this he believed that supporters would flock to their anointed King. On 22 August 1642 he raised his standard at Nottingham but few volunteers came forward. Fortunately, his army grew considerably with the accession of a large number of Welsh recruits when he arrived at Shrewsbury. By the beginning of October both the King and Parliament were ready for the one battle that both believed would decide all. How wrong they were to be proved.

The First Campaign

Both armies continued to recruit and organise. In September Parliament's main army, commanded by the Earl of Essex, advanced on Worcester. It was here that the first clash between Essex's and the King's armies took place. On 23 September a small force of Royalist cavalry was surprised by Essex's advance guard at Powick Bridge. Prince Rupert, the Royalist commander, immediately mounted his men and led them in a furious charge that totally routed the Parliamentarian troopers. It was the start of Prince Rupert's legend of invincibility, which he would reinforce over the coming months.

In mid-October the two armies began to move. The King intended to march on London and put his unruly Parliament in its place. On the other hand, Essex intended to do no more than prevent him from reaching the capital. Both armies were untested, with only a few officers experienced in European warfare. Scouting was rudimentary and both armies groped their way through the Midlands until the evening of 22 October. Royalist troopers, looking for quarters near the village of Edgehill, captured several Parliamentarian quartermasters, who informed them that Essex's army lay only a short distance away at Kineton. Essex must have had an even greater surprise when he realised the King's army lay between him and London. This was the first of several occasions when Essex allowed the King to come between him and his base. The morning of the 23rd was spent in gathering the King's army on Edgehill. Below them, at Kineton, the Parliamentarian Army began to form its line of battle. When Essex refused to attack with his army up the steep western slope of Edgehill the King moved his army into the valley. Late in the afternoon the Royalists began to advance. The first major battle of the Civil Wars had begun.

Both sides formed with infantry in the centre and cavalry on both flanks. As the battle opened, both flanks of the Royalist horse charged fiercely and swept away their opponents in short order. Unfortunately for the King his second line cavalry regiments had joined in a general pursuit of the Parliamentarian horse, and of several regiments of Essex's foot, which had joined in the rout. While the Royalist horse chased their opponents from the field the two bodies of foot came to grips. Unbeknown to the King, Essex had held two regiments of horse, Balfour's and Stapleton's, in reserve and at an opportune moment these joined in the infantry fight and their intervention was almost decisive. The Royalist foot was forced back and the King's Standard was captured, although it was later retrieved. It was only the return of some of Rupert's troopers and the fall of night that saved the King's infantry from defeat. Both armies claimed the victory. Essex claimed it because he had held the field, the King's army having withdrawn up Edgehill for the night. Strategically, the King's army had a greater advantage: Charles was still between the Earl of

Essex and London, and when the latter withdrew to Warwick this advantage was increased. Not for the last time would the King squander such an advantage.

Advancing slowly south the King received the surrender of Banbury on the 29th, then continued south through Oxford and Reading and arrived at Brentford on 12 November. The Royalist commanders must have been surprised to find two of Essex's regiments, Brookes and Holles, defending the town. The King ordered Rupert to storm the defences and this he duly did, capturing both regiments. The King then continued his advance on London. On the 13th the King arrived at Turnham Green to find a mass of Parliamentarian troops awaiting him. The remainder of Essex's army and the London Trained Bands had adopted a defensive position among the hedges and closes. The Royalists' slow march south had allowed Essex to march on a more easterly route and arrive at London before them. Greatly outnumbered by an enemy in a strong defensive position, the King decided against an attack. Over the next few days he withdrew first to Reading and then to Oxford, which became his capital and main base for the remainder of the First Civil War. With the King's withdrawal both armies went into winter quarters and began to garrison towns, castles and houses. As things quieted in the centre the northern and western flanks came to life.

The Three-Pronged Attack
During 1643 there developed a three-pronged Royalist attack on London. The first prong was Hopton's Western Army, which advanced from the West Country and through the Southern Counties. It would be opposed by Sir William Waller's army. The second prong was the King's Oxford Army, which, as its name suggests, was based on Oxford. It vied with the Earl of Essex's army for control of the Thames Valley and the Western Midlands. In the north the Earl of Newcastle's army faced that of Lord Fairfax and fought for control of Yorkshire. By the end of the year all three armies had been successful and had brought pressure to bear on London. There is no indication that this three-pronged assault was a deliberate plan but it seems to have come about almost accidentally. It was the high point of the Royalist cause.

The South West
In Cornwall Sir Ralph Hopton, supported by the local gentry, had raised an army. While Cornwall seems to have been staunchly Royalist, Devon, in the main, supported Parliament. Hopton first had to fend off a Parliamentarian offensive into Cornwall during the early part of 1643. On 19 January Hopton's army engaged a Parliamentarian force commanded by Colonel Ruthven, a

Scots officer, at Braddock Down. Although outnumbered Hopton went on the offensive. Two hidden guns opened fire on the Parliamentarian foot, disordering them. Then Sir Bevil Grenville, commander of the Cornish foot, led them into the attack. The redoubtable Cornish pikemen drove back Ruthven's centre and when Hopton launched his horse the rout was complete.

In due course Sir Ralph received orders to move his army out of Cornwall and to join the King's army in Somerset. The Earl of Stamford attempted to stop Hopton carrying out this order by crossing the Tamar and advancing to Stratton. Stamford's army defended a hill to the west of Stratton village. On 16 May Hopton attacked Stamford's position. Although outnumbered he divided his army into four bodies, which attacked the hill from four different directions. Once again Grenville's Cornish pikemen won the day. Stamford was captured and his army shattered.

With his victory at Stratton, the way was open for Hopton to advance into Somerset. There he was joined by a force of Royalist horse under the command of Prince Rupert's younger brother, Maurice. The combined army captured Taunton and Bridgewater and in early July advanced towards Bath. There another army waited to oppose them. It was commanded by Sir William Waller, a close friend of Hopton. This illustrates a poignant aspect of any civil war: friends torn apart and fighting one another on a point of principle. Both men seemed to have had similar political views but Sir Ralph Hopton could not bring himself to fight against his King. On the other hand, Sir William could not bring himself not to. Their two armies met at Lansdown Hill on 5 July. Sir William held a strong position on the top of Lansdown Hill. Sir Bevil Grenville once again led his Cornish pikemen in a column up the road towards the top of the hill. To their flanks bodies of musketeers skirmished with Waller's men who were lining the hedges. The Royalist attack stalled against determined opposition. Sir Bevil, leading by example, drove his men on again and gained the summit of the hill. Much beloved by his men, Sir Bevil was killed during this final attack.

Although they had gained another victory the Royalist situation deteriorated after the battle when Sir Ralph was badly injured by a powder wagon exploding close to him. After this his army withdrew into Devizes. Even though it had been defeated, Waller's army was in a better condition than Hopton's and followed it to Devizes, where it besieged the Royalists from a commanding position on Roundway Down. The Royalist forces were short of powder and had resorted to using bed cords as match for their muskets. In the nick of time a force of cavalry, under the command of Henry Wilmot, detached from the Oxford Army, arrived to save them. Arriving by forced marches Wilmot's men surprised Waller on 13 July. The Parliamentarian force had little time to form up before the Royalist horse attacked. Waller's cavalry, including Haselrig's fully armoured 'Lobsters', were quickly beaten. Dozens of routing troopers were killed as they galloped over the 'Bloody Ditch', a precipitous slope at the western end of Roundway Down. Hopton's infantry had formed up, marched onto the Down, and saw off the remainder of Waller's army.

Over the next few months Hopton's army advanced through Wiltshire (aiding Rupert at the storming of Bristol) into Hampshire, and by the end of the year was in winter quarters around Winchester. Arundel Castle was held for the King and a small garrison held Alton, although this was retaken by Waller on 13 December after a sharp fight around the town church, which still bears the scars. The first prong of the triple assault was thus poised to continue its advance upon the capital in the New Year.

The Midlands

The King's Oxford Army spent much of 1643 consolidating its position in the Midlands. A number of Parliamentarian garrisons were taken by Prince Rupert. On 2 February Cirencester fell and then Rupert marched north to take Lichfield on 20 April. In June Rupert led a raid into the Thames Valley and routed a Parliamentarian force at Chalgrove Field on the 18th. One of the results of this small action was the death of John Hampden, one of the five members King Charles had attempted to arrest in January 1642.

On 23 July Rupert's army combined with Hopton's Western Army near Bristol and the combined force then laid siege to the town. Prince Rupert does not seem to have liked lengthy sieges and often stormed fortified towns. Bristol was summoned on the 24th and its governor, Nathaniel Fiennes, refused to surrender. For the next two days the Royalist cannon bombarded the town. Before dawn on the 26th Rupert ordered his troops to storm the defences. The garrison put up a determined defence and caused grievous casualties on the Royalist troops, but Bristol's defences had a 5-mile circumference and eventually a weak point was found. Colonel Washington's men opened a gap in the defences, which allowed Rupert's troopers to enter the outer town. The inner town had another shorter line of works. The defenders, driven from their outer defences, manned this inner line. Beyond these works lay the castle, a strong final defensive position. Although Bristol's defences were still formidable Rupert had his blood up. Sending for reinforcements from Hopton's army he prepared to continue the assault. Fortunately for Rupert's men, Fiennes' position was untenable. His men were short of powder and the inhabitants of Bristol beseeched him to surrender before Rupert's men stormed and sacked the town. Rupert agreed to the garrison's surrender. Bristol was a great boon to the King's cause: not only was it a major port but it was also an arms-manufacturing centre, something the King lacked. But as great a victory as the storming of Bristol was, it had been paid for with the blood of many of Rupert's and Hopton's men.

With the taking of Bristol, the King's position in the Midlands was much more stable than it had been at the beginning of the year. Only Gloucester remained in Parliament's hands and this became the King's next objective. Leaving a strong garrison in Oxford, the King's army marched to Gloucester, arriving there on 10 August to begin laying their siege lines. Prince Rupert wanted to storm the town but the King wished to avoid a similar effusion of blood as had taken place at Bristol. By the end of the month the town's defenders, commanded by Colonel Massey, were in dire straits. They could not hold out for much longer but help was on the way. On 22 August, the anniversary of the raising of the King's Standard, the Earl of Essex led his army from Hounslow Heath on its long march to Gloucester. His men carried twelve days' rations with them. On 5 September Essex's army arrived on the downs above the town where his cannon fired a salute, which was answered by the defenders. Essex expected to have to fight his way into the town but when his army advanced early on the 6th they found that the Royalist siege lines were empty. Not wishing to be trapped between Essex's relieving force and a sally from the garrison the King had withdrawn his army. Gloucester had been relieved.

Having achieved his objective Essex now had to march his army back to London. Moving to Tewkesbury he began his return journey on 15 September. The King's army marched on a parallel route across the Cotswolds, with Rupert's cavalry snapping at the heels of Essex's army and attempting to slow its progress. Finding little success with this tactic Rupert engaged Essex's vanguard of horse on Aldbourne Chase on the 18th. Having been badly mauled the Parliamentarian horse fell back on their foot. Unsupported, Rupert made little progress and the battle ended in a draw but he had succeeded in his main objective: he had allowed the King to overtake Essex. On the following day Essex crossed his army to the south bank of the Kennet and headed for Newbury. His men were short of supplies. The inhabitants of Newbury were staunch supporters of Parliament and Essex expected to be able to resupply his troops and quarter them in the town. His surprise must have been great when, arriving before the town, he discovered the King's army waiting for him.

The First Battle of Newbury is one of the most confusing actions of the Civil Wars. Fought among enclosures, open hills and narrow lanes to the west of Newbury it ended in a tactical draw. In hard fighting neither side gained much ground on their opponents. By the close of 20 September Essex's army had been brought to a halt. Short of supplies, and with an enemy force between him and his main base, Essex had no choice but to continue the fight on the morrow. If he failed to break through the Royalist lines his options would be extremely limited. The King had an excellent opportunity to destroy Parliament's main army and end the war. Unfortunately, the Royalists had problems of their own: they were virtually out of gunpowder. In a council of war Rupert wanted to await the arrival of a powder convoy from Bristol, which was expected any day. The more cautious members of the King's council demanded a withdrawal and the King agreed to this. Essex was able to resupply his army at Newbury and then march on to London, while the King's army returned to Oxford.

With the end of the Newbury campaign the fighting between the King and Essex quietened. Both armies occupied their quarters and awaited the New Year. No decisive action had taken place but the King's position was much stronger. With the exception of Gloucester, the towns of the Severn Valley were garrisoned by his forces. With his rear protected he could concentrate on the destruction of Essex's army in the new campaigning season.

The North
In the north, particularly in Yorkshire, Royalist fortunes had soared during the summer of 1643. The previous year had ended with a series of small actions for possession of key towns, namely Bradford, Leeds and Tadcaster. This fight for the West Riding would set the tone of the campaign for the first half of the New Year. On 22 February the Queen landed at Bridlington. The Earl of Newcastle's army was marching towards the east coast but Newcastle was unsure of where the Queen would land. Having sent a message to Newcastle on the 22nd, the Queen had taken up residence in Bridlington. In the early hours of the morning of the 24th a squadron of Parliamentarian ships commenced a bombardment of the town. The house the Queen was staying in received several hits and the Queen and her ladies had to take shelter in a ditch. Help came from an unexpected source. The Queen had been escorted by the Dutch Admiral van Tromp. Having remained in the area, van Tromp demanded that the Parliamentarian ships cease fire or he would be forced to engage them. This threat, and the falling tide, persuaded the Parliamentarian commander to withdraw his ships. By 7 March Newcastle had escorted the Queen and her convoy of arms and powder to York.

On 25 March Parliament's cause received a stunning blow when Sir Hugh Cholmley and the entire garrison of Scarborough defected to the Royalist side. With this defection the whole of the East Riding, with the exception of Hull, came under Newcastle's control. Lord Fairfax, Parliament's commander in Yorkshire, decided that his position around Cawood and Selby was untenable and decided to withdraw to Leeds. The withdrawal began early on the 30th. To cover the retreat of the main force Lord Fairfax's son, Sir Thomas, led a raid against Tadcaster. The Royalist garrison quit the town and withdrew to York. Sir Thomas then spent three or four hours slighting the town's defences before beginning his withdrawal towards Leeds.

Newcastle reacted quickly to news of this raid and despatched Colonel George Goring with a force of twenty troops of horse and dragoons, possibly 1,000–1,200 men. Fairfax's force comprised only three troops of horse and an indeterminate number of foot. Although he had more men than Goring their fighting capability was limited by lack of pikes. Fairfax had to withdraw across two large areas of open ground separated by enclosed fields. Having successfully negotiated the first open expanse Fairfax was caught and badly defeated while crossing the second, Seacroft Moor. Although his force was shattered, as many as 800 being captured, Sir Thomas arrived safely at Leeds.

Newcastle followed up this victory by advancing on Leeds. Having spent several days in an abortive siege of the town, Newcastle proceeded south to Wakefield, which he garrisoned with 3,000 men before he continued his march south to Rotherham. After a two-day siege the town fell on 4 May. On the 6th the garrison of Sheffield abandoned the town and Newcastle took possession. Things seemed to be going well for the Royalists until 21 May, when news reached Newcastle that Wakefield had been stormed by Sir Thomas Fairfax in a surprise attack. Arriving before the town in the early hours of the morning Fairfax's men assaulted the defences at the ends of Northgate and Warrengate. After a short, fierce, fight the Royalist garrison surrendered. Much to their surprise the Parliamentarian commanders realised they had stormed a town defended by twice their own numbers. Lord Fairfax stated that it was more a miracle than a victory.

Expecting an immediate reaction from Newcastle, Sir Thomas withdrew his force to Leeds. Instead of marching straight to Leeds the Earl of Newcastle tamely withdrew to York. He had good reason to do this as the Queen was still in York. Before he could open a full campaign against Lord Fairfax and his West Riding garrisons, he had to escort the Queen from Yorkshire as she travelled south towards Oxford. By 16 June the Queen had left Yorkshire and had arrived safely at Newark. This left Newcastle free to turn his attention on the West Riding.

His first move was against Bradford. Marching to Howley Hall, between Bradford and Wakefield, his army successfully stormed it on 21 June. Having spent several days resting his army at the Hall, Newcastle took his next step. On the morning of the 30th his army set off for Bradford. In the enemy camp, Lord Fairfax had decided that Bradford was untenable. His men had succeeded in a surprise attack against the enemy garrison at Wakefield, could they not do the same against the enemy quarters at Howley? With this in mind Fairfax's army also left its quarters on the morning of the 30th. Both armies were marching in opposite directions along the same road and were bound to collide. This collision took place at Adwalton Moor.

At Adwalton Moor Lord Fairfax came very close to defeating Newcastle's much larger army. Having driven the Royalist vanguard back on their main force, deployed on Adwalton Moor, Fairfax's men began to make progress from the enclosures they occupied onto the moor itself. Although heavily out-numbered, Sir Thomas's horse held a narrow gap against the Royalist horse. After defeating a second attack Sir Thomas counter-attacked onto the moor and almost captured Newcastle's guns. This, combined with an attack by Parliamentarian musketeers onto the moor, led to the start of a Royalist withdrawal. Throughout the battle Newcastle's pikemen had remained un-engaged on the moor. Colonel Posthumous Kirton asked permission to lead a body of them forward, which was granted, and the subsequent attack com-pletely changed the course of the battle. The Royalist pike, followed by a body of horse, shattered the Parliamentarian centre. Within minutes the bulk of Lord Fairfax's men were streaming back towards Bradford. Having been cut off from the Bradford road Sir Thomas and his men withdrew in good order to Halifax.

Newcastle continued his advance to Bradford and began his bombardment on 1 July. Lord Fairfax and the bulk of his remaining troops had withdrawn to Leeds during the night of 30 June and Sir Thomas had assumed command of the garrison of Bradford. At a council of war during the night of 1/2 July it was decided that the town could not be held and that a withdrawal to Leeds should be attempted. Many of the Parliamentarian troops were captured or forced back into Bradford. After a short fight, during which his wife was captured, Sir Thomas broke through the Royalist lines and arrived at Leeds. Lady Fairfax was treated with all honour and returned to her husband at Hull. The in-habitants of Bradford waited for the morning with dread, as the Earl of Newcastle had declared the town was to be stormed and no quarter was to be given. He spent the night at Bolling Hall and local tradition has it that he was visited during the small hours by an apparition begging him to 'Pity poor Bradford.' The room where this visitation took place still exists in the Hall. True or not, by the morning of the 2nd Newcastle had changed his mind and his army occupied Bradford without any trouble.

In another council of war Lord Fairfax decided that Leeds could not be held. The only garrison left in Yorkshire was Hull. Fairfax had received intelligence that Sir John Hotham, Hull's governor, had been corresponding with

Newcastle and might change sides at any moment. Would his remaining troops be allowed entrance into the town? In the nick of time news reached him that the Hothams, father and son, had been arrested and the town was secure. With this it was decided that an immediate retreat to Hull was in order. After a brief skirmish at Selby the Parliamentarian Army, or what was left of it, reached the safety of the town. Shortly afterwards a body of Royalist horse arrived before the town and the Second Siege of Hull had begun.

By 3 July the Earl of Newcastle controlled the whole of Yorkshire, with the exception of Hull. His next step was to besiege the town. Unfortunately for Newcastle, Parliament had control of the sea and the town could be readily supplied. Its defences were strong, both natural and man-made. The First Siege of Hull lasted until 27 July. Newcastle then pushed part of his army into Lincolnshire and fought a number of small actions against elements of the recently raised Army of the Eastern Association. Returning to Hull on 2 September a third siege followed, lasting until 12 October. Once again Hull refused to fall and the siege was broken off. Newcastle then moved south into Lincolnshire and Derbyshire, where his army remained until the end of the year.

Newcastle, now elevated to the title of Marquis after his victory at Adwalton Moor, had been presented with an ideal opportunity to march south and reinforce the King. Unfortunately, his Yorkshire supporters would not leave the county while Hull still remained in Parliament's hands.

Parliament in Trouble

By the close of 1643 Parliament was in trouble and the situation had been worsening month by month. Two of its three main armies had suffered major reverses and the third, Essex's, had only just held its own against the King's army. Steps were taken to improve this situation. A new army, under Waller, would face Hopton's army in Hampshire. In the East Midlands Newcastle's army would be counteracted by Manchester's Army of the Eastern Association, should it march south into the heart of the Association. Both the King and Parliament had looked further afield for assistance. The King had tried to reach an agreement with the rebel Irish Confederation. If such an agreement was reached English troops serving in Ireland could be brought back to the mainland. Both the King and Parliament had talks with the Scots – the defeat at Adwalton Moor had prompted Parliament into this course of action. On 25 September these talks bore fruit for Parliament. Members of the House of Commons and the Scottish Estates signed the Solemn League and Covenant. As part of this agreement Parliament would introduce the Presbyterian faith as England's state religion. In return the Scots would raise an army of over 20,000 men and invade the North of England. Although many members of Parliament already followed the Presbyterian faith, many others were opposed to its introduction. These 'Independent' members, as they became known, managed to get the agreement worded in such a way as to be able to avoid its implementation. This, in due course, would lead to conflict with the Scottish nation, but that was in the future.

The Scots began to raise their forces throughout the nation. Twenty-one regiments of foot, seven regiments of horse, two independent troops of horse and one regiment of dragoons were to be raised by mid-January, when the invasion was scheduled. Some areas raised troops more speedily than others and to encourage the laggards the Committee of Estates took drastic measures:

> The Committee of States fearing the slownesse of the Counties in leavy-ing our Forces in this season of the yeer, and perceiving that the sitting of the Session, and other ordinary Judicatories, did much hinder the setting forward of our Army, did adjourn them upon the 23 of December, to the first of February; and sent further Instructions to all the Shires, ordaining the Committees of the severall Shires, Colonells, and all other Officers, to raise as many as they could for the present, and give those free Quarter upon the rest of the County, till they had their full number in readinesse: withall, assuring those Counties who should be first in readinesse, That the Counties who were last in sending their Regiments to the place of Rendevouz, should be liable to the whole expence and charge they should be put to in attending those Shires, who should not come about the time appointed.[1]

With this command the Convention of Estates placed the expense of the quickly-raised regiments squarely onto the shoulders of the more reticent counties. On 9 January the Convention appointed four commissioners to go to London and sit on the Committee of Both Kingdoms. The four were the Earl of Loudon, Lord Maitland, Lord Wariston and Robert Barclay. The latter two were to depart at once, while Loudon and Maitland were to leave at the earliest opportunity after the beginning of February. On the 13th the Convention moved to Berwick, where the main army was gathering under the Earl of Leven. By the 18th the invasion force was in place. Some regiments marched from Dunbar to Berwick on that day in atrocious weather conditions:

> And upon the 18, severall Regiments marched from Dunbar and the adjacent villages, thorow a Heath 10 miles long, to Barwick, being in all 18 Scottish miles, when it was knee-deep Snow, and blowing and snowing so vehemently, that the Guides could with great difficulty know the way, and

it was enough for the followers to discern the leaders; notwithstanding whereof, they were very cheerfull all the way; and, after they had been a little refreshed at night, professed, They were willing to march as far to morrow.[2]

The hardiness of the Scots soldiers is vouched for by Sir James Turner who writes, 'I found the bodies of the men lustie, well clothed and well monnied, but raw, untrained and undisciplined; their officers for most part young and unexperienced'.[3] John Rushworth included a list of Scots regiments, including their senior officers, in his account of the campaign in the north, part of his monumental work published in 1692 (see Appendix I).[4] From this list it can be seen that although many of the lieutenant colonels and majors had experience from the Thirty Years War, few of the regimental commanders had. Many of the company officers, captain and lieutenants, would have been too young to have had much, if any, experience in the art of war. Most of the soldiers had been recently recruited and had not long been subjected to military discipline. This said the Scots Army marched under strict articles of war (see Appendix II). Stringent rules for requisitioning supplies and quartering troops were also enforced (see Appendix III). Hardy but raw, the Scots invasion force had completed its deployment along the border by 19 January. Other regiments would move to the border over the following days. On the morrow the Tweed would be crossed and enemy territory entered.

Chapter 2

The Scots Invasion

The raising of the Army desired by the Parliament ...

The Scots intended to cross the border in three separate columns. The first, commanded by the Earl of Leven, would march south from Berwick. The second, under Lieutenant General Baillie, would cross the Tweed at Kelso. The third, much smaller, column would march south from Coldstream. In due course all three columns would converge at Alnwick and then proceed south via Morpeth to Newcastle. On the morning of 19 January 1644 these movements began. Leven's column, comprising three regiments of foot and thirteen troops of horse, marched a few miles south from Berwick and then halted at Haggerston. During the night a letter was drafted by the representatives of the Committee of Both Kingdoms with the Scots Army, Argyle and Armyne, and duly despatched to Sir Thomas Glemham, the Royalist commander in Northumberland. This letter[1] stated that the Scots Army had crossed the border at the behest of Parliament to preserve and reform religion, to preserve the honour and happiness of the King and to restore the peace and liberty of his dominions. It goes on to blame the Roman Catholic Church for causing all the present troubles in the two kingdoms and ends with a warning that supporters of their objectives would be treated as friends, while those opposed to them would know what to expect.

Sir Thomas Glemham had been expecting the Scots invasion for several weeks and had sent Colonel Sir Francis Anderson and his regiment of horse to the border. During the morning of the 20th Sir Thomas received a letter from Colonel Anderson informing him that the Scots had crossed the Tweed.[2] Close to Colonel Anderson's headquarters at Wooler a small column of Scots had crossed the border, comprising a body of foot, possibly part of Lord Maitland's regiment, and Michael Weldon's regiment of horse. This is an interesting unit. First, it was one of only two regiments of horse partly armed with lances, and second, its commander was an Englishman. The regiment was intended to remain in Northumberland and form the cadre of a new Parliamentarian Army to be raised in the county. By nightfall on the 19th two

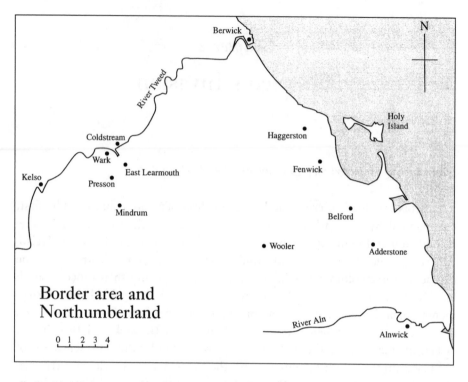

Border area and Northumberland

of the three invasion columns had crossed the border. The third column, Baillie's, had not been able to cross the Tweed at Kelso and was unable to do so for several days.

On the 20th the Scots Army kept to its quarters with the exception of two regiments of foot, which marched from Berwick to join Leven at Haggerston. There was good reason for this inactivity: Leven and Argyle were waiting for an answer to their letter and did not wish to commence hostilities until they were sure that Sir Thomas Glemham and the local gentry would oppose them. They received a reply very quickly.[3] Sir Thomas was unable to give them an answer until he had gathered his officers and the 'Gentlemen of the County' at Alnwick and discussed the matter with them. Once a decision had been reached by this council he would send them a reply immediately. Being a man of his word, Sir Thomas promptly called his officers and gentlemen to Alnwick and a meeting was held on the 22nd. According to one Scots source[4] three questions were discussed at this meeting. First, what should be done to the areas of the county not yet controlled by the Scots but which the Royalists would be unable to defend? Second, what answer should be given to the letter of the Committee of Both Kingdoms? Third, should they actively oppose the Scots in Northumberland?

The council was divided in its answer to the first question. Many of Sir Thomas's officers were Yorkshiremen and put forward a scorched earth policy. Militarily, this was a sound plan. It would deny locally gathered supplies to the Scots and at this time of year their supply lines would be somewhat precarious, with roads alternating between deep snow and even deeper mud. This obviously did not meet the approval of the local gentry. Understandably they were concerned that this scorched earth policy would be carried out on their lands. Furthermore, when the Scots had occupied Northumberland during the Second Bishops' War they had behaved well: surely it was better to submit to a second Scots occupation than to see their lands laid waste? As will be seen later some of the local gentry actually took this policy of cooperation one step further and joined the Scots Army.

With regard to the second question, once again the council was divided. One group believed that such a fair letter should be given a fair reply, while a second group suggested that it was too grave a subject to be answered by them and should be referred to the Marquis of Newcastle. A final group thought that as the letter was from a foreign invader it should be referred to the King himself.

Only on the third question were they unanimous: the Scots Army would not be opposed in its advance towards Newcastle. The small Royalist army comprised only sixteen troops of horse and two regiments of foot, in all probability less than 2,000 men. It was opposed by an army with a combined strength of almost 20,000. It is easy to see why the council reached a unanimous decision. They would retreat to Newcastle and there reinforce the garrison and attempt to hold the town until the Marquis had arrived with his army. As they marched south they would destroy any bridges to impede the Scots advance. With their discussions complete Sir Thomas sent a reply to the Committee of Both Kingdoms.[5] In it he refuted the Scots reasons for invading England and quite categorically claimed that their intention of preserving England's state religion was, in fact, an attempt to innovate it. After berating the Scots as supporting traitors, if not actually fomenting their treason, he went on to warn them to withdraw to their own country before 'the Sword be unsheathed, or the breach be made too wide'.

Having received Sir Thomas's unequivocal reply the Scots resumed their advance on the 23rd. Leven's main column was reinforced by two more regiments of foot from Berwick before it advanced and quartered around Adderstone and Fenwick. Baillie's column was finally able to cross the Tweed. The river had been impassable until, on the nights of the 21st and 22nd, there 'was so great a frost (the like whereof we have not seen) that in two nights the River of Twede froze so strong, that our Army and Ammunition which was at Kelso marched over upon the Ice, which otherwise could not have yet come over'.[6] This column, comprising six regiments of foot and one of horse, then proceeded to Wooler, where it quartered during the night of the 23rd.

On the 24th the Scots remained in their quarters while Leven awaited the arrival of his 'great gunnes'. Due to the state of the roads these had to be shipped to Berwick before proceeding south in the wake of the army. In a letter written from Leven's quarters on the 24th one Scots correspondent optimistically predicted that the army would be quartered around Newcastle by 27 January.[7] He goes on to detail the dispositions of the Scots Army on the 24th:

> There is a Regiment of Foot at Barwick, and other three upon the Border, which are to march over as soon as the other Regiments march forward, for otherwise they can have no Quarters. There are likewise two Regiments of Horse, some of them with the Artillery, some in Barwick, and others of them upon the Border, all to march over at Barwick on Thursday and Friday; and from Kelso 2 Regiments of Foot, and a Regiment of Horse. There are in all eighteen thousand foot, and three thousand Horse, and betwixt four and five hundred Dragoons, besides Baggage-Horse, and the Garrison at Barwicke, already within this Kingdom, and within a dayes march of the Borders. There be likewise two Regiments of Foot, and a Regiment of Horse coming from the North.

Including the troops already in England this gives a total of twenty-one regiments of foot and seven of horse, which is in agreement with Rushworth's list (see Appendix I). With the exception of Lord Maitland's regiment of foot and Weldon's regiment of horse there are no details of where individual regiments were deployed. During the 24th Leven sent an order to Baillie to rendezvous with him at Alnwick on the following day.

As the Scots advanced on Alnwick Sir Thomas Glemham began his withdrawal, his troops destroying its bridge as they left the town. Proceeding south towards Morpeth, Sir Thomas attempted to demolish the bridge over the River Coquet at Felton. This did not quite proceed the way Sir Thomas had expected, as is recounted by a Scots correspondent:

> Sir Thomas Glemham did intend to cut Feltam Bridge, but the Masons and workmen which hee brought thither for that purpose, were so affrighted by reason of the exclamations and execrations of the Countrey women upon their knees, that while Sir Thomas went into a house to refresse himselfe they stole away, and before hee could get them to return, hee received an alarum from our Horse, which made himselfe to flee away with speed to Morpeth, where hee stayed not long but marched to Newcastle.[8]

The Scots proceeded to occupy Alnwick on the 25th. The Marquis of Argyle then led a small force to attack the Royalist garrison on Coquet Island. The garrison surrendered after the first shot was fired at them. The whole garrison of seventy officers and men plus all of their arms and ammunition, seven brass guns and enough food to supply the garrison for a year were captured for no loss.[9] The march south continued on the 26th and by the 27th they were quartered at Morpeth, where they remained for several days. Their march south had been 'a hard and difficult march in respect of the thaw, which so swelled the waters (whereof there were not a few in their way) that oftentimes it came to the middle, and sometimes to the Arme pits of the Foot'.[10] The hardiness of the soldiers, both Scots and Royalist, is to be admired and their ability to continue in such foul weather, with heavy freezes followed by rapid thaws, is almost beyond belief.

The Scots remained at Morpeth until 1 February. Leven's intention was to arrive at Newcastle on the 2nd but once again the weather played its part, slowing the Scots advance. The Scots Army quartered around Stannington on the night of the 2nd and then marched to Newcastle on the 3rd. But they had arrived a day too late: the Marquis of Newcastle had thrown his army into the town hours before the Scots arrived.

Newcastle Moves North

The Marquis of Newcastle (he had been raised from Earl to Marquis after his victory at Adwalton Moor) spent the final weeks of 1643 in winter quarters in Derbyshire. A Scots invasion was expected early in the New Year, and with this in mind, he had despatched Sir Thomas Glemham into Northumberland as his lieutenant. In early January he received an invitation from the gentry of Yorkshire to return into the county. They promised him 10,000 new recruits to help him fight the Scots but these were not forthcoming when he arrived at York on, or around, 15 January. News from the north warned him that the Scots Army was massing along the border and, expecting their invasion at any time, he began preparations to march north. Due to the recent death of Sir William Saville, who had been Governor of York and commander of the Royalist forces in Yorkshire, a replacement had to be found. Colonel John Belasyse was ordered north from Oxford and assumed the post.

While awaiting his arrival, Newcastle continued to recruit troops to march north with him and to garrison Yorkshire in his absence. On the 28th Newcastle wrote a letter to Prince Rupert.[11] In this letter he stated that he had less than 5,000 foot with which to march north and that his cavalry were ill equipped. He also passed on news from the north: the Scots had advanced as far as Morpeth with 14,000 men.

On the 29th Newcastle marched north. Sir Charles Lucas reports Newcastle's departure and his intention to continue recruiting on the march:

> The Marquis is himself, the 29th of this last month, advanced against the Scots. Having sent the greatest part of his Army before, the number of his foot is yet uncertain, because many are to come in to him as he passes through the bishopric; yet I believe they are going out of these parts, above five thousand foot and above three thousand horse.[12]

Sir Charles's estimate of numbers for the Marquis' marching army is much in agreement with Newcastle's own. On the 29th Newcastle marched north with 5,000 foot and 3,000 horse. Newcastle detailed his march north in a letter to Prince Rupert on 13 February:

> We remained there not above a fortnight, but the Scots had invaded the kingdom with a very great Army, although the season of the year and a great snow at the very instant did persuade us that it was impossible for them to march. Yet not trusting to that, my Lord-Lieutenant-General hasted away with all expedition with such horse and foot as were quartered nearest to those parts, and, receiving intelligence of the Scots continuing their march, he hasted to Newcastle in his own person some days before his forces could possibly get thither; where truly he found the town in a very good posture, and that the mayor, who had charge of it, had performed his part in your Majesty's service very faithfully; and all the aldermen and best of the town well disposed for your service. And though our charge was very tedious, by reason of floods occasioned by the sudden thaw of the snow, yet I came thither the night before the Scots assaulted the town.[13]

As Newcastle marched north his Lieutenant General, Lord Eythin, marched before him. Eythin arrived at Newcastle with a small body of troops to organise its defence but found that the Mayor and his council had matters well in hand. Gathering troops to him as he advanced, Newcastle arrived at the town on the night of 2 February, notwithstanding the state of the roads. In five days he had marched from York to Newcastle. This was a very quick march in comparison with that of the Scots over the same period and in similar conditions.

Newcastle Is Summoned

At about noon on Saturday 3 February the Scots Army approached Newcastle and formed into line of battle before summoning the town. The Marquis of Argyle's trumpeter was sent into the town with a letter offering a parley. The letter once again stated why the Scots had invaded England and that if the citizens of Newcastle agreed to their objectives they would be treated as friends. If they did not agree or refused to parley they would be responsible for 'those manifold Inconveniences and Calamities that may be the fruit of those forcible ways you will thereby Constrain us to'.[14] To reinforce his point Leven decided on a show of strength.

The Scots sent a body of commanded musketeers to capture an unfinished work near the entrance to the Shieldfield. This was quickly carried, the Royalist garrison withdrawing to a more substantial work, described as a sconce or fort, close to the north gate. A number of accounts, both Scots and Royalist, describe the subsequent attack against this work.[15] Leven sent two bodies of musketeers to attack the sconce from the east and west sides. The Royalist troops, commanded by Sir Charles Slingsby, held the Scots for some time. The Scots were pinned down by both musket and cannon shot. The Royalist garrison, having lost a number of men, decided to withdraw into the town. To cover the withdrawal eight troops of horse advanced from the north gate. These were charged by David Leslie and five troops of Scots horse. The ground on which this cavalry skirmish took place was scattered with coal pits and spoil heaps, which constrained the fighting somewhat. Having succeeded in covering the retreat of Sir Charles Slingsby and his men, the Royalist horse withdrew into the town. Their retreat was in turn covered by the guns of the town, which fired an ineffective bombardment against the pursuing Scots horse. Losses on both sides were light. In the cavalry fight not a man had been lost by either side, although two Royalist horsemen had been captured. The Royalist defenders of the fort had lost eight men, while their attackers had lost either ten or fourteen men, depending on which source is believed. One of the Scots casualties was Patrick English, the Captain Lieutenant of Lord Lindsey's regiment. It can be assumed from this that Lindsey's regiment supplied at least some of the musketeers in the assault force.

The stiff Royalist resistance must have come as a surprise to the Scots leaders. A further surprise awaited them when they received a reply from the Mayor of Newcastle, John Marley, who wrote that the town council was unable to reply to their letter as the King's General was in residence in the town. He went on to add that if Newcastle had not been in the town they still could not have given a satisfactory answer to the Scots as they could not 'Betray a Trust reposed in Us, or forfeit Our Allegiance to his Majesty'.[16] To further reinforce their intention to defend the town the Royalists set fire to the suburbs lying close to the walls. The Scots called this barbarous but it made sound sense. If these buildings had been left standing the Scots would have had covered approaches to the walls. With the Royalist intention to hold the town made abundantly clear, the Scots moved into quarters surrounding the northern side of the town on 4 February.

Holding the Tyne

With the exception of Newcastle, North Shields and Tynemouth Castle, the whole of the coastal plain of Northumberland was under Scots control. By 4 February the Scots had moved into quarters around Newcastle. One Scots account lists quarters at Morpeth, Seaton, Hexham, Ogle Castle and Prudhoe.[17] The Scots could do very little against Newcastle until their heavy guns arrived and these had to be transported by sea from Berwick to Blyth as the roads were in an appalling state, as one Scots writer relates:

> The weather hath been extreme stormy, the ways are unpassable with Carriages, and our Ammunition hath been long in coming: The uncertainty of the season of the yeer, and the swelling of the River by sudden rains, makes our passage more difficult: The windes have not served to bring Ships with provision from Scotland, and the Countrey is burnt and wasted in many places.[18]

The Scots supply lines were in a shambles. This presented the Marquis of Newcastle with an opportunity to worsen their situation by raiding their quarters and depriving them of any available supplies. The Royalists conducted regular raids and as can be seen from the above passage large areas of Northumberland were 'burnt and wasted'. But not all these raids were successful. Thomas Riddell, an officer from the garrison of Tynemouth Castle, led a force of fifty musketeers to destroy supplies of corn in the Scots quarters but they were set upon by a body of twenty-five Scots horsemen, commanded by Major Montgomery, major of the Earl of Eglington's regiment of horse. Several Royalists were killed and the remainder taken prisoner. The Earl of Leven returned all but two of these prisoners to the Marquis of Newcastle, who thanked him and hoped he would have opportunity to return the favour.[19]

On the whole, the Scots soldiers behaved well during their occupation of Northumberland. They were regularly paid and this allowed them to pay for any supplies taken from the local inhabitants:

> They doe carry themselves so civelly and orderly that the Countrey doe even admire them, taking not the worth of a penny from any man but what they pay fully for, and they are not come unprovided, for every souldier hath 2 or 3 peeces in his pocket, and there hath thousands come into them, and taken the Covenant, and their Army doth exceedingly increase.[20]

It could easily be believed that the mention of thousands of inhabitants taking the Covenant and joining the Scots Army was a piece of propaganda but a similar theme is mentioned in a Royalist source. The Marquis of Newcastle, in a letter to Prince Rupert, writes that the Scots had withdrawn into their quarters, 'where they have remained ever since quartered in strong bodies, and raising the whole country of Northumberland, which is totally lost, all turned to them, so that they daily increase their Army'.[21]

On Tuesday 6 February the Scots guns finally arrived at Blyth by ship. By the 7th they had reached the main army. At this point Leven had a decision to make. Although he outnumbered the Marquis' forces in Newcastle and he had his heavy guns with the army, would his army be able to take Newcastle? In the fighting on the 3rd the garrison had shown its determination to hold the town. Although Leven's troops closely blockaded the walls of the town, its south side, the River Tyne, was still open. This would enable the Royalists to move men and supplies into the town unhindered. Leven decided that to take Newcastle he had to move part of his army onto the south bank of the river, thus completely surrounding the town. It was decided that an attempt would be made to bridge the river on the night of the 8th. The Tyne still contained many ships and boats of varying sizes. Its mouth was blockaded by a Parliamentarian squadron and the boats lying along its banks provided ready made pontoons for the Scots. During the 8th a raid was made on this shipping and a number of boats and lighters (flat-bottomed barges) were captured. On the night of the 8th the Scots made their first attempt to cross the river. Sir James Turner, an eyewitness, wrote a succinct account of this attempt:

> The Scots main care was, how to get over Tyne, never caring to possess themselves of a pass on that river for their retreat, so much did they trust their own valour and success. While I was there, they endeavoured one night to bring boats from the glass houses, or above them, to the river, and so make a bridge. But fearing the King's forces should fall out upon them that were at work, Argile and his committee sent over Colonel [William] Steuart [The Galloway regiment], with 1200 foot, to stand between the workmen and the town. They had but a little narrow bridge to pass in their going and coming, and if 2000 had fallen stoutly out of the town on them, they had killed and taken them every man, for retire they could not. Argile hearing this was my opinion, which was seconded by others, asked Deare Sandie [General Hamilton], Sir James Lumsdaine and myself, what was best to be done. We were unanimous that false alarms should be given about the whole town, to divert the enemy from falling too strong upon Steuart, for the town's outer guards of horse had certified them

within of his approach. I was sent with this message to the General, whom I found going to supper. When I returned, I was ashamed to relate the answer of that old Captain; which was, that he feared the brightness of the night (for it was moonshine) would discover the burning matches to those on the walls. I told him, the moonshine was no prejudice to the design, for it would hinder the matches to be seen; for the more lunts [lights] were seen, the better for a false alarm. However, the alarms were made in several places, which were taken so hotly where I was beside the workmen, that though I called often to them, it was our own people, yet some great persons, whom I shall not name, called eagerly for their horses, and when they were on them rode away. The work was left undone, because it was neap tide, and Steuart returned safely, to the great disgrace of these within.[22]

Sir James's account needs little explanation. The Scots attempt to cross the Tyne is definitely open to criticism and Sir James goes on to do this:

I have often made myself merry with that night's work, first to consider how the Committee of Estates, especially their president Argile, who was a good seaman, did not advert it was neap tide, before they attempted the removal of the boats: secondly, how they adventured to face a town wherein there was six thousand horse and foot, with 1200 men, and no way for them to retreat; thirdly, of General Leven's impertinent answer to my message; fourthly, to see men afraid at their own shadow, men run away for an alarm themselves had caused make; and for a farce to the play, to hear my old Colonel Steuart, when he was returned to his quarters, vapour and brag of the orderly retreat he had made without the loss of a man, when there was not so much as a foot boy pursuing him.

Sir James was obviously not impressed with the Scots Army's performance. With this failure to cross the Tyne the Scots settled into a period of inactivity.

On 16 February the Marquis of Newcastle wrote a letter to the King.[23] In it he sums up his situation: his army was beset by enemy forces; before him at Newcastle was the Scots Army; Newark, one of his southern most outposts, was strongly besieged by Sir John Meldrum; Lord Fairfax had begun to make inroads into the East Riding and his son, Sir Thomas, was bringing pressure to bear in the West Riding. The Marquis' position was unenviable but he put forward a number of suggestions. First, that the Scots were the King's main problem. Troops, particularly foot, should be sent north to reinforce the Marquis' army. Once the Scots were beaten the King's 'game' would be won. Second, Newark should be relieved and the Earl of Manchester's army drawn away from it. Finally, Cheshire and Lancashire should be ignored for the time being. In this letter can be seen the seeds of the plan that led directly to the field of Marston Moor. In the meantime, Newcastle planned a great raid across the Tyne. It would be the biggest attack on the Scots quarters yet planned and would take place on 19 February.

The Battle of Corbridge

The Marquis of Newcastle's objective was no less than the destruction of almost one-third of the Scots horse. Two regiments, the Earl of Leven's and Lord Kirkcudbright's, were quartered at Corbridge in a very exposed position. Corbridge lay close to several fords across the Tyne and was in the outer line of Scots quarters. Newcastle intended to take advantage of this by a dawn attack. Sir Marmaduke Langdale would lead twenty-five troops of horse and several hundred musketeers across the river near Hexham. While Langdale's men attacked Corbridge from the west a second column of ten horse troops, commanded by Colonel Brandling, would cross the river to the east of Corbridge and engage the Scots horse from the rear. To divert the Scots attention from the attack at Corbridge, and prevent support reaching the Scots troopers, a third column would cross the Tyne at Prudhoe. This column was commanded by Colonel Dudley and comprised horse and dragoons, although no indication is given of its size. This was a very complicated plan, and in an age of poor communications, was prone to error.

Several contemporary accounts of the battle, both Scots and Royalist, exist.[24] In general they are very much in agreement and vary only in small details. Langdale's column did not cross the river as early as had been intended. They were observed in their passage and this allowed the Scots regiments to form up to receive them. The Scots formed a body of fifteen troops of horse and three troops of dragoons. The Earl of Leven's regiment had eight troops and was commanded by its Lieutenant Colonel, James Ballantine. Four troops of the regiment were armed with lances. Lord Kirkcudbright commanded his own regiment of seven troops. The brigade was commanded by Lord Balgoney, the Earl of Leven's son, and amounted to no more than 800 men. Langdale's troopers, amounting to 1,000–1,200 men, advanced to the attack. The Scots did not wait to receive them. Lieutenant Colonel Ballantine led his men forward in a counter-charge and the Scots horse drove the Royalists back towards the support of their musketeers, taking a number of prisoners as they went. The Marquis of Newcastle specifically mentions that the Scots lancers were the cause of his men's retreat. Both sides reformed and charged once more. Yet again the Scots had the better of the fight but Ballantine seems to have got carried away with his success and charged a third time. Once again the Royalists fell back, this time as far as their musketeers. The fire support of the Royalist shot changed the course of the battle and Langdale led a successful counter-attack, which broke the Scots, who retreated rapidly towards Corbridge, losing 150 prisoners in their retreat. By this time Brandling's column should have reached the field and completed the defeat of the Scots but was nowhere to be seen. After a short pursuit Langdale reformed his men and withdrew to the south bank of the Tyne, taking his prisoners with him.

Colonel Brandling's column splashed across the Tyne much later than planned. As they moved towards Corbridge a body of Scots horse advanced eastwards. So late was Brandling's column that they met the retreating Scots horse coming towards them! Although the Scots had reformed by this time a charge by Brandling's men would probably have seen them on their way again. Instead of forming his men and leading them forward, Brandling decided to challenge a Scots officer, Lieutenant Elliot, to a single combat. Having discharged pistols at each other they drew their swords and charged. As Brandling tried to turn his horse it lost its footing and Elliot, who was very close to Brandling, hauled him from his saddle and took him prisoner – whereupon Brandling's men turned tail and fell back towards the river. Seeing this, the Scots troopers took heart and charged them, pursuing them to the ford. Some Royalists were killed, others taken prisoner and yet more drowned as they fled across the Tyne.

As the to-and-fro fight at Corbridge was going on Colonel Dudley led his men across the Tyne at Prudhoe. Surprising an enemy quarter Dudley took fifty-five prisoners and caused chaos in four other surrounding quarters. With enemy pressure growing, Dudley began to retreat towards the river. On the way his men surprised and captured eight Scots horsemen. Dudley successfully withdrew to the south bank, his only loss being four dragoons who were taken prisoner because their horses were too tired to ford the river. Cavalry operations at this time of year must have taken a savage toll on the horses, particularly dragoon horses, which were of much lower quality than those of the horse regiments.

On the whole the Royalists had the better of the day. Casualties were about even, although the Scots lost more prisoners than the Royalists. It is interesting to ponder whether the Marquis did return Leven's favour by returning the prisoners to him. If so, he did not return them all, as Sir Henry Slingsby reports the arrival of Scots prisoners from the Corbridge fight at York.

The one concrete result of the fighting on the 19th was the contraction of the Scots quarters into a much smaller area. Obviously this provided more security but brought its own problems. A smaller quartering area would produce fewer supplies. The roads were still a shambles and supplies by wagon or ship must have been rare. The Scots needed to establish a secure supply base. Their choices were limited. Newcastle was holding firm against them and Berwick was too far away. The only viable choice was Sunderland but the town lay south of the Tyne. Yet again the Scots would have to attempt a crossing of the river. This time they decided on a crossing using the fords to the west of Newcastle. Newburn Ford, the scene of their victory in 1640, was strongly held. Several other fords around Ovingham and Bywell showed more promise. It was decided to attempt a crossing at these fords: but would the Marquis of Newcastle oppose them? Newcastle provides his own answer to this question:

> First after I had made true inquisition of the passes over the river Tyne, I found there was so many fordable places betwixt Newcastle and Hexham, about 12 miles distant one from the other, that it was impossible with my small number of foot to divide them so as to guard and make good every place, but to hazard the loss of them at any one place, and yet not do the work; so I resolved of two evils to choose the less, and left them to their own wills.[25]

Newcastle had decided that he didn't have enough men to defend the Tyne. If the Scots wanted to cross, so be it.

Chapter 3

The Fight for County Durham

So great a power hath the Cathedral here ...

The Scots began their march towards the Tyne crossings on 22 February 1644. Sir James Lumsden remained to blockade Newcastle with six regiments of foot – the Earl Marshall's, Lord Coupar's, the Levied regiment, Lord Gask's, Sir David Home of Wedderburn's and Douglas of Kelhead's – and 'some Troops of Horse'.[1] Although not specifically mentioned, the troops of horse almost certainly belonged to Michael Weldon's regiment, as this regiment did not march south with the main army in April. The main Scots Army, fifteen regiments of foot and six of horse, marched to Heddon-on-the-Wall and quartered very near to the ford at Newburn, where they had crossed the Tyne and beaten the English in 1640. On the 23rd they continued their march towards Corbridge and quartered along the north bank of the Tyne close to the fords at Ovingham and Bywell. Several bodies of Royalist horse were observed on the south bank of the river around Hexham but during the night they marched away. On the following day the weather broke and a terrible snowstorm prevented the Scots from continuing their march. One Scots writer gives praise for the two days of clear weather, the 22nd and 23rd, which had enabled the Scots to march to their crossing points.[2]

By the 28th the snow had cleared enough for the Scots Army to begin its crossing of the fords at Ovingham, Bywell and Eltringham. Although the fords were deep the Scots were able to cross and spent the night quartered in the villages around the crossings. They had crossed the Tyne in the nick of time. For the next eight days the river could not be forded due to the snow melting in the hills to the west. On the 29th the Scots continued their march and reached the River Derwent near Ebchester. The river was in spate and the only crossing was a 'narrow Tree-bridge'.[3] Half of the Scots foot was able to cross during the day and the whole army spent a very cold night in the fields around the crossing. By the next morning the river level had fallen and the rest of the Scots Army, including its wagon train, was able to cross. The day was cold and miserable but this did not prevent the Scots from continuing their march as far as Chester-le-Street.

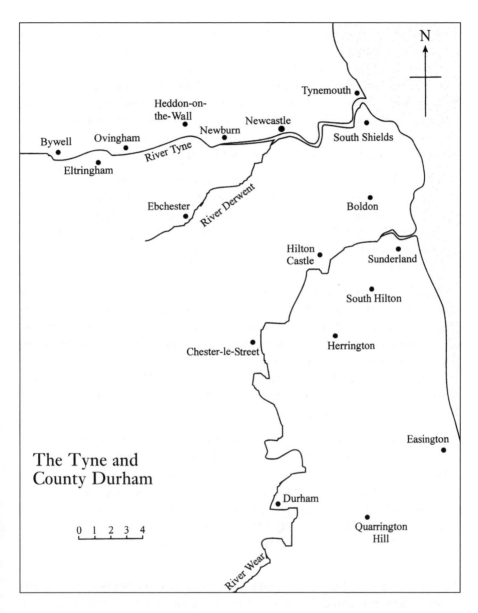

The Tyne and County Durham

On Saturday 2 March the Scots passed the final obstacle before reaching their objective, Sunderland. Crossing the River Wear at the Newbridge, near Lumley Castle, the Scots marched to Herrington, only 4 miles from Sunderland. Here the Earl of Leven received some good news when his scouts informed him that Sunderland was not being held against him and that the Royalist Army was nowhere to be seen. The Scots had been marching for five days without a break and Leven decided to spend the Sunday in his quarters around Herrington to rest his men. On the Monday they continued their march to Sunderland and established their quarters.

The Scots now had a secure supply base. There were two methods for the Scots to gain supplies. First, they could forage in the surrounding areas but the amount of supplies to be garnered in this way was likely to be limited. The situation seems to have been made even worse by the attitude of the local inhabitants, as a Scots correspondent describes:

> All that day, and the day following, was spent in taking care to supply the Army with Provisions; which we obtained with no small difficulty, being the enemies Countrey; for so we may call it, the greatest part of the whole Countrey being either willingly or forcedly in Arms against the Parliament, and afford us no manner of supply, but what they part with against their wills.[4]

A second Scots account[5] is very much in agreement with this but ascribes the reason for the inhabitants' hostility to the power of Durham Cathedral over the area. The second method was by ship. The Scots would have to rely on Parliament's control of the sea to provide them with supplies but would the North Sea, and the weather, allow this?

As the Scots had been marching across County Durham what had the Marquis of Newcastle been doing? One Scots author writes of his surprise at Newcastle's lack of action:

> In this March from Tine to Sunderland, notwithstanding the many straight and disadvantagious passages (which were so narrow, that sometimes the people were constrained to march one by one, as in a string: and if God had given our enemies hearts, we might have beene cut in peeces, or stopped) but we found no opposition from the enemy, and scarcely obtained a sight of them, onely a Body of Horse appeared upon our Reare, at our passing over the River Weare, at New-Bridge, but interrupted us not.[6]

The very nature of the terrain, which had constrained the Scots to 'march one by one', had prevented Newcastle from attacking them. Newcastle's main advantage was his experienced regiments of horse. Although he was heavily outnumbered in foot, he had a larger number of horse than Leven, and these regiments were better mounted and more experienced than the Scots troopers. Leven had kept his army moving through heavily enclosed terrain and had chosen his quarters carefully. Newcastle writes: 'I could by no means march to them, for the situation of these quarters gave them great advantage against our approaches.'[7] Now that the enemy had reached Sunderland, Newcastle would attempt to draw them into a battle where his horse would prove a major advantage. On 6 March he made his first attempt.

The Battle of Hilton

The actions of 6, 7 and 8 March hardly deserve the title of 'battle'. The Scots adopted a defensive stance on the hills to the west of Sunderland, while the Marquis of Newcastle tried to draw them into more open terrain by man-oeuvring towards the town. On the 6th the Marquis gathered his troops and advanced towards Sunderland, crossing the Wear at Newbridge. His army had been reinforced by a body of horse commanded by Sir Charles Lucas and by 1,500 foot from Cumberland. A number of contemporary accounts exist of the day's action, the Marquis of Newcastle's being by far the most detailed.[8] The Royalist Army formed on Worm Hill. A body of Scots horse appeared on the hill opposite and advanced towards the Royalists but was driven back by Royalist musketeers. The Scots horse then withdrew but reappeared in greater numbers shortly afterwards. Newcastle reinforced his advance guard with part of Colonel Dudley's brigade and moved forward but the Scots withdrew as the Royalists approached them. This seems to have ended the day's fighting and both armies fell back to their respective hills. The two armies remained in the field throughout the snowy night, which was bitterly cold.

The snow continued to fall during the morning of the 7th and, although both armies formed up, little movement took place. Late in the morning the skies cleared. The Scots showed no indication of advancing so Newcastle decided to draw them out. Advancing north up the Wear valley he attempted to march around the northern flank of the Scots and either occupy Sunderland or gain an open area close to the town. If he succeeded in either objective the Scots would be forced to fight him on ground of his choosing. The terrain through which the Royalists advanced was heavily enclosed and Newcastle's pioneers had to cut a path through the hedgerows crossing their route. The Scots were able to keep pace with Newcastle by marching along the hills. The Marquis describes this attempt to outflank the Scots:

> The convenient passage we could find to it being through some fields of furze and whin bushes, where we were to make our way with pioneers through three thick hedges with banks, two of which they had lined with musketeers, there also being a valley betwixt us and them, besides they had possessed themselves of a house, wherein as we guess they had put 200 musketeers and a drake, which flankered those hedges which were betwixt us, and from thence there ran a brook, with a great bank, down to

the River Wear; behind these places was this plain above-mentioned, where they stood in their best postures to receive us, having the sea behind them and on the left hand the town, the hill and inaccessible places, by which we must have fetched so great a compass about, that they would have been upon the same hill again to have received us that way.[9]

Once again the Scots had adopted a strong defensive position. To assault it the Marquis would have required a larger force of foot than the defenders had. Unfortunately, this was a luxury Newcastle did not possess. The Scots had refused to be drawn into an open fight, where Newcastle's superiority in horse would be a decisive factor. It is interesting that the two Scots accounts of the day's proceedings both mention that they wished to fight but were prevented from doing so by the terrain, and not by a wish to remain on the defensive.[10] The two armies had reached an impasse. By this time night was rapidly approaching and both armies pulled back and spent another cold night in the field.

Having spent two nights in the open with very little gain, Newcastle decided to withdraw to his main base at Durham. During the night of the 7th he had sent his guns back. His foot then left early in the morning, while his horse covered their retreat. The Scots realised Newcastle was in the process of withdrawing and sent a body of horse in pursuit. Scots writers speak of the fighting that followed as 'some little Skirmishes' but Newcastle adds a few more details.[11] Newcastle sent 120 horse to confront the Scots. Two hundred Scots troopers, supported by a body of Fraser's dragoons lining a hedge to their rear, faced them. The Scots did not expect the Royalists to attack them, having to charge into the teeth of the dragoons' muskets. But charge the Royalist troopers did, and the Scots horse promptly fled. In the pursuit Newcastle's men killed a number of Scots and captured 100 prisoners. The Royalist horse was in turn attacked by a large body of Scots, including lancers. This indicates that the Earl of Leven's regiment was part of the Scots force. The Royalists withdrew rapidly, losing all but twenty of their prisoners. It was later discovered that three of the Scots prisoners were, in fact, Englishmen. One of them – a deserter from Newcastle's army – was immediately hanged.

The Scots then realised that Newcastle was retreating and sent a large force of horse and musketeers in pursuit. The Scots horse formed into three bodies in a large field, supported by their musketeers. Newcastle decided to turn the tables on them. He sent a body of musketeers along a hedgerow that ran past their flank, while a body of Royalist horse fronted them. With their attention fixed on the horse to their front it must have come as a great surprise to the Scots horse when a volley of musket shot tore into their ranks from behind their flank. With this the Scots withdrew and allowed Newcastle to complete his retreat, covered by another snowstorm and the smoke from the villages the Royalists fired along their route. Destroying these villages may seem cruel but it was a sound move to deny supplies and shelter to the Scots.

So came to an end the Battle of Hilton. Newcastle's first attempt to draw the Scots into an open fight had failed. Both armies had suffered terribly from spending three days and two nights in the open, although the Royalist horse seem to have suffered worst of all and required a period of rest before the next round of fighting.

Expanding of Quarters

Although the Scots had obtained a secure base of operations their supply situation was still precarious. Ships attempted to reach Sunderland from both Scotland and London, with varying degrees of success. Five barks in a convoy from Scotland had all been lost, sometime between 4 and 12 March.[12] Three of them were lost at sea and the other two had been driven into the Tyne and captured by the Royalists. The guns of Tynemouth Castle and a fort at South Shields effectively blocked the entrance to the river. Any ship entering would be unable to leave. This was a problem the Scots would address in due course. Some ships did make it safely to Sunderland. On the 10th two ships carrying meal arrived from Scotland and Captain Carres' ship from London arrived with a cargo of cheese and butter.[13] Even with the steady trickle of supplies provided by the arrival of these ships the Scots rarely had more than twenty-four hours' rations available for their army, while fodder for the horses seems to have been in even shorter supply.[14] In a letter to a friend in London a gentleman, with the initials W.R., who was resident with the Scots Army, suggests which commodities captains should carry to Sunderland:

> For the present you may know that we are Masters of a vast quantity of Coals belonging to this Port, most of it appertaining to Delinquents, which wilbe (I hope) a comfortable supply to London: But if you have any friends that intend hither for Coales, advise them to bring some provisions for the Army, especially six-shillings Beer, Hay, or Oates.[15]

Sunderland lay at the heart of a rich coal mining area. Before the commencement of hostilities London, and much of the south, had been supplied by coal carried from Sunderland and Newcastle. Obviously, with the North East in Royalist hands, this source of supply had dried up. The Londoners had spent a very cold winter and the price of wood and other fuel stuffs had rocketed as temperatures had fallen. Vast amounts of coal, belonging to Royalist supporters, had been captured. Here was a chance for entrepreneurial sea captains to turn a fast profit by sailing with provisions, which were readily available in the south, and selling them at a profit to the hungry Scots Army. They could then purchase coal with the profit and sell it at an even greater gain back in London. It is interesting to note the type of provisions the writer suggests: beer for the men and fodder for the horses – obviously both were in short supply. It should be noted that in the days before a ready supply of clean water, beer was the staple drink for both soldiers and civilians.

With the unreliable flow of supplies from the sea, the Scots had to look for other sources to sustain their army. The immediate area had been bled dry by previous Scots foraging expeditions and by the depredations of the Royalists, who had taken all that could be removed and burnt all that could not. That said, the areas to the north and south of the Scots quarter were relatively untouched. As the Royalists had withdrawn into Durham to recuperate, the Scots were presented with an ideal opportunity to expand their quartering areas. Two regiments of foot were left to garrison Sunderland, while seven more regiments crossed to the north bank of the Wear. The remainder of the army marched south towards Durham on either the 12th or the 13th. This move south provided the Scots with horse fodder for several days. Once this supply had been exhausted the Scots returned to Sunderland on the 16th.

The Scots commanders were still worried about the security of their base, which was in the process of being fortified. They did not want to move their army too far away in case a Royalist raid threatened it. On the 12th the Royalists burnt the Newbridge. This did not affect the Scots, as their eventual move south would be along the coast, but did provide them with a modicum of security for their western flank. With the return of the main army to Sunderland it was decided that the troublesome fort at South Shields should be attacked.

The Capture of the Fort at South Shields

The first attempt to take the fort at South Shields took place in the early hours of Saturday 16 March. The Scots attack hardly seems to have started before they withdrew.[16] In a Royalist account of the attack William Tunstall, in a letter to his father-in-law, writes:

> The Scotes set upon a litel fort at the Sheldes and was forsed backe, but the horse would not let the foute rune. Upon the place where they first asalted it there laye maney deade bodeyes. Upon the next asalt, being the same daye, they brought of there men, but with greate losse to them, Tinmouth Castle and the fort playing hotley upon them, and it was thought they lost towe hundred men that daye.[17]

The Scots accounts and Tunstall's vary somewhat. The Scots advance was halted by the guns of Tynemouth Castle and the fort, but the assault force was prevented from retreating by a body of Scots horse. After an abortive second attack the Scots withdrew, having suffered some losses, although the 200 men mentioned by Tunstall are highly unlikely. On the 19th the Scots held fast and in the early hours of the 20th returned to the assault.

Although the fort was not particularly large it was well constructed. Its surrounding ditch was 12 feet across and 11 deep. The ramparts of the fort rose 9 feet above the ground, giving a total height of 20 feet from the bottom of the ditch to the top of the rampart. It contained five iron guns, the smallest of which fired a 9-pound ball. These guns would usually cover the river but had been moved to the fort's landward side. It could also rely on the support of the guns in Tynemouth Castle and a ship, described as a frigate or a pinnace, moored close to it. The fort had a garrison of 100 men – seventy musketeers and thirty pike – commanded by Captain Chapman, a local man.

The Scots plan of attack involved two phases. First, a forlorn hope of 140 men, armed only with swords, would assault the fort. Some would be carrying ladders and others fascines – bundles of twigs or straw. Once the fascines had been used to fill the ditch, the ladders would be raised and the assault would begin. A second wave of attackers, musketeers supported by pikemen, would reinforce the forlorn hope at this point. The assault force was commanded by Colonel Stewart, Colonel Lyell, Lieutenant Colonel Bruce and Lieutenant Colonel Johnston. From the names of these officers it can be assumed that elements of at least three regiments took part: the Galloway regiment (Stewart), Lord Livingstone's regiment (Bruce) and the Master of Yester's regiment (Johnston). For the encouragement of his men the Earl of Leven was present and observed the assault.

Several contemporary accounts describe the attack.[18] Most agree in general but differ in the amount of detail they provide. The Scots forlorn hope reached the ditch and cast their bundles into it. They then set the assault ladders against the wall, although not all of them reached its top due to parts of the ditch not being as well filled as others. The forlorn hope then began the task of climbing the ladders and gaining a foothold inside the fort. Their support troops quickly followed them into the ditch and carried on the assault. The Royalist defenders fought bravely and held the Scots for over an hour, during which the Scots in the ditch were subjected to both musket fire and grapeshot. But the artillery was relatively ineffective once the Scots had reached the ditch, as their muzzles could not be brought to bear on the troops below. After an hour the Scots managed to gain the ramparts. At this point the bulk of the Royalist defenders began to withdraw down the beach towards the moored frigate. They were covered by a small group, a lieutenant and five men, who subsequently surrendered. The victorious Scots pursued the retreating Royalists down the beach but this pursuit was quickly halted by the fire of the waiting frigate.

In a hard-fought assault the Scots had captured the fort. In it they captured five iron guns, several barrels of powder and the defenders' colours. The Scots reported sixteen Royalists killed while they had lost only seven men and a number of others wounded (once again Tunstall gets a little carried away and writes of 300 Scots dead, almost certainly a gross exaggeration).

With the capture of the fort the Scots had opened the mouth of the Tyne for their shipping and closed it to that of the Royalists. It was also an excellent jump-off point for raiding the Royalist ships moored further upstream. On the 23rd the Scots took advantage of this and captured seven ships, two of them carrying salt, an important commodity.[19]

The assault on the fort at South Shields was not the only Scots success on the 20th. Lieutenant Colonel Ballantine, who had led the Scots cavalry charge at Corbridge, carried out a successful raid against a Royalist quarter at Chester-le-Street. Having gained information that a troop of Royalist horse were quartered there, he quietly led his men into the town and surprised the Royalists, capturing two captains of foot and twenty horsemen, along with forty horses.[20] It would not be the last time that Lieutenant Colonel Ballantine's name would be connected to such exploits.

The Battle of Bolden Hill

While the Scots had been busy taking the South Shields fort and raiding Newcastle's quarters, the Marquis had remained at Durham, resting and recuperating his men. On the 15th the Marquis of Montrose arrived at Durham and requested Newcastle to provide him with men for a crackpot scheme – no less than the invasion of Scotland. Newcastle had few men to spare but placed 200 of his horsemen under Montrose's command, after the Battle of Bolden Hill. With these Montrose departed, probably much to Newcastle's relief. When Montrose eventually reached Scotland he carried out a highly successful 'shoestring' campaign, tying up a large number of government troops with an army that never exceeded a few thousand men.

With his men and horses rested, Newcastle decided on another attempt to draw the Scots into an open battle. The bulk of the Scots Army was now on the north bank of the Wear, although Sunderland was heavily garrisoned. On 23 March Newcastle marched his army to Chester-le-Street with the intention of attacking the enemy on the following day, which was a Sunday. He hoped to gain an advantage by attacking them while they were celebrating the Lord's

Day. But his troops were not the only ones on the move. Sir James Lumsden, who had been left to blockade Newcastle, had crossed the Tyne with three regiments of foot, two of which must have been Lord Coupar's and Douglas of Kelhead's, as these two regiments marched south with the main army in April. Lumsden's force arrived at Sunderland on the 23rd. On the 24th Newcastle continued his march along the north bank of the Wear and faced the enemy near the village of Bolden, close to Hilton Castle. This has caused some confusion. The fighting of the 6th to 8th took place near the village of South Hilton, on the south side of the Wear. The fighting of the 24th and 25th was close to Hilton Castle but takes its name from the villages of East and West Bolden, and a hill lying close to the villages, Bolden Hill.

In contemporary accounts of the fighting on the 24th and 25th there are many contradictory statements.[21] The Scots provide much more detail on the infantry fighting of the 24th, while the Royalists do the same for the cavalry fight and withdrawal of the 25th. Even though the Royalists advanced under the cover of a foggy morning the Scots had prior warning and had time to draw up on Bedwick Hill. They had a few light guns with them but their larger field pieces were across the river in Sunderland. One of these heavy guns was ferried across the river by some Scots seamen who then dragged it into position. The falling tide prevented any further movement of the Scots ordnance.

Finding the Scots in position awaiting them, the Royalists drew up on Bolden Hill, to the west of the Scots position and close to Hilton Castle. The valley between the two armies was full of small enclosed fields and ditches. Once again it would largely be an infantry fight. At about five o'clock in the afternoon the guns of both sides opened a loud, but ineffective, bombardment of the lines opposite. Shortly afterwards Fraser's dragoons fired the opening shots against the Royalist forlorn hope. Newcastle sent four regiments of foot into the valley, while Leven reinforced Fraser with six regiments of foot. The Royalist guns attempted to support their outnumbered infantry in the valley but, once again, had little effect on the enemy. Numbers began to tell and slowly but surely, the Scots forced the Royalist foot back from one hedgerow to the next. This fighting went on for some time, ending between eleven o'clock on Sunday night and the early hours of Monday morning, depending on which account is believed.

Eventually the Royalist foot withdrew to the brow of Bolden Hill and the Scots were left in possession of the valley and a quantity of powder and ammunition left behind in the withdrawal. The Scots had lost a number of men dead and a larger number of wounded, including Patrick Leslie, the Lieutenant Colonel of the Earl of Lothian's regiment. Their claims to have caused more enemy casualties seem to be well substantiated. They possessed the ground the

Royalists had held and could see the number of dead and wounded they had left behind. They also had a report from the Constable of Bolden, who informed them of a convoy consisting of seven wagons sent back towards Durham by the Marquis of Newcastle, full of dead and wounded.

Newcastle must have been very frustrated by Leven's refusal to come out into the open to fight. During the night of the 24/25th he came to the conclusion that Leven would continue to hold his ground. The enclosed nature of the battlefield put Newcastle at a grave disadvantage and he had no option but to withdraw. He attempted to conceal the movement of his army by building two positions for his guns. Under the cover of this work the army began its retreat, and it was not until after noon that the Scots realised their enemies were actually pulling back. Leven then sent his regiments of horse in pursuit. The Scots horse caught Newcastle's rearguard of 500 troopers and badly mauled them, killing and capturing a number of officers and men – thirty according to a Royalist account – and capturing a cavalry standard. This was the opportunity for which the frustrated Royalist horse had been waiting. Sir Charles Lucas turned his brigade and charged the pursuing Scots horse. Although outnumbered, the Royalist troopers sent their Scots opponents packing, back to their main body on Bedwick Hill. As the Royalist horse resumed their withdrawal the Scots guns opened a fierce fire, which proved ineffective. The Scots horse, suitably chastened, followed the Royalists at some distance until nightfall, allowing the Marquis' army to complete its withdrawal to Durham unmolested.

The Scots Move South

After the Battle of Bolden Hill things quietened down for several days. As April approached, and the weather improved, the Scots supply situation had improved considerably. Leven decided that it was time to put pressure on the Marquis of Newcastle by marching towards Durham. In the meantime Newcastle had been busy writing to Prince Rupert. On the 25th he wrote the following letter:

> In the first place I congratulate your huge and great victories, which indeed is fit for none but your Highness. For all the affairs in the North I refer your Highness to this bearer, Sir John Mayne, who can tell your Highness every particular; only this I must assure your Highness that the Scots are as big again in foot as I am, and their horse, I doubt, much better then ours are, so that if your Highness do not please to come hither, and that very soon too, the great game of your uncle's will be endangered, if not lost; and with your Highness being near, certainly won: so I doubt not but your Highness will come, and that very soon.[22]

Newcastle was congratulating Rupert on his victory at Newark on 21 March. It is frustrating that the bulk of the message was sent by word of mouth, although from a security point of view it is understandable. In a second letter written on the 29th he writes:

> All your commands are obeyed, and ever shall be by me; and I give your Highness humble thanks for commanding me. They say Sir Thomas Fairfax is coming into Yorkshire for certain, which will much disturb his Majesty's affairs here. Could your Highness march this way it would, I hope, put a final end to our troubles: but I dare not urge this, but leave it to your Highness's great wisdom.[23]

Newcastle was keeping a weather eye on proceedings in Yorkshire. His fears were well founded. Both these letters urge Prince Rupert to bring his army north to defeat the Scots and this seems to be a recurring theme in Newcastle's correspondence with the Prince.

On 31 March the Scots began to move south. By the night of 1 April they were encamped at Easington, east of Durham. Hartlepool was one of Newcastle's main supply points and the Scots camp at Easington effectively blocked this supply route. On the 8th the Scots marched to Quarrington Hill, within a few miles of Durham. During the night of the 10th, Lieutenant Colonel Ballantine led another successful raid, capturing twenty men and thirty horses along with their equipment.[24] During the 12th Newcastle received a shattering piece of news: Selby had fallen to Lord Fairfax. His Yorkshire army had been destroyed, with the bulk of it being captured, including its commander, Colonel Belasyse. During the early hours of the 13th the Royalist Army marched south from Durham. The race for York was on.

The Scots did not discover Newcastle's absence until three o'clock in the afternoon. Upon learning this Leven immediately decided to follow Newcastle's army south into Yorkshire. The Royalists reached Bishop Auckland by nightfall on the 13th, while the Scots quartered at Ferry Hill. On the 14th both armies continued south, reaching Barnard Castle and Darlington respectively. John Somerville writes of a successful attack on the Royalist rearguard by a body of Scots horse:

> Our major commandit the pairtie; he with his pairtie tuik fourtie men and many horses, and slew many of their straggillars, and gatt two thousand merkis worth of silver plait, and mikill cheis, pork and bread.[25]

Both armies continued their march. On the 15th the Scots reached Northallerton and by the following day they were at Thormanby. On the 17th they marched to Boroughbridge and continued on to Wetherby on the 18th. They were visited in their quarters by Lord Fairfax and his son, Sir Thomas. On the 19th Leven reciprocated by visiting Lord Fairfax's army in its quarters. During this visit it was decided that the combined army should close on York. Tadcaster was to be the rendezvous and this was reached on the 20th. Having continued south, the Marquis of Newcastle reached York in the nick of time, arriving there on the 19th.[26] Within two days the armies of Lord Fairfax and the Earl of Leven would be before York's walls. In less than two weeks the whole situation in the north had changed. How had this come to pass?

Chapter 4

The Reconquest of Yorkshire

Absolutely the seat of the war will be in the north ...

As the Marquis of Newcastle marched north the situation he left behind in Yorkshire was very fluid. On the surface the Royalist position in Yorkshire was very strong but events conspired to prove that the strength of the Yorkshire Royalists was illusory. Newcastle held the whole of Yorkshire with the exception of Hull and his forces garrisoned parts of Lincolnshire, Derbyshire and Nottinghamshire. Lord Fairfax had been penned inside the defences of Hull since early in July 1643. His son, Sir Thomas, had joined with the Earl of Manchester's army in Lincolnshire. In late December 1643 he was ordered into Cheshire to assist Sir William Brereton against the local Royalists, commanded by Lord John Byron, and was still there as the campaign began.

Before his departure the Marquis attempted to put the troops he would leave behind in some semblance of order. A lack of time was not his only major problem. The Yorkshire gentry had promised him 10,000 recruits if he marched back from Derbyshire into Yorkshire[1] but these recruits were not forthcoming and the Marquis had to begin raising troops himself. By the time of his departure he had 5,000 foot and 3,000 horse in his marching army and was able to leave 3,000 foot and 1,500 horse in scattered garrisons throughout Yorkshire. Not only did the Marquis have a shortage of men, he also had no officer to leave as his commander. Sir William Saville, the obvious choice for the post, had recently died. Sir Thomas Glemham, another possible candidate, was commanding Newcastle's forces in Northumberland. To solve this problem Colonel John Belasyse was despatched from Oxford.[2] Belasyse was an experienced officer and had served with the King's army from the outset of the Edgehill campaign. He had commanded a brigade of foot at the Battle of Edgehill and had continued in command throughout 1643, leading the brigade at the first Battle of Newbury. It is known that Belasyse had arrived in York by 25 January, as he issued recruitment orders to a number of officers in the North Riding.[3] On the 29th, within a few days of Belasyse's arrival, Newcastle departed.

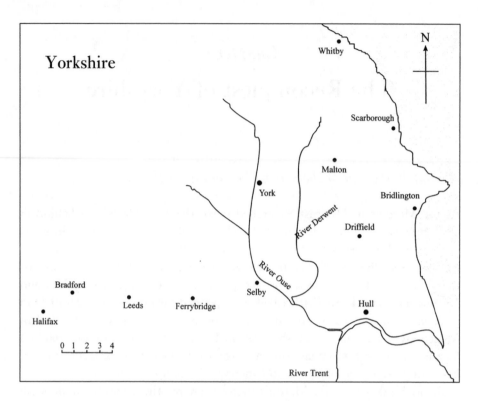

Upon his arrival at York Belasyse found that the state of the Royalist forces in the county left much to be desired. His secretary and biographer writes:

> Upon my lord's arrival at York he found great disorders amongst the King's party, by reason of the factions and discontents occasioned by the ill government and discipline of my Lord Newcastle's army.[4]

This seems a little at variance with the Duchess of Newcastle's account of the same events. She writes that her husband set about recruiting troops and 'when he had settled the affairs in Yorkshire, as well as time and his present condition would permit, and constituted an honourable person Governor of York and Commander-in-Chief of a very considerable party of horse and foot for the defence of the county' he marched north.[5] It should be borne in mind that both these accounts are written by partisans and the truth may lie somewhere between the two. Newcastle had begun the reorganisation of his Yorkshire forces but time and the Scots invasion conspired to prevent him from completing it.

Belasyse continued Newcastle's work upon his arrival and the Marquis' departure. A number of tasks faced him. First, he had to complete the reorganisation of the Yorkshire forces. To achieve this he began gathering his scattered garrisons to form a more cohesive defence. With these troops he had to cover possible incursions from three directions: Lord Fairfax's forces in Hull, Sir Thomas Fairfax's troops in Lancashire and the resurgent Parliamentarians in Nottinghamshire. Sir Charles Lucas, who had been sent north from Oxford with 1,000 horse and dragoons, had several small engagements against these Nottinghamshire troops. On 2 February he wrote a letter to Prince Rupert from Doncaster.[6] In it he warns of the possible consequences of leaving South Yorkshire bare of troops and the possibility of Newark's being cut off. He states that he had been left behind by the Marquis to prevent this happening. In due course Sir Charles would be called north by the Marquis and his prediction about Newark would come true.

As well as reorganising his own forces and defending Yorkshire from possible Parliamentarian incursions, Colonel Belasyse had a second task: to provide supplies and recruits to Newcastle's army in the north. Moone writes:

> Besides the care incumbent on him to preserve the country, my Lord Newcastle had imposed that of providing for his Army on the bishopric with money, provisions, ammunition and recruits of horse and men, so as no difficulty could possibly be greater to any person in His Majesty's service than those he was involved in through this employment.[7]

Belasyse had been set a Herculean task. Would he be up to it?

Caracoling in the East Riding

The Royalist situation in Yorkshire began to deteriorate very quickly. In a letter to the King, written from Newcastle and dated 16 February, the Marquis of Newcastle sums up the situation in the north:

> These enclosed will let your Majesty see that absolutely the seat of the war will be in the north, a great Army about Newark behind us, and the great Scotch Army before us, and Sir Thomas Fairfax very strong for the West Riding of Yorkshire, as they say, and his father master of the East Riding: so we are beset, not able to encounter the Scots, and shall not be able to make our retreat for the Army behind us.[8]

The summary given in this letter is not entirely accurate but within a few weeks would give a true picture of Belasyse's position in Yorkshire. On the 29th Sir John Meldrum, with an army of 7,000 men, laid down his siege lines around Newark. About the same date Colonel John Lambert, with the vanguard of Sir Thomas Fairfax's forces, had appeared in the West Riding and by the end of the month Lord Fairfax had gone a long way towards gaining control of the East Riding. Although his letter was written two weeks before the above actions took place, Newcastle had accurately predicted the course of events in Yorkshire.

As Colonel Belasyse gathered his scattered garrisons an opportunity presented itself to Lord Fairfax. In early February he ordered Sir William Constable to lead a raid into the East Riding and the Parliamentarian troops reached as far as Pickering. Belasyse despatched all his regiments of horse and a body of foot, all commanded by Sir Charles Lucas, to force Constable back into Hull. The Royalist scouts were unable to find Constable's force and this enabled him to surprise one of their quarters on or around 10 February. Three regiments of Royalist horse, Sir Walter Vavasour's, Sir John Key's and Sir Thomas Slingsby's, were attacked at Colham, possibly Kilham or Cowlam. Constable captured a large number of prisoners, including the major of Sir Thomas Slingsby's regiment, before returning to Hull.[9]

Pressing his advantage, Sir William did not remain in Hull for long. By the 12th he was at Bridlington, which he took with its garrison of 250 men. At some time between the 13th and the 19th he fought another successful action at Driffle.[10] Driffle is difficult to identify. Vicars describes it as lying between Malton and Scarborough. The only town in the East Riding whose name bears any resemblance to Driffle is Driffield, but this town lies 13 miles south of a direct line from Scarborough to Malton. Another Parliamentarian source identifies Constable's two fights as being at Cowlam and Burton Agnes.[11] Burton Agnes is close to Driffield, so Vicar's 'Driffle' could be correct, although his geography is a little out. Bypassing Scarborough, which was held for the King by Sir Hugh Cholmley, Constable next struck at Whitby on the 20th. Once again he successfully gained the town plus 500 officers and men and a large number of guns taken from ships in the harbour.[12] Swinging inland towards York, Constable surprised the garrison of Stamford Bridge, capturing three guns, on or around the 22nd. This is confirmed in a letter written from Bradford by Colonel Lambert on 11 March.[13] He then returned to Hull.

Towards the end of the month Lord Fairfax received an interesting letter from the Committee of Both Kingdoms.[14] As mentioned in Chapter Three, the state of the North Sea had caused major problems with supplying the Scots Army at Sunderland. It was also causing considerable problems with maintaining communications between London and the Scots Army. They requested that Lord Fairfax attempt to open an overland line of communication with the Scots, while the forces in Lancashire would open another. By the end of February Lord Fairfax had control over much of the East Riding and had succeeded in opening a line of communications with the Scots. It was now time for his son to move back into the West Riding.

Lambert at Bradford

Sir Thomas Fairfax had been despatched into Cheshire in late December 1643. His objective was the relief of Nantwich, besieged by Lord Byron. Several Parliamentarian forces were in a position to carry out this task and Sir Thomas considered his the least prepared:

> But in ye Coldest season of it, I was ordered by ye parlamt to goe & raise ye seidge of Nantwich, wch ye Lord Byron wth ye Irish Army had reduced to great extremity, I was ye most unfit of all ye Forces, being ever ye worst pd, my men sickly, & almost naked for want of clothes. I desired ye parlamt they would please to supply those wants (not to excuse myselfe, as some, who hade no will to stir, though well enough accommodated wth all these, & a businesse of so much Importance).[15]

The Committee of Both Kingdoms was adamant that Sir Thomas carry out his orders. He paid for new clothing for 1,500 of his men out of his own pocket, and set off across the Pennines on 29 December. Stopping at Manchester he gathered a small force of Lancashire troops and continued his march towards Nantwich. On 24 January Lord Byron raised the siege and marched to face Fairfax's approaching force. On the 25th Sir Thomas defeated Byron's Royalist troops, forcing them to withdraw to Chester with heavy losses in casualties and prisoners. Sir Thomas's victory was to have a great effect on the campaign in the north. As a direct consequence of Byron's defeat, the King despatched Prince Rupert to Shrewsbury. In due course Rupert would continue his march north through Lancashire and on into Yorkshire. In the short term Sir Thomas's victory swung the balance of power in Lancashire to the Parliamentarian side. With the exception of Lathom House, held in her husband's absence by the Countess of Derby, the whole of Lancashire came under Parliamentarian control.

By the end of February Sir Thomas was ready to move back into Yorkshire. In preparation for this he despatched his vanguard, under Colonel John Lambert, into the West Riding. It is difficult to ascertain exactly the date of Lambert's march. Captain John Hodgson, a Bradford man who accompanied Lambert, writes that the Parliamentarian force marched through Sowerby Bridge to Halifax, then to Keighley and finally into Bradford.[16] The town was held by a small Royalist force and this was driven out by Lambert's men. There has been much confusion about the actions in West Yorkshire in February and March 1644. Writers from the time of the Civil War report a single action at Bradford and this has led to modern historians perpetuating the error. Peter Newman was the first author to write of two actions at Bradford, one on 3 March and another on the 25th.[17] Although the present author disagrees with the date for the first action, Newman's evidence for two separate actions is convincing. The lynchpin of Newman's evidence is the movements of Sir Charles Lucas, as will be shown.

Two accounts exist of Lambert's arrival at Bradford.[18] The Parliamentarian troops quickly drove a small garrison from the town. As the horse pursued the retreating Royalists they were met by a body of Royalist horse commanded by Sir Charles Lucas. Lucas drove Lambert's troopers back into Bradford but was stopped by Lambert's foot and driven from the town. It is difficult to put an exact date to these events. What is known is that Lambert was in possession of the town by 6 March. On that day he wrote a letter to Sir Thomas Fairfax reporting a successful raid against Hunslet, in which a large number of Royalist troops were captured.[19] Obviously, for Lambert to have felt secure enough to start raiding local Royalist garrisons, the fight for Bradford must have happened several days before. Another factor that points to a date in late February or early March is the whereabouts of Sir Charles Lucas. Three separate contemporary accounts of the Battle of Hilton mention Sir Charles being at Durham, with the Marquis of Newcastle, by 6 March.[20] It would have taken several days for Lucas to march from Bradford to Durham, so the 3rd is possibly a little too late and the 1st more likely. Whatever the actual date of the first action at Bradford, Colonel Belasyse had a serious problem on his hands and had to move quickly to stabilise the situation.

The Royalists Reorganise

In response to the Parliamentarian incursions into the East and West Ridings, Colonel Belasyse began a reorganisation of his forces. He divided his horse into three bodies.[21] One at Leeds would cover the West Riding, another at Malton would cover the East Riding, and a third at York would protect the North Riding. The body at York was also ideally suited to support the other two, should the need arise. Garrisons of foot were placed in Halifax, Leeds, Doncaster and Stamford Bridge. This obviously occurred after Lambert's march to Bradford, as his force passed through Halifax on its way to its objective and no fighting was reported there. John Lambert reports the movement of Royalist troops to Leeds: 'The enemy is fortifying Tadcaster; and even now I hear that he is marched towards Leeds with eighteen colours of foot and the demi-cannon.'[22]

At about the same time Belasyse seems to have gathered a force of 1,500 horse and 5,000 foot at Selby, which he made his headquarters.[23] All these moves seem to be perfectly reasonable, with garrisons covering the approach routes of both Parliamentarian forces arrayed against him. Selby was particularly important as a crossing over the River Ouse. It was also an obvious rendezvous for a force advancing from the direction of Bradford and Leeds and another moving north-west from Hull. Colonel Belasyse's objective was to prevent Lord Fairfax and his son, Sir Thomas, from combining their forces and he had been ordered to adopt a defensive posture as the Duchess of Newcastle writes:

> For the Governor whom he had left behind with sufficient forces for the defence of that country, although he had orders not to encounter the enemy, but to keep himself in a defensive posture; yet being a man of great valour and courage, it transported him so much, that he resolved to face the enemy.[24]

It is difficult to imagine Newcastle having given an order not to engage the enemy, if the opportunity to do so with numerical superiority presented itself, and towards the end of the month this is exactly what Belasyse did.

*   *   *

While Colonel Belasyse had been reorganising his forces what had the Parliamentarian commanders been doing? The Fairfaxes seem to have been busy recruiting and preparing their forces for their forthcoming advance. As mentioned earlier, Colonel Lambert busied himself raiding nearby Royalist quarters. In London the Committee of Both Kingdoms began despatching a series of orders to their Northern commanders. On 5 March similar letters were sent to both Lord Fairfax and his son.[25] The Committee desired the two commanders to combine their forces and bring pressure to bear on the Royalists in Yorkshire, which would prevent Belasyse from sending reinforcements to the Marquis' army at Durham. If possible they were to move towards the Tees to assist the Scots Army, which had recently arrived at Sunderland.

On the 8th two further letters were despatched to Sir Thomas. The first was very similar to the letter sent on the 5th.[26] He was to march into the West Riding with all his horse and two regiments of Lancashire foot. Contained in this letter were two letters for the colonels of the Lancashire regiments, which would accompany Sir Thomas.[27] The names of the two colonels were left blank so that Sir Thomas could choose which units he would take. The second letter of the 8th ordered Sir Thomas to detach six troops of horse to the Earl of Denbigh in Shropshire.[28] This is a good example of political interference and further examples will be shown in a later chapter.

By the 20th the Committee of Both Kingdoms had sent Sir Thomas duplicates of the letters of the 8th but had changed their minds about the despatch of the six troops to the Earl of Denbigh:

We now think fit that those six troops then appointed to go for Shropshire shall march with you into Yorkshire, and that for that purpose have sent you six letters which you are to direct to those captains of horse that you will have to go with you in that service.[29]

On the same day, the Committee sent a letter to Lord Fairfax reiterating their earlier communications.[30] They also promised him a reinforcement of 200 foot and the return of his own foot regiments serving at Newark with Sir John Meldrum. How many of these reinforcements arrived is open to debate. On the following day, the 21st, Prince Rupert surprised Meldrum's besieging army at Newark and forced it to surrender. Meldrum's defeat allowed a body of 1,000 Nottinghamshire horse, under Sir Gervase Lucas and Colonel George Porter, to reinforce Colonel Belasyse.[31] The arrival of these reinforcements allowed Belasyse to move against Lambert at Bradford, before he could be reinforced by Sir Thomas Fairfax.

Once again it is difficult to give an exact date for the second action at Bradford. It must have been between 21 March, the date of Meldrum's defeat at Newark, and 2 April, when Sir Samuel Luke reported an action at Bradford 'last week'.[32] Allowing a couple of days for their march north, Lucas and Porter could not have reinforced Belasyse before the 23rd. Allowing another two days for the combined force's march from Selby to Leeds and then on to Bradford gives a date of 25 March. This date is put forward by Peter Newman and must be close to the actual date of the action.[33]

Belasyse left Selby with a force of 1,000 foot and 500 horse and was met en route by Lucas and Porter with another 1,000 horse. Contemporary accounts are in agreement as to the main events of the fight at Bradford.[34] Lambert sallied out of the town with his horse to oppose the Royalists' advance, but being badly outnumbered he was forced back into his works. The Royalist foot gallantly assaulted the town but were held by the Parliamentarian garrison. Vicars reports that towards evening the garrison began to run out of powder.[35] Lambert called a council of war and it was decided that a breakout to Halifax would be attempted. Lambert's troops successfully defeated a body of Royalist horse, commanded by Colonel Porter, capturing Colonel William Bradshaw in the process, and continued their withdrawal to Halifax. Although the Royalists had taken the town they too had run out of powder. With this in mind, Belasyse decided to withdraw to Leeds.

By nightfall both sides were withdrawing and Bradford was left to its own devices. When Lambert realised that the Royalists had not occupied the town he returned and re-established his garrison. Colonel Belasyse continued his withdrawal to his starting point at Selby, where he awaited events. Porter seems to have got the blame for the Royalist failure at Bradford: taking offence, he joined forces with Sir Gervase and marched back to Newark.

The Storming of Selby

On 1 April the Committee of Both Kingdoms despatched two orders, one to Lord Fairfax and the other to Sir Thomas Fairfax.[36] Sir Thomas was to march with his horse and dragoons without delay and combine with his father's forces. The combined army was then to march to the Tees to assist the Scots. Lord Fairfax received a similar command. He was also to march without delay, with any troops that were ready, to join his son. But by the time these orders arrived, Lord Fairfax and Sir Thomas had put another plan into action.

On 9 April the two commanders met at Ferrybridge. Lord Fairfax had left Hull on the 7th and had a difficult march through the marshes 10 miles below Selby. On the 9th Sir Thomas received his orders from the Committee of Both Kingdoms, but chose to delay his departure:

> Here I received another command from ye Parlamt to march Immediately wth my Horse & Dragoones into Northumberland to Joyne wth ye Scotts Army. The E. of Newcastle who was yn, at Durham, being much stronger in Horse yn they; for want of wch they could advance no furthur. But it being resolved, wthin a day or 2 to storme Selby, I stayed till yt businesse was over; wch proved as effectual for ye Releife of ye Scotts Army.[37]

On Wednesday 10 April Lord Fairfax's army began its approach to Selby. Lord Fairfax, in a letter to the Committee of Both Kingdoms, reports that the Parliamentarian force comprised 2,000 horse and dragoons and 2,000 foot.[38] He also reports the strength of the Royalist defenders as 1,500 horse and 1,800 foot. The only other contemporary writer to give a figure for the Royalist force was Sir Thomas Fairfax, who put Belasyse's total force at 2,000 men.[39] As will be seen from the number of prisoners taken, Lord Fairfax's figure is probably the closer. As the Parliamentarian force approached the town Colonel Belasyse ordered a body of horse to intercept it. Lord Fairfax's advance guard of horse quickly drove the Royalists back into the town, taking a number of prisoners, and by nightfall the Parliamentarian Army was in position to attack the town on the following morning.[40] Lord Fairfax sent a summons to surrender, which Colonel Belasyse promptly refused.[41] As night fell both armies waited to see what daylight would bring.

Although it was not a fortified town, nature had made Selby a difficult place to attack. The town was almost surrounded by water obstacles. Along its north side ran the River Ouse, while to the west was Selby Mill Dam, which ran into the Ouse. To the east the fishponds of the old abbey covered the approaches to the town. Both the Mill Dam and the fishponds had a tendency to flood at certain times of the year and this seems to have been the case in early April 1644. The only approach not covered by a water obstacle was from the south, between Gowthorpe and Brayton Lane. But what nature had failed to do, man had done. During his occupation of the town in 1643 Lord Fairfax had completed its water defences by digging a ditch between the town's two southern entrances. Four roads ran into the town and because of the water obstacles these were the only entry points. On the eastern side of the town Ousegate ran alongside the river, as its name suggests. This was the widest road into the town and, as will be seen, the weakest point in the defences. Gowthorpe entered the town from the south-west and was joined by Brayton Lane, coming from the south-east, several hundred yards below the market place. The final road into the town was Mill Gate. This ran in a northwesterly direction towards Cawood. With the exception of Mill Lane all the entrances to the town were barricaded and defended. Mill Lane was considered too narrow to need defending and this is borne out by Lord Fairfax not attacking it.

Lord Fairfax planned to attack the town in three places: Ousegate, Gowthorpe and Brayton Lane. He divided his forces into three bodies, each comprising horse and foot. The foot would assault the defences and once they had cleared a gap the horse would attack into the town. Lord Fairfax commanded the troops attacking along Ousegate and his son commanded their supporting horse. The other two bodies were commanded by Sir John Meldrum and Colonel Needham, although which body attacked along Gowthorpe and which attacked along Brayton Lane is not clear.[42]

Several accounts exist of the engagement and, for once, they are very much in agreement.[43] The Royalists fought bravely and held their lines for several hours. Finally, Lord Fairfax's regiment gained the barricade at the end of Ousegate. One Royalist officer, Captain Wilson, was blamed for the Parliamentarian success and was later tried and condemned. The Parliamentarian foot were unable to make further progress because of the threat of the Royalist horse further up Ousegate. Sir Thomas Fairfax's men cleared the barricade and charged the Royalist horse, which quickly broke and fled over the bridge of boats towards York. Sir Thomas was then counter-attacked by another body of horse, commanded by Colonel Belasyse himself. This time the Parliamentarian troopers were driven back. Sir Thomas was unhorsed and found himself in the midst of Belasyse's men. Fortunately, Sir Thomas's men rallied and charged to their commander's rescue. Once again the Royalist troopers broke and galloped across the bridge of boats towards York. Colonel Belasyse and some of his officers found themselves surrounded. Belasyse fought gallantly but was wounded twice and unhorsed. It was only the quality of his armour that prevented his being killed. Belasyse was taken prisoner and Lord Fairfax's own surgeon tended his wounds.

With the capture of their commander, and the Parliamentarian entry into the town along Ousegate, the Royalist defenders broke, allowing Fairfax's men to enter the town at all points. The defenders – or at lease those who were able – fled the town towards York and Pontefract, pursued closely by Sir Thomas's horse. Few of the Royalist foot escaped from the town, most of them being captured. Reports of the number of prisoners taken vary. Two contemporary accounts list the officers captured by name. The first list names eighty officers and reports 1,600 common soldiers being taken as prisoners.[44] The second names 104 officers but also gives 1,600 as the number of other ranks captured.[45] Interestingly, the names differ slightly between the two lists. Sir Henry Slingsby gives the number of prisoners taken as '80 officers besides Comon souldgiers',[46] while *Hulls Managing* reports '100 Officers besides, and more than 2000 common Souldiers'[47] captured. Although the numbers differ slightly between these accounts, it can be seen that Belasyse's army had virtually ceased to exist. Lord Fairfax also reports the capture of a large quantity of arms and ammunition: four brass guns, 2,000 arms, seven barrels of powder and sixteen bundles of match.[48] The captured supplies would have been a great boon to Lord Fairfax, as his army often operated on a 'shoestring'. He also reports the capture of a large number of horse and foot standards, although his men do not seem to have been very forthcoming with them.

With the fall of Selby the situation in both Yorkshire and the north-east changed considerably. As was shown in Chapter Three, Belasyse's defeat caused the Marquis of Newcastle to withdraw from Durham and race south to York. The Scots Army pursued him closely and by the 18th had arrived at Wetherby. On the 20th the Scots Army met Lord Fairfax's force at Tadcaster. This Allied Army then marched on to York, arriving in quarters before its walls on the 22nd. During the night the Marquis of Newcastle took the sensible precaution of despatching the bulk of his horse southwards, under the command of Sir Charles Lucas. The Marquis had decided to stand a siege. Sending his horse south had two advantages: first, horses were of limited use in a siege and consumed precious food supplies; second, the horse troopers would be far more effective operating in the open, possibly forming part of a relieving army. Although the Royalist horse managed to escape to the south, the Allied cavalry was sent off in pursuit, killing and capturing a number.[49] Meanwhile, the Allied Army began digging its siege lines and the Siege of York began.

Chapter 5

The Siege of York

Having closely besieged the city on all sides ...

On 22 April 1644 the Allied Army moved into position close to York. The Scots Army covered the area on the south bank of the River Ouse. Their main quarters were at Bishopthorpe and Middlethorpe. Lord Fairfax's army moved onto the north bank of the Ouse and covered the area between the Ouse and the Foss. His main quarters were at Fulford and Heslington. The Allied Army did not have enough men to complete the encirclement of the town, so the area between the north bank of the Ouse and the west bank of the Foss was left open. Initially, cavalry patrols were used to attempt to close off this area and prevent men and supplies from entering the city. These patrols do not seem to have been particularly successful, as Sir Henry Slingsby reports: 'Thus we were blockt up upon two sides of ye town, & the rest we had open for about 3 weeks, until, such times as my Ld Manchester came with his Norfolk men.'[1]

Sir Henry is a little out in his estimate of the time before the Earl of Manchester's army arrived. Five weeks elapsed before his arrival, on 3 June, as opposed to three as Sir Henry states. He also mentions the building of a 'bridge of boats' across the Ouse to connect the two armies. One of the Allies' main worries at this time was their vulnerability to a sudden attack from the besieged garrison, for the Marquis of Newcastle was operating on interior lines and his men could quickly pass from one part of York to another via the city's bridges. Having concentrated his men he could swiftly strike before his enemy could gather to oppose him. In order to counter Newcastle's advantage, the two Allied commanders kept their forces concentrated – thus leaving the north side of the city open – and built a bridge of boats to allow each army to support the other in the event of a major attack from the city. The fact that no such attack took place speaks volumes about Newcastle's caution, as opposed to the Allied commanders' lack of preparation. When Newcastle sent the bulk of his horse south, during the night of the 22nd, the likelihood of a major sally from the city became even less likely. And yet, to make doubly sure they would not be surprised, the Allies fixed their lines some distance from the city walls, as one

Parliamentarian source writes:

> Our Guards being at such a distance from the City, they cannot well sally
> forth in any parties to our prejudice, for first our men have more time to
> make ready, and then while they assault one quarter, the two next can
> more easily strike in betwixt them and home, to intercept their retreat.[2]

As will be seen in due course this plan seems to have worked well, for the few
sallies from the city had little effect.

The supply situation in York was good. Sir Henry Slingsby writes 'of provisions we had in good store in ye town',[3] while the author of *Hulls Managing*
reports that the Royalists were 'much straitned for flesh, meat, & salt, but of
corne they have no lack'.[4] One of the reasons for Newcastle's despatch of the
bulk of his horse was to conserve supplies, for several thousand horses, and the
men they carried, would quickly deplete even a plentiful supply of corn.

The Allied commanders found themselves in a similar position to the
Scots when they had arrived before Newcastle in early February. They were
besieging a well-fortified city with an ample garrison. Their force could not
completely surround the city and, until it could, the city could not be starved
into submission. More troops were needed to complete the ring around York,
but could they be found? Fortunately for Leven and Fairfax, another army was
operating not far to their south, in Lincolnshire. If the Earl of Manchester
could be persuaded to bring his Army of the Eastern Association to York, then
a real siege could begin. With this in mind, a deputation, comprising the Earl of
Crawford-Lindsey and Sir Thomas Fairfax, was sent to discuss the matter with
him. Fortunately for the Allied commanders, Manchester readily agreed to
move northwards once Lincoln had been taken. Until his arrival the Allied
commanders would do their best to pin Newcastle's forces inside York and
prevent supplies reaching him from the north.

The March of the Northern Horse

As a brief aside from the Siege of York, it is worth discussing the movements of
the Northern Horse, as Newcastle's cavalry will be referred to. As has already
been mentioned, Newcastle ordered Sir Charles Lucas to take his men from
York to the south. Lucas's orders were to march into Derbyshire, Nottinghamshire and Leicestershire and keep his men supplied.[5] His other objectives
would have been to raise recruits to enable him to march to York's relief or to
attach himself to Prince Rupert's army if the Prince moved north with the same
objective. Whether Rupert would move north, or march into the south to support the King, was still not known. The Northern Horse's march from York
was not without incident. Even though the march was undertaken at night they

were pursued by the Allied horse. Their rearguard was overtaken and in a brief running fight the Allies took sixty prisoners. Fortunately for Sir Charles, the bulk of his men escaped into South Yorkshire.

The next report of the movements of the Northern Horse is from the Siege of Lincoln. John Rushworth writes:

> Next day [4 May] they had notice, that a great Body of Horse, to the Number of five or six thousand, under Colonel Goring's command, were coming to relieve the City, this hastened Manchester into a Resolution to storm them [Lincoln] that afternoon, and to that instant the Scaling Ladders were brought forth, and the Foot were ready to set on; but understanding the said Horse could not come up that Night, it was put off till next Morning; and to prevent the Relief expected, Cromwell with two thousand Horse was sent to meet them.[6]

The two bodies of cavalry do not seem to have come into contact, with the Royalists withdrawing at Cromwell's approach. Colonel Goring could not have commanded this abortive relief attempt. He had been captured at the storming of Wakefield on 21 May 1643[7] and had not been exchanged until early April 1644. He left Oxford with a regiment of horse on 10 May and assumed command of the Northern Horse shortly afterwards. Simeon Ash, chaplain to the Earl of Manchester, reports a clash between a large body of horse and the Eastern Association horse, commanded by Cromwell.[8] The date of this action is not given but in the context of Ash's letter it seems to have taken place after Manchester had begun to move his army north, towards the end of May, and not before Lincoln had fallen on the 5th.

After this clash the Northern Horse moved into Leicestershire and began to raise recruits and money. On the 25th the Committee of Both Kingdoms sent a letter to the Earl of Manchester:

> We have certain intelligence of the great damage done to the counties of Leicester and Stafford, and those parts by Lord Newcastle's horse that have come from York, and how they have recruited themselves to a very great strength, raised at least 1,000 horse and 10,000 l. [£10,000], and are now about 3,000 horse and dragoons near Uttoxeter in Staffordshire, which we hear with 1,000 horse might have been wholly prevented. They still increase their force, raise much money, and ruin those that depend on protection from the Parliament.[9]

As well as informing the Earl of the movements of the Northern Horse this letter is also mildly rebuking him for not preventing the depredations committed against Leicestershire and Staffordshire.

On 28 May Sir John Meldrum, commander of the garrison of Manchester, reports the presence of a body of horse with Goring, Lucas and Langdale in Derbyshire.[10] Sir John wrote another letter on the 31st, to the Earl of Denbigh, informing him that 'the Marquis of Newcastle's horse, not exceeding 3,000 as I am credibly informed, and 100 foot, without ordnance, lying upon the frontiers of Yorkshire, betwixt Woodhead and Stopford [Stockport]'.[11]

On 1 June the Earl of Manchester replied to the Committee of Both Kingdom's letter.[12] In answer to their rebuke he wrote that his horse had been unable to interfere with Newcastle's men because they could not get across the Trent due to heavy rains having swollen the river. Manchester's horse had moved towards Nottingham, where they would be able to cross the Trent. This movement had caused the Northern Horse to move further westwards, crossing the Trent at Burton and then moving on to Uttoxeter. They had then moved north towards Sheffield, but once again had moved towards the west when Sir Thomas Fairfax had approached them. Sir John Gell, the Parliamentarian commander in Derbyshire, reported Goring's approach towards Sheffield and that the Royalists had left their baggage train at Sheffield Castle before attempting to cross through the Peak District into Cheshire, in a letter to the Committee of Both Kingdoms, dated 1 June.[13]

The final report of Newcastle's horse as an independent body comes in a letter from the three Allied commanders at York on 5 June.[14] In it they report that 'on Monday Last we hear that General Goring with all or part of his horse are joined to Prince Rupert's army at Bury'. This is confirmed by a Royalist source, which states that Goring and his men joined Prince Rupert at Bury on 30 May.[15] The further movements of the Northern Horse as part of Prince Rupert's army will be discussed in the next chapter.

Manchester Moves North

With the fall of Lincoln on 5 May the Earl of Manchester was free to move against the enemy as he saw fit. After a meeting with the Earl of Crawford-Lindsey and Sir Thomas Fairfax, Manchester had decided to join his army to those of the Earl of Leven and Lord Fairfax, who were besieging York. His first task was to find a good crossing point on the Trent. With this in mind he sent two regiments of foot with some guns to Gainsborough. His pioneers built a bridge of boats there and this would be his main crossing point. In siege operations his regiments of horse would be of limited use and with this in mind he despatched Lieutenant General Oliver Cromwell, with 2,000 horse, across the Trent towards Bawtry, Retford and Tuxford. Cromwell was to combine with a body of Scots horse and shadow the movements of the Northern Horse. The remainder of Manchester's army would march north to York.

On Friday 24 May Manchester's army marched from Lincoln to Gains-borough. It was a tough march. Simeon Ash, who accompanied the army, writes that: 'we were compelled to leave our greatest Ordinance behind us, the wayes being deep, by reason of great rain which hath been in these parts.'[16] On the following day the army crossed the River Trent and marched into the Isle of Axholme. The Sunday was used to provide much needed rest for the army after two days' marching on muddy tracks. Manchester, however, did not rest, but visited Cromwell and his other commanders of horse. On the Monday the army continued to Thorne. Once again Manchester did not remain with the army but rode to York to consult with the Earl of Leven and Lord Fairfax, returning to meet his army at Selby on the Tuesday evening.

Manchester's army remained at Selby for several days. On the 31st a meeting was held at Eskrick, at the house of Lord Howard. The three Allied commanders discussed the siege at York and Manchester's prospective role in it. It was decided that Manchester's army would fill the gap in the encircling lines – the area between the north bank of the Ouse and the west bank of the Foss. An officer was despatched to find quarters for the army to move into. Once the decision had been taken Manchester began to move his forces. On Saturday 1 June part of his army marched north towards York. The remainder of his men continued their stay at Selby. From there Manchester wrote to the Committee of Both Kingdoms.[17] He informed them that Sir John Meldrum had been despatched from the leaguer at York with two regiments, one of which was Scots. He was to reinforce the garrison of Manchester and oppose Prince Rupert's march through Lancashire. Manchester also informed them of the Allied commanders' resolution to continue the Siege of York:

> I believe we shall use all means to give some speedy issue to this siege of York, that so all our forces may be ready to oppose any enemy whereso-ever they are, for the engagement is such now, and the consequences of carrying this place so great, as they cannot undertake any other action until this be finished.

This was the first warning from the triumvirate of commanders that they would not split their forces, or abandon the Siege of York, to react to Prince Rupert's movements. This would become a continuing theme throughout the siege.

While Manchester moved from Lincolnshire towards York, the Earl of Leven and Lord Fairfax had not rested on their laurels. Much of their horse had been despatched into the West Riding to cover the movements of the Northern Horse. The two generals had also been reinforcing their position by capturing a number of enemy positions. In a letter from the Committee

of Both Kingdoms to Sir William Waller, who was marching through the
Midlands in pursuit of the King's army, they report the capture of two such
positions:

> Good success in Yorkshire; Cawood, a strong castle near York, is yielded,
> and 140 prisoners taken, most of whom have taken the covenant and bear
> arms for the Parliament. A fort at Aire-mouth, which commands a con-
> siderable pass upon the West Riding, is also taken.[18]

Cawood Castle was an important position. It lay on the west bank of the Ouse
between Selby and York. The importance of the position was not missed by the
Royalists who later attempted to recapture it. A party of horse from Pontefract
Castle launched a surprise attack on the castle but were prevented from
capturing it by the vigilance of the sentries.[19] Although the attempt had failed a
number of prisoners escaped in the confusion.

On Monday 3 June Manchester's army completed its march into its quarters
to the north-west of York. It was a long march 'little lesse then 12 Northerne
miles',[20] in heavy rain during the morning. The men completed the march with
few complaints and Manchester dismounted from his horse to march most of
the way on foot with his men. As Manchester's troops filed into their quarters a
body of Royalist horse attempted to break out towards Scarborough. The
author of *Hulls Managing* reports the consequences of this sally:

> In particular upon Munday the third of Iune instant, a partee of horse
> sallyed out towards our Quarters at Clifton, intending to breake through
> and advance towards Scarborough, being discovered our horse divided
> themselves into three Squadrons, the middle charged them, the other two
> wheeled about upon their right and left, and charged them in the reare,
> and so having encompassed them, cut most of them off; took 67 horse,
> very few escaped to carry the news to Yorke.[21]

The Royalist horse had been caught in a classic pincer movement from which
few escaped. With the arrival of Manchester's army the ring around York had
closed and the siege proper began.

The Great and Close Siege

It would be expected after their long march on the 3rd, that Manchester's men
would have spent the 4th in resting. Although many did rest others were more
active. Simeon Ash writes: 'some of them upon their owne accord went up to
the walls of Yorke, and fetched out of the Pastures there oxen, kine and some
horse.'[22] Obviously, some of Manchester's men were eager for the fray. The
three Allied commanders held a meeting to decide the course of the siege.

Over the next few days the decisions taken at this meeting became evident. Throughout the day there were a number of small skirmishes between the Allied troops and the defenders of York. Although few details were recorded of these skirmishes, the Duchess of Newcastle writes of an attempt by Allied troops to clear the city gates as the Royalist defenders attempted to block them.[23]

The first of the decisions taken on the 4th was put into action on the 5th. The Scots Army and that of the Earl of Manchester formed into battle lines and advanced on the city, as if intent on assaulting it. In fact this was merely a diversion. While the attention of the defenders was drawn to the northern and western walls of the city, Lord Fairfax's men raised a battery of five guns 'upon ye Windmill hill, which lay close to Walmgate Bar, in the direction of Hesslington'.[24] Simeon Ash mentions that this battery was 'within lesse then Musquet shot of the Towne'.[25] Fairfax's men also captured the suburbs outside Walmgate Bar and planted two guns in the street opposite it. A third gun was positioned close to 'ye Dovecoat', obviously a local landmark at the time.[26] The ability of Fairfax's soldiers to plant guns so close to one of the city's main gates shows a major deficiency in the Royalists' defensive planning. At Newcastle, in February, the suburbs of the city had been burnt down on the approach of the Scots Army, to deny them a covered approach to the city. The same should have been done at York but was not. Belated attempts were made to rectify this, as will be shown, but were unsuccessful. Because of the Royalists' failure to burn the suburbs the Allied troops had a covered approach to at least two of the main gates: Bootham Bar and Walmgate Bar.

The Allied commanders were still under pressure from the Committee of Both Kingdoms to provide support for the defenders of Lancashire who, by this time, were under severe pressure from Prince Rupert. The Committee had despatched Sir Henry Vane to the leaguer at York to ascertain the true situation and the ability of the Allied forces to send such assistance. On 5 June the Allied commanders once again wrote to the Committee to sum up their situation:

> For by this accession of forces Prince Rupert's Army is so increased as we think it not safe to divide our men, and send a part to encounter him in Lancashire. If we should raise our siege before York and march with all our forces against him, it is in his discretion to avoid us, and either pass by another way than we take, and so come into Yorkshire, or else retire into Cheshire, whither if we should pursue him, it would be in the Marquis of Newcastle's power, in our absence, to recover all Yorkshire again and increase his Army to as great a strength as ever it was.[27]

This refusal to divide their forces made sound strategic sense and it is easy to imagine the disaster that would have taken place if part of their force had been sent into Lancashire to face Prince Rupert.

On 6 June the Allied troops continued to move into the suburbs. Simeon Ash reports two separate attacks by the Earl of Manchester's army.[28] The first was a raid by a small force led by a 'Corporal of Horse'. Having entered the eastern suburbs they killed five of Newcastle's men, for no loss, and returned to their own lines with 'some goods'. This raid was just Manchester's men flexing their muscles and enriching their pockets. The second attack was part of the siege plan. Manchester's troops attacked into the suburbs along Bootham. The attack was successful and, for the loss of five or six men, Manchester's army had begun its approach to Bootham Bar and the King's Manor.

The 7th seems to have passed quietly, although the guns on both sides kept up a steady bombardment of the enemy lines. In the early hours of Saturday 8 June, the first major action of the siege took place. To the west of York lay three small forts. These forts prevented the Scots from approaching the city walls and had to be taken. Two accounts exist of the Scots assaults, interestingly one Royalist and the other Allied.[29] The first fort the Scots attacked had a garrison of 120 men, of which sixty were killed and the rest captured. The second fort was also taken with the loss or capture of its garrison of fifty men. The third fort was saved by the sally from Micklegate Bar, the only gate not sealed up, of a strong force of horse and foot. One of the captured forts was demolished and the other garrisoned. The Royalists had lost about 170 men killed or captured. Scots losses are not as clear. Simeon Ash reports ten officers and men killed but 'many others wounded'. Sir Henry Slingsby belittles the Scots effort. He writes that, other than the casualties, it had little effect on the Royalist situation and that they were still able to graze their cattle and horses outside the city walls.

With the Allied lines slowly but surely closing in, Newcastle made another attempt to fire the suburbs. Although his men had a few small successes many of them were captured. Simeon Ash describes some of these prisoners:

Upon Saturday the 8 day in the morning, a souldier of the Marquess of Newcastle was taken in the Earl of Manchesters leager: he was in a red suit, he had pitch, flax, and other materials upon him for the fiering of the suburbs there, as yet free from the wasting flames. Some more of the Marquesse his souldiers were taken prisoners also; they had white coats (made of the plundred cloath taken from Clothiers in these parts) with crosses on the sleeves, wrought with red and blew silk, an ensigne as wee conceive of some Popish Regiment.[30]

He also goes on to describe an attempt by Manchester's men to burn the wooden gate at Bootham Bar, although this was stopped by the defenders throwing grenades – ceramic spheres filled with gunpowder – from the walls.

The Marquis of Newcastle's position was beginning to deteriorate and his army was firmly sealed inside the walls of York. Sir Henry Slingsby writes that he was unable to get news of his wife and children at 'Red House', near the village of Moor Monkton, a few miles from York, as his messengers were taken either leaving the city or trying to return.[31] In a letter to the Committee of Both Kingdoms the Earl of Manchester reported: 'We are on all sides very near the town walls, and I hope within a few hours Sir James Lumsden and myself will have our mines ready, if not hindered by the tempestuous rainy weather.'[32] Sir James Lumsden had been sent with a brigade of Scots foot to reinforce Lord Fairfax. The Allies were digging two mines: one at Walmgate Bar and the other under St Mary's Tower, part of the King's Manor. Both of these mines were near to completion. The tunnels for the mines were relatively short, as the Allies had possession of the suburbs close to their targets. Yet again Newcastle's failure to burn the suburbs had returned to haunt him.

Newcastle had to gain some time to allow Prince Rupert to attempt his relief and he opened communications with the Allied commanders. On the evening of the 8th he despatched two identical letters: one to the Earl of Leven, the other to Lord Fairfax:

> I cannot but admire that your Lordship hath so neere beleagured the Citie on all sides, made batteries against it, and so neere approached to it, without signifying what your intentions are, and what you desire or expect, which is contrary to the rules of all military discipline and customes; therefore I have thought fit to remonstrate thus much to your Lordship, to the end that your Lordship may signifie your intentions and resolutions therein, and receive ours, and so I remain my Lord.[33]

It was usual for a defended location to be summoned before it was attacked. Leven had summoned the town of Newcastle before his attack on the Shieldfield fort and Fairfax had done likewise before his attack on Selby. Newcastle expressed his surprise that the Allied commanders had not done so and asked what their intentions were. This letter began a series of communications that gained Newcastle seven days. The Earl of Leven sent his reply on the same day:

> At this distance I will not dispute in points of militarie discipline, nor the practice of Captains in such cases, yet to give your Lordsh. satisfaction in that your letter desires from me, your Lordship may take notice, I have drawn my forces before this citie with intention to reduce it to the

obedience due to the King and Parliament, whereunto if your Lordship shall speedily confer me, it may save the effusion of much innocent blood, whereof I wish your Lordship to bee no lesse sparing then I am, who rest . . .[34]

With this reply Leven had cast down the gauntlet. He would not discuss the niceties of the disciplines of war with Newcastle and his intention was to bring York back into the obedience of the King and his Parliament (throughout the First Civil War the Scots and Parliamentarian forces stated quite firmly that they were not fighting against the King and were his loyal subjects – they were fighting against his evil counsellors). In a meeting held by the Allied commanders it was discovered that the Earl of Manchester had received no communication from Newcastle. The Marquis was informed of his error and on the 9th sent a letter to Manchester, complete with copies of his correspondence with Leven and Fairfax:

> The inclosed is the effect of two letters I writ yesterday, one to the Earle of Leven, and the other to the Lord Fairfax, and I had done the like to your Lordship then, if I had had any assurance of your Lordship being in these parts in your own person. But since I am now satisfied of your Lordships being here, I have thought fit to present the same to your Lordships consideration, with this desire that I may receive your Lordships resolutions therein, and so I remain . . .[35]

It is surprising to find that, almost a week after the Earl's arrival, Newcastle was unaware of Manchester's presence – or was this just another sign of how well the Allies had kept the Royalists penned inside the city? Manchester replied immediately and informed Newcastle that he was well acquainted with the letters that the Earl of Leven and Lord Fairfax had received. He also stated that he was in complete agreement with the other two commanders. Another meeting was held by the Allied generals, during which an agreement to discuss the surrender of the city with Newcastle was reached. A message to this effect was sent to the Marquis, who said he would reply on Tuesday the 11th.

On the 10th, while they waited for Newcastle's decision, a meeting was held between the three commanders and Sir Henry Vane, the Committee of Both Kingdom's representative. In a long letter to the Committee Sir Henry sums up the situation in the north and makes the following statement: 'The truth is I could not satisfy my own judgment that anything considerable could be done for Lancashire by these forces until the business of York were decided.'[36]

The Committee's own representative was in agreement with the Allied commanders and the Committee now left the three generals to prosecute the war as they saw fit. While the Allied commanders had their discussions with Sir Henry, the Royalists attempted to break out with two separate bodies of horse.[37] Two hundred horsemen sallied out to the north of the city but were quickly driven back inside. In the meantime a smaller body, only eighty strong, left Micklegate Bar and headed towards the south-west, to Acomb, but had as little success as the first body.

True to his word, Newcastle sent his reply to the Allied commanders on the 11th:

> I have received your Lordshipps Letter with the names of the Commissioners appointed by your Lordshipps, But since your Lordshipps have declared in your Letter to allow a Cessation of Armes only on that side of the Towne during the time of the Treaty, I finde it not fit for me to incline to it upon those conditions, and had returned your Lordshipps this answer long before this tyme if some weighty affaires had not retarded my desires in that particular, I am ...[38]

Newcastle would not agree to a parley with the Allied commissioners, as the three commanders would not agree to a total ceasefire for the duration of the conference. To add insult to injury, he informed them that he would have replied sooner if he had had the time. This seems to have riled the Allied commanders and their reply to Newcastle was a straightforward ultimatum:

> We the Generalls of the Armies raised for the King and Parliament, and now imployed in this expedition about Yorke, That no further effusion of blood be done, and that the City of Yorke and Inhabitants may be preserved from ruine; We hereby require your Lordship to surrender the said City to us in name and for the use of King and Parliament within the space of 24 houres after the receit hereof, which if you refuse to doe, the inconvenience ensuing upon your refuseall must bee required at your Lordships hands, seeing our intentions are not for blood or destruction of Townes, Cities, and Counties, unlesse all other meanes being used, we be necessitated hereunto, which shall be contrary to the mindes and harts of ...[39]

Newcastle had been given twenty-four hours to surrender or the blood spilt when the town was stormed would be upon his head. On the morning of the 13th Newcastle sent his reply:

> I have received a Letter from your Lordships dated yesterday about four of the clock in the afternoon, wherein I am required to surrender the City to your Lordships within 24 hours after the receipt; but I know your Lordships are too full of honour, to expect the rendring the City upon a demand, and upon so short an advertisement to me, who have the Kings

Commission to keep it, and where there is so many generall persons, and men of honour, quality and fortune concerned in it. But truly I conceive this sad demand high enough to have been exacted upon the meanest Governor of any of his Majesties Garrisons: And your Lordships may be pleased to know, that I expect Propositions to proceed from your Lordships, as becomes Persons of honour to give and receive one from another; and if your Lordships therefore think fit to propound honourable and reasonable terms, and agree upon a generall cessation from all acts of hostility during the time of a Treaty, then your Lordships may receive such satisfaction therein, as may be expected from persons of honour, and such as desire as much to avoid the effusion of Christian blood, or destruction of Cities, Towns, and Counties as any whatsoever, yet will not spare their own lives, rather then to live in the least stain of dishonour, and so desiring your Lordships resolution.[40]

Once again Newcastle assumed the moral high ground. All he required from the Allied commanders was a cessation of arms for the duration of the conference and he would discuss terms with them like men of honour. Leven, Fairfax and Manchester quickly replied to the Marquis and agreed to a ceasefire and a parley on the following day.

On the 14th the parley took place. It was scheduled for three o'clock and would continue until eight. There would be a ceasefire from three hours before the parley until three hours after its completion and this ceasefire would cover the whole of the city. The commissioners would meet in a tent between the lines and would be allowed 100 musketeers as an honour guard. The Marquis named seven commissioners: Lord Widdrington, Sir Thomas Glemham, Sir Richard Hutton, Sir William Wentworth, Sir Robert Strickland, Sir Thomas Metham and Master Robert Rockley.[41] The Allied commissioners came from all three armies and were: the Earl of Crawford-Lindsey, Lord Humbey, Lieutenant General Baillie, Sir William Fairfax, Colonel Hammond, Colonel Russell and Colonel White.[42] The conference began with the Royalist commissioners stating the conditions under which the Marquis would consider rendering the city to them. Simeon Ash reports these in full:

Propositions made to the three Generalls by the Earl of Newcastle, concerning the rendering of the City of York, entitled, Propositions to be tendered to the Enemy.

I. That the town shall be rendered within twenty dayes, in case no relief come to it by that time from the King or Prince Rupert, upon these conditions:

That the Marquess Newcastle with all officers and souldiers therein have free liberty, to depart with colours flying and match light, and to take with them all Arms, Ammunition, Artillery, Money, Plate, and other goods belonging to them; for which end, that carriages be provided them, and victualls and other provision for their march.

That they be conveyed with our Troops to the King, Prince Rupert, or any other garrisons of the Kings where they please; And that they be not forced to march above 8 miles a day.

That they shall have liberty to stay or appoint others to stay 40 dayes in the town for sale of such goods, or for conveying of them to other places which they shall not be able to carry away with them.

That no Oath, Covenant, or Protestation be administred to any of them, further then is warranted by the known lawes of the land.

II. That the Gentry herein have liberty to go to their houses, and there be protected from violence, and not questioned for what they have done to the other partie: that no Oath or Covenant be tendered them as above said.

III. That the townes-men injoy all their priviledges and libertie of trade and merchandice, as before, and not to be questioned for any things they have done against the Parliament; and that no Oath be tendered to any of them, &c.

That the Garrison to be sent into York be only Yorkshiremen.

That all the Churches therein be kept from prophanation, and no violation offered to the Cathedral Church.

That the service be allowed to be performed therin as formerly had bin.

That the Revenues of the Church remain to the Officers thereof as hath done, and that the Prebends continue their Prebendaries and other Revenues as formerly according to the Lawes.

IV. That all Ministers and other Ecclesiasticall persons therein, of what countrey soever, have liberty to depart with the Army, or to their own livings, there to serve God and to enjoy their estate without disturbance.

That no oath or covenant be proffered them as aforesaid, nor they questioned hereafter, for what they have done to the Kings party.

That good Hostages be given, and to remain in their custodie: And that Cliffords Tower (the chiefe Fort in York) be still kept garrisoned by them, untill the Articles abovesaid, and some others then offered with them, be punctually performed. And then the said Garrison, and all Armes, Ammunition and Cannon therein, be safely conveyed to what Garrison of the Kings they pleased.[43]

The Allied commissioners could not agree to such conditions. Three of them left to discuss the situation with their commanders and returned one and a half hours later. They had with them a paper containing counter-propositions, signed by Leven, Manchester and Fairfax. These conditions were as follows:

That the City of York and all the Forts, together with all Arms, Ammunition, and other warlike provisions whatsoever in and about the same be tendered and delivered up to us for and to the use of King and Parliament, upon the conditions following, viz.

That the common souldiers shall have free liberty and licence to depart and go to their own homes, and to carry with them their clothes and their own money (not exceeding 14 days pay) And shall have safe conduct and protection of their persons from violence, they promising that they will not hereafter take up Arms against the Parliament or Protestant Religion.

That the Citizens and ordinary inhabitants of the said City shall have their persons and house protected from violence; and shall have the same free trade and commerce as others under obedience of King and Parliament, And that no Regiment or Companies shall be admitted or quartered in the Town of York, except for those that are appointed for the Garrison thereof.

That the Officers of all qualities shall have liberty to go to their own homes with swords and horses, and shall have licence to carry their apparell and money along with them (the money not exceeding one months means for every severall officer.

Any officer who shall be recommended by the Marquess of Newcastle shall have a pass from one of the Generalls to go beyond the seas, they promising not to serve against the Parliament and Protestant Religion.

That the Gentry and other inhabitants of the County of York, now residing in the City of York, shall have liberty to go to their own homes, and shall be protected from violence.

That a positive Answer be returned to these Propositions by 3 of the clock tomorrow afternoon, being the 15 instant; And in case they shall not have been accepted, we shall not hold our selves bound to them, and in the mean time we declare there is no cessation after the 3 hours already granted.[44]

One of the main differences between the two sets of propositions is the existence of Newcastle's army. The Royalists demanded that the army be allowed to march with all its arms, ammunition and baggage to join Prince Rupert, the King or another, as yet unnamed, garrison. It is obvious that the Allied commanders could not agree to this. If Rupert's army was reinforced by Newcastle's men it would pose an even more serious threat as it rampaged through Lancashire. The Allied demand was for the disbandment of Newcastle's army. Needless to say, the Royalist commissioners could not accept this. In fact, so angry were the Royalist commissioners at these propositions that they left the negotiations immediately and refused to take a copy of the Allied demands back to the Marquis. With the departure of the Marquis' commissioners the parley came to a close. On the following morning a drummer was sent to the city with a copy of the Allied propositions. It was obvious that Newcastle would also refuse to accept them and his reply must have been expected by the Allied commanders:

> I have perused the Conditions and demands your Lordship sent, but when I considered the many professions made to avoide the effusion of Christian blood, I did admire to see such propositions from your Lordshipps, conceiving this not the way to it, for I cannot suppose that your Lordshipps doe imagine that persons of honour can possibly condescend to any of these propositions, and so I remaine . . .[45]

With Newcastle's refusal to accept their propositions the Allied commanders declared the ceasefire at an end. On the night of the 15th the Royalists lit signal fires on the top of the Minster tower and these were answered by fires on Pontefract Castle.[46] This was taken by the Allies as a warning that Prince Rupert was heading towards York.

On 16 June Sir Henry Vane was busy writing a letter to the Committee of Both Kingdoms to inform them of the progress of the siege.[47] He writes of the completion of two mines and the repair of the largest siege gun the Allies possessed, which fired a 64-pound shot. After continuing to provide the Committee with further information he writes the following lines:

> Since my writing thus much Manchester played his mine with very good success, made a fair breach, and entered with his men and possessed the manor house, but Leven and Fairfax not being acquainted therewith, that they might have diverted the enemy at other places, the enemy drew all their strength against our men, and beat them off again, but with no great loss, as I hear.

There are a number of accounts of the assault on the King's Manor at St Mary's Tower.[48] Strictly speaking the Manor was not part of the city. Originally it had been a walled abbey, outside of the city walls. With the demise of the large religious houses during Henry VIII's reign the abbey fell into ruins. The King's Manor was built inside the abbey grounds. It was still outside the main city walls but the Manor's grounds themselves were walled. At their north-western corner stood, and still stands, St Mary's Tower and it still shows the scars left upon it by the explosion of the Parliamentarian mine. Lawrence Crawford, Major General to the Earl of Manchester, had command of the Allied lines adjacent to the Manor walls and St Mary's Tower. A battery had been raised against the north-western wall of the Manor, which had been breached. The Royalist defenders had barricaded the breach with a wall of earth and sods. At noon on the 16th Crawford ordered the mine to be blown without giving notice to any of the other commanders. Why did he do so? Simeon Ash writes that he had no choice as the mine was beginning to flood, due to the heavy rain.[49] This is a distinct possibility. Sir Henry Slingsby reports a similar situation in the mine at Walmgate Bar: 'Ye Scots [Sir James Lumsden's men] were all ye while busie about the mine, & we as busy in countermining, but at length both give over being hinder'd by water.'[50]

But Sir Thomas Fairfax gives a rather different reason for the blowing of the mine: Crawford was 'Ambitious to have the honor, alone, of springing ye myne'.[51]

Whatever Crawford's reason for blowing the mine when he did, there was no excuse for his not informing the other Allied commanders. It is almost beyond belief that the mine was flooding so quickly that it had to be blown before Crawford had chance to send messengers to Leven and Fairfax. If he had informed the other commanders they would have been able to provide diversions while he attacked the King's Manor. By not doing so he brought the weight of the Royalist defenders down upon his assault force.

As the smoke cleared from the exploding mine the outer section of the tower collapsed into Bootham. Crawford ordered his assault force of 600 men forward. While some attacked the tower, others attacked the breach and a third group scaled the wall, using ladders. The stunned Royalist defenders fell back and Crawford's men gained possession of the bowling green behind the tower (the area is still a bowling green today). Sir Phillip Byron, the Royalist commander on the spot, rallied a few men and led a counter-attack onto the bowling green. When Sir Phillip was killed his men fell back. By this time several hundred of Crawford's men had broken into the Manor and proceeded to take possession of it, but their success was to be shortlived. With the remainder of the Allied forces remaining within their lines, the Royalists were able to concentrate a large force – up to 2,000 men – against the assault force. The Marquis of Newcastle led a body of his 'Whitecoats' in this counter-attack. One body of Royalist troops sealed the breach and Crawford's assault force was cut off from any support. There lay Crawford's second mistake: so confident was he of the success of his initial assault, he had provided no support for it. His men fought gallantly until they had exhausted their ammunition, when the bulk of them were forced to surrender.

With the exception of the Duchess of Newcastle's, the contemporary accounts give similar numbers for losses. Crawford lost thirty-five dead and about 100 wounded, both inside and outside the walls. He also lost 200 prisoners, although Simeon Ash expected them soon to be restored once York had fallen.[52] Royalist casualties were not reported but probably equalled the Parliamentarian losses. They had also lost 100 prisoners in the initial assault but these would have been recovered when the Allied attackers surrendered. On the following day some of Manchester's men approached the tower and heard the cries of the wounded still laying among the ruins of the tower. They began to dig among the ruins and recovered two survivors and one body but were stopped by fire from the city.[53] It was not until Wednesday the 19th that the Royalists gave permission for Manchester's men to recover the bodies of their dead comrades for burial.[54]

With the failure of Crawford's attack the siege seemed to grind to a halt. Prince Rupert had begun to move towards York and both sides held their breath in anticipation. Lord Fairfax's efforts at Walmgate Bar also seem to have stalled, for, as already mentioned, Sir James Lumsden's mine had been flooded out. The Allied bombardment had reduced the height of the gate to that of the city walls, but the Royalists had filled in the gate with earth. Just in case the Allies managed to break through at the Bar a number of houses behind it had been demolished and barricades built. One of the reasons for the lack of activity by Lord Fairfax's men was a lack of supplies. Lord Fairfax summed up his supply situation, and that of the Scots Army, in a letter to the Committee of Both Kingdoms written on the 18th:

> I must solicit you for a speedy supply of gunpowder, match, and bullet for my own and the Scotch armies in very large proportions, otherwise the service of these armies will be much retarded, contrary to our desires and your expectations. For my own particular I must intreat a supply of muskets, pistols, and carbines, concerning which I have often written. I am necessitated still to move you to acquaint the Parliament with my want of money, for my men are like to mutiny and many run away, whom I cannot in justice punish having nothing to pay them withall, while Manchester's men are very well paid, and a considerable supply furnished to the Scott's Army. I beseech you to consider what it is to have an Army and nothing to give them, while joined with other armies that are well paid. The pay of my Army comes to 15,000 l. a month, and I have received only 10,000 l. for these four months past at least.[55]

Once again Lord Fairfax's Northern Association army was playing the poor relation. This had been the case throughout the previous two years of the First Civil War.

The next event of note took place on 24 June. In the early hours of the morning, at about four o'clock, a large body of commanded musketeers sallied out of Monk Bar to attack Manchester's quarters.[56] The Royalist musketeers had little success and were driven back into York with some loss. One Parliamentarian writer reports twenty dead and twenty prisoners on the Royalist side and three of Manchester's men killed, although he does qualify this statement by saying 'this is reported somewhat diversely.'[57]

With the defeat of this sally the siege returned to its usual round of skirmishing and cannon fire. Then on 30 June definite news reached the leaguer of the arrival of Prince Rupert at Knaresborough. The Allied cavalry had been watching the passes through the Pennines in an attempt to block Rupert's relief attempt. In a rapid march to the north Rupert had swung around the northern flank of the Allied horse. The Allied commanders were in a difficult position. They did not have enough men to maintain the siege and face Prince Rupert. In a meeting during the night it was decided that their main task would be to stop Prince Rupert relieving York. The besieging army would leave its lines and rendezvous with the horse on Hessay Moor, near Long Marston, and block the main route to York from the west. During the early hours of Monday 1 July the Allied Army marched from its lines around York to its rendezvous on Hessay Moor. Sir Henry Slingsby writes of a skirmish between the garrison and the rearguard of the Allied Army:

> Sr James [Gamaliel] Dudly yt command'd at Waingate [Walmgate] barr, sends out over ye Wall 12 foot men & as many horsemen, wch they might lead over an earth work att ye end of ye stone wall yt is towards ye Castle Mills, to discover wt became of ye enemy. Wn these went, there was no stay, but all ye Troop would go, & a great many more of ye foot: they find their Hutts empty; their horse command'd by Major Constable advanceth further towards fowlforth [Fulford]; about half ye way distance they perceiv'd some horse in ye Town, & presently ye trumpet sounds to charge. Our horse was forc'd to stand, yt our foot might ye better retreat to ye walls, & stays so long till they were forc'd to charge, & presently mingl'd one wth another; in this charge they took some of ours prisoners, & we kill'd a Cornett of theirs wch they said should have marry'd [Colonel] Sr. Tho. Norclift [Norcliffe] his sister, & they shot Capt. Squire a Yorkman in ye back. Thus they part'd, we to our Garison, & they to their Randevous on Knapton Moor, where all of ym meet, & for haste had

lost a boat load of shoes & other provisions wch they could not carry away.[58]

Finding Lord Fairfax's siege lines to be empty, a body of Royalist horse and foot moved out to find the enemy. They soon found them on the road to Fulford, now the A19. The Allied horse charged the Royalist troopers, who fought a hard defensive action to cover their foot as they pulled back to Walmgate Bar.

Out on Hessay Moor the Allied commanders awaited the arrival of Prince Rupert's army. A body of Royalist horse appeared, but later in the day marched out of sight to the west. Then shattering news reached the three generals: Rupert had, yet again, outflanked them. He had swung north, putting the Ouse between his army and the Allies. York had been relieved. With this piece of news the Allied Army settled for the night around Long Marston and waited for morning.

Chapter 6

Prince Rupert's March

This fierce thunderbolt which strikes terror among the ignorant ...

On 16 May 1644 Prince Rupert began his move north, towards Lancashire. It was the start of a march that would, six weeks later, lead to Marston Moor. As Rupert began his advance York had been under siege for almost a month. The armies of Lord Fairfax and the Earl of Leven lay before the city's walls. Prince Rupert's plans for the forthcoming campaign are not known but several letters exist that may shed some light on the subject. On 7 March the Earl of Derby wrote to Prince Rupert.[1] The Earl's house at Lathom had been besieged by Parliamentarian forces since the end of January 1644, in the aftermath of the Battle of Nantwich. Sir Thomas Fairfax reports that Lathom House was the only Royalist garrison holding out in Lancashire, and that it was being besieged by Lancashire forces.[2] The Countess of Derby gallantly inspired the garrison and this was of great concern to her husband, the Earl. In his letter to Prince Rupert he writes:

> I have received many advertisements from my wife of her great distress and imminent danger, unless she be relieved by your Highness, on whom she doth more rely than any other whatsoever, and all of us consider well she hath chief reason so to do. I do take the boldness to present you again my most humble and earnest request in her behalf, that I may be able to give her some comfort in my next. I would have waited on your Highness this time, but that I hourly receive little letters from her, who haply, a few days hence, may never send me more.

A heart rending plea! The Earl bemoans the fact that Lord Byron and the local Royalist forces were unwilling to offer any assistance to his wife. It is hardly surprising that Byron was loath to leave the shelter of Chester, as he was still trying to reorganise his army after its defeat at Nantwich in January. The Earl then writes of the situation in Lancashire and how Liverpool and Warrington were weakly held and that a large part of the Manchester garrison had marched to the siege lines around Lathom House. If Rupert were to threaten any of

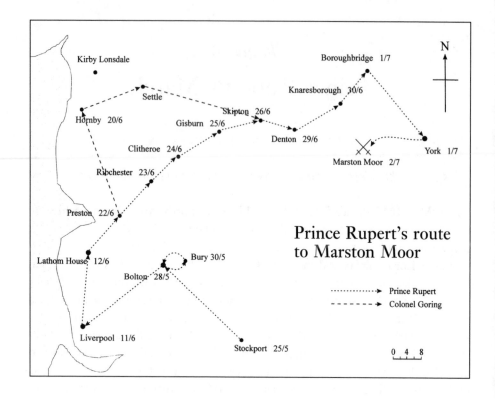

Prince Rupert's route to Marston Moor

these towns then the siege at Lathom might be raised, or so weakened that supplies might be got into the house.

On 8 March Lord Digby wrote a letter to the Prince reinforcing the need to relieve Lathom House, although not at the risk of being unable to assist his uncle, the King.[3] Towards the end of March the Prince received two letters from the Marquis of Newcastle. The first, written on the 25th, stated: 'that if your Highness do not please to come hither, and that very soon too, the great game of your uncle's will be endangered, if not lost; and with your Highness being near, certainly won.'[4] The second letter, dated the 29th, followed in a similar vein: 'Could your Highness march this way it would, I hope, put a final end to our troubles: but I dare not urge this, but leave it to your Highness's great wisdom.'[5]

As can be seen from the four letters mentioned above a great amount of pressure was being applied to Prince Rupert for a march into Lancashire and then to aid the Marquis of Newcastle. Two of the letters quoted also had references to other messages being passed by word of mouth.[6] It would be intriguing to know what information these verbal communications contained, as it would to have all of Prince Rupert's correspondence for the period leading up to his march into Lancashire.

As well as the pressure being applied to the Prince, it made sound strategic sense to move into Lancashire. The county had been a rich recruiting ground for the King, particularly in the Earl of Derby's lands. The King's supporters had been cowed by their defeat at Sabden Brook at the end of May 1643 and the supply of men had dried up. In fact, the Parliamentarians had recruited a large number of troops, some of whom had marched into Yorkshire with Sir Thomas Fairfax. Another source of troops for the King was the English Army in Ireland. Some of these troops had already landed at Chester and had been involved in the siege and battle at Nantwich. Liverpool was an ideal port to land these reinforcements and, according to the Earl of Derby, was weakly defended. An attack into Lancashire would almost certainly raise the Siege of Lathom House and stood a good chance of raising the Siege of York. It all depended on whether the Allied commanders at York could ignore Rupert's attack into Lancashire and concentrate on the siege. Would they send part of their forces to oppose the Prince? If so he would defeat them then march into Yorkshire to finish off the remaining forces at York. Would they raise the siege and march their whole force into Lancashire? If this happened then the Prince could fight them or draw them into Cheshire, allowing Newcastle to raise his army anew. Their third option was to ignore Rupert and continue to prosecute the siege. As was shown in the previous chapter this was the choice that Leven, Manchester and Fairfax took, but as the Prince prepared to move north he did not know this would be the case.

Passing the Mersey

On 16 May Prince Rupert marched out of Shrewsbury and by the 25th had reached Stockport. A document exists that records Prince Rupert's daily marches and this has been used as the main source for what follows.[7] The Prince had marched from Shrewsbury to Petton, near Wem, on the 16th. On the 18th he continued to Whitchurch, where he was close to the Parliamentarian garrison at Nantwich. Swinging to the east he marched to Market Drayton (20th), Betley (21st), Sandbach (22nd) and finally to Knutsford, arriving there on the 23rd. At Knutsford he rested his army for a day, after having marched for four consecutive days in bad weather and along poor roads.[8] Several sources, both Royalist and Parliamentarian, give Rupert's army a strength of 8,000 men – 2,000 horse and 6,000 foot.[9] At the time of the Civil War there were three crossings of the Mersey: Hale Ford, Warrington, and Stockport. Rupert decided on the bridge at Stockport and on the 25th his army advanced on the town.

One Royalist document sums up the action at Stockport as follows: '25 Satterday. Stopford passe wonne, Latham seige reysed.'[10] Fortunately, other accounts exist of the action on the 25th, which give much more detail.[11] Stockport lies on the south, Cheshire, bank of the River Mersey. It was garrisoned by 3,000 locally raised troops, who seem to have been in some disorder at Prince Rupert's approach. The garrison manned the hedges surrounding the town. The Prince sent Colonel Washington and his dragoons forward to clear the defenders. After a brief fight the Parliamentarian troops abandoned their positions and fled back into Stockport. With the way clear, Prince Rupert now led his troopers into the town. This was the last straw and the defenders fled across the bridge towards Manchester, 6 miles away. The Royalist horse pursued them but nightfall curtailed the pursuit. With this the Royalist soldiers fell to plundering the town – a sign of things to come. Casualties were light, although one Royalist source states that there were no casualties on either side, which is difficult to believe.[12] The Parliamentarian defenders lost several hundred prisoners, all their cannon and baggage, and many arms were found where they had been abandoned. Prince Rupert had gained his passage just in time. Sir John Meldrum arrived in Manchester on the 26th with two regiments of foot and two troops of horse. If these reinforcements (1,200 to 1,500 experienced troops) had arrived twenty-four hours earlier the Prince's crossing would have been much more difficult. Such are the fortunes of war.

On the 27th the Committee of Both Kingdoms wrote to Lord Fairfax with a warning about the situation in Lancashire:

> They have received some late information concerning Lancashire, where affairs are in some uncertainty and many suspicions that correspondence may be held between some in the Parliament's service there and Prince Rupert's forces, which may tend to a great disturbance of that county and be of ill consequence to the northern parts.[13]

It is doubtful whether the Committee had heard news of the fall of Stockport but was already worried about the effect Prince Rupert would have on the war in the north. As if to reinforce their fears the Prince began his move towards Bolton on the same day as the Committee was writing to Lord Fairfax. His army quartered around Eccles on the night of the 27th and on the morning of the 28th marched on to Bolton.

The Storming of Bolton

'28 Tuesday, Bolton taken by assault.' This is how one Royalist account sums up the events of 28 May 1644, one of the darkest days in the history of the Civil

Wars.[14] On the afternoon of the 28th Prince Rupert's army assaulted Bolton, a large market town. What followed left a black stain on Rupert's reputation. Is this stain deserved and what reasons did the Royalists have for treating the inhabitants of Bolton in such a manner? The contemporary accounts, both Royalist and Parliamentarian, shed some light on the events of that Tuesday afternoon.[15]

On the morning of the 28th Colonel Rigby, commander of the besieging forces at Lathom House, arrived at Bolton with 2,000 men. In the town were many ill-armed clubmen – civilians who had armed themselves with any weapon to hand. The numbers given vary between 500 and 1,500: an inhabitant of Bolton, who was an eyewitness to the day's proceedings, reports 500;[16] but in a letter to the Committee of Both Kingdoms the Allied commanders at York put the number at 1,500,[17] and as this information had come from Colonel Rigby, it is probably a more accurate estimate of the number of armed civilians involved. But not all the civilians in the town were inhabitants of Bolton. With Prince Rupert's advance many refugees had fled there from the towns and villages in his path.[18] The town had no defensive works except for barricades blocking its entrances. Colonel Rigby attempted to fortify the town, in the time remaining to him but the inhabitants 'hindred their better fortifying of the same'.[19]

At about two o'clock in the afternoon Prince Rupert's army was seen approaching from the south-west, across the moor. An eyewitness describes their approach: 'They appeared at first like a wood or cloud.'[20] By the time Rupert's army marched to Bolton it had grown, with the aid of the Earl of Derby, to between 10,000 and 12,000 men. As the army neared the town it divided into several bodies ready for an assault. Colonel Rigby's men manned the perimeter of the town, lining hedges, occupying buildings and manning the barricades at the street ends. Rupert's first attack went in and was repulsed after hard fighting. According to one Royalist source four regiments were involved in this attack: Warren's, Prince Rupert's, Tyldesley's and Ellis'.[21] During the attack the defenders had taken a number of prisoners, among them an Irish Catholic. As one of the regiments involved in the attack had recently returned from Ireland this is a distinct possibility. He was promptly hanged in full view of the Royalist Army. This action is reported in two contemporary accounts. Prince Rupert's Diary says: 'During ye time of ye Attaque they took a prisonr (an Irishman) and hung him up as an Irish papist.'[22] Interestingly, the second account is a Parliamentarian one. John Rushworth writes: 'That the Prince sending an Officer to summon the Town, they not only refused, but in defiance caused one of the Prince's Captains whom they had taken not long before, to be hanged in his sight.'[23]

Rushworth goes on to qualify this comment by stating that he had been unable to find the name of the captain involved and that his Parliamentarian witnesses denied it. A third account of this incident exists.[24] Although written in the middle of the eighteenth century it was almost certainly taken from original sources. Seacome served as steward to the ninth Earl of Derby and had access to the family's papers. He writes:

> His Highness being greatly Irritated and Ruffled by this Repulse, but especially with the Barbarous Cruelty of the Enemy, who murdered his Soldiers taken in the Storm in Cold Blood upon the walls before his eyes.

Bolton had a reputation for being a staunchly Protestant town. A minister from Manchester, while writing a letter to his wife about the storming of Bolton, stated that the town was 'the next Towne for Religion to Manchester in all the Countie'.[25] Having just repulsed a major attack against them it is not beyond belief that the defenders of the town, finding a foreign Catholic, particularly an Irish Catholic, among their prisoners, hanged him as an example to the other Irishmen in Prince Rupert's army, and as a gesture of defiance to the Prince himself.

With his blood up, Rupert ordered a second attack, which was carried out by Colonel Broughton's regiment. During this attack a body of Royalist horse was led into the town by a local inhabitant, at an area on its north-west side called the 'Private Acres'.[26] With Royalist foot pressing them closely from the front and Royalist horse inside the town to their rear, the defenders broke and fled. With their entry into Bolton the Royalist troops let loose their anger. The enemy troops were hounded through the surrounding countryside and anyone caught under arms in the town was killed. Parliamentarian accounts talk of men killed after quarter had been given, women abused and houses plundered. A full eyewitness account of the events after the Royalists stormed the town is given in Appendix III.

It is difficult to ascertain losses for the two sides. The Royalists lost 300 men in the first assault and must have lost some in the second. Parliamentarian losses were much higher. Royalist accounts talk of between 1,000 and 2,000 casualties. Colonel Rigby reported to the Allied commanders at York that he had lost only 200 of his own men.[27] This number seems a little low. By far the largest number of casualties was among the local inhabitants. In a letter written from Manchester, one Parliamentarian correspondent speaks of 1,500 dead being buried over the two days after the action.[28] In the parish register only seventy-eight names are recorded, including two women.[29] This is a surprisingly low figure. There are two possible reasons for this. Contemporary accounts speak of many of the losses being in the surrounding countryside and these bodies may have been buried close to where they fell. Many of the defenders were from nearby towns and villages and they may have been returned home for burial. In addition to those killed, 500 prisoners were taken sheltering in the town church.

The complete story of the storming of Bolton will probably never be known. Contemporary accounts show the prejudices of both sides. The Royalists write of it as a great victory, while the Parliamentarians talk of a bloody massacre. The Royalists talk of killing large numbers of enemy soldiers, the Parliamentarians of the death of large numbers of civilians. Are the two sides reconcilable? Both sides admit to a large number of clubmen defending the town. When does an armed inhabitant, who has recently been shooting at his attackers, become an unarmed civilian? How does a victorious attacker tell the difference between the two? The defenders of Bolton had refused a summons to surrender. This alone meant that the town was subject to plunder, according to the disciplines of war at the time. The attackers had suffered a bloody repulse, with the loss of many of their comrades, and this would have angered them considerably. Add to this the possibility of one, or more, of their comrades being hanged by the defenders and it is hardly surprising that the Royalist attackers went on the rampage, and in the process spilt innocent blood. Such circumstances bring out the worst in mankind.

The Siege of Liverpool

Having rested his men on the 29th, Prince Rupert moved his army to Bury on the 30th. Here he received a large reinforcement of horse when he was joined by Colonel Goring and the Northern Horse.[30] The next few days were spent in raising and training recruits. In a letter written by Sir John Meldrum, from Manchester, to the Earl of Denbigh on the 31st, Rupert's strength is given as 4,000 horse, 7,000 foot and fourteen guns of various calibres.[31] He mentions the 3,000 men of the Northern Horse as a separate body. Obviously news of their joining with the Prince's army had not reached him. Troops were drawing towards Rupert from much of the north of England. In a letter to the Committee of Both Kingdoms Sir John Gell, Parliamentarian governor of Derby, reports the movement of a body of Derbyshire Royalists towards Prince Rupert's army:

> Our country Colonels Fretchwell [Fretchville], Eyre, and Millward, with their chief force of horse and foot, after several marches to Sheffield and back again with their carriages and most of their strength, on Thursday [30 May] and yesterday [31 May] marched after Goring; they have quitted Chatsworth, the Earl of Devonshire's house, but they still keep the rest of

their garrisons in this country; Fretchwell took along with him eight colours of horse, averaging about 20 to a colour, but his foot were not many; the other Colonels had about 100 horse, 30 dragoons, and 220 foot.[32]

As Prince Rupert gathered his forces at Bury the Parliamentarian commanders attempted to work out his next move. In a letter from the Committee of Both Kingdoms to the Earl of Essex, the Committee successfully predicted Rupert's plans: 'Prince Rupert is thought to have an eye on Liverpool as a place of great advantage in order to their designs of Ireland.'[33] On 4 June Rupert returned to Bolton. On the 5th he continued his march towards Liverpool, quartering at Wigan. From here he despatched Colonel Washington and his dragoons to reconnoitre the defences of the town. On the 6th the army marched to Prescot and on the 7th carried on to Liverpool.

The contemporary accounts of the Siege of Liverpool are fairly unanimous as to the course of events between 7 and 11 June 1644.[34] Colonel Moore, the Parliamentarian governor of Liverpool, had at his disposal 600 men of his own command plus the sailors from the ships in the harbour, who seem to have taken an active part in the defence of the town. He had recently received 300 or 400 English and Scots reinforcements from Manchester. These troops had marched to Warrington then been taken downriver by boat to Liverpool. The town was much better fortified than either Stockport or Bolton. Seacombe writes that: 'it was well fortified with a strong and high mud wall, and a ditch of 12 yards wide, and near 3 yards deep.'[35]

Between the 7th and the 9th the Royalists bombarded the town's walls. Their fire was answered by the guns of the town and those of the ships in the harbour. By the 10th the ditch had almost been filled by the collapsed walls, close to one of the town's gates, and the Royalists prepared to assault the town. About noon the Royalist troops attacked but were held by Colonel Moore's defenders, who were supported by sailors from the ships. The fighting continued for an hour before the Royalists were repulsed with some loss. Although his men had held the line of the wall Moore decided the town was untenable. During the remainder of the day and throughout the night, Moore evacuated his men from the town onto the waiting ships, complete with their arms, ammunition and largest guns. He also loaded goods of any value from the town: particularly, as his enemies claimed, his own! As a decoy he planted twelve colours along the walls. Early on the 11th, Colonel Tillier, whose men were closest to the sea, realised what was afoot and led his men into the town. The Royalist troops were furious that little had been left to plunder and the few enemy stragglers were killed out of hand. All that had been left for the Royalists were fourteen small guns and twenty-six small vessels.

The March to York

On 12 June Prince Rupert and the Earl of Derby rode to Lathom House and while there the Prince presented the Countess with the standards taken at Bolton. On the 13th he returned to Liverpool. On the same day the Committee of Both Kingdoms wrote to their representatives resident with the Scots Army at York.[36] Moves were afoot to oppose Rupert's movements in Lancashire. The Committee had ordered the Earl of Denbigh to gather his forces and march north to Manchester to combine with forces there, under the command of Sir John Meldrum. If he was unable to reach Manchester he was to try to prevent Rupert's force passing back into Cheshire from Lancashire. The Committee also communicated with other local commanders in the north. In one letter Colonel Hutchinson, the governor of Nottingham, was requested to join the Earl of Denbigh with 200 horse and 300 foot.[37]

Rupert's army remained at Liverpool until 20 June, as did their commander, with the exception of another visit to Lathom House on the 18th. On the 19th Rupert received a letter from the King.[38] This is one of the most controversial letters of the Civil Wars and also one of the most confusing. Historians have argued for many years as to its meaning and whether or not it was a direct order to fight the Allied Army at York. It is included in full in Appendix IV. Whether or not it was a direct order, Rupert believed it to be one, and acted on it by ordering his army to march towards Yorkshire. By the 22nd the Prince's men were at Preston, ready to begin their crossing. The Northern Horse would cross by a more northerly route, via Hornby and Settle to Skipton. On the 20th Goring wrote a letter from Hornby to Sir Phillip Musgrave, the King's commander in Cumberland and Westmorland, requesting any troops that Musgrave could spare from his forces at Kirkby Lonsdale.[39]

On the 23rd Prince Rupert began his crossing of the Pennines. That night the army quartered at Ribchester. On the 24th it continued to Clitheroe. During the day a part of the army took White Hall, a small Parliamentarian garrison.[40] On the 25th the Prince continued to Gisburne and then on the following day reached the security of the garrison at Skipton Castle, where the whole army gathered. Once again part of the army attacked a small Parliamentarian garrison at Thornton Hall.[41] Having rested his army on the 28th, the Prince marched to Lord Fairfax's house at Denton, near Otley, on the 29th. By the evening of the 30th he had reached Knaresborough. In a rapid march Prince Rupert had outflanked the Parliamentarian cavalry forces blocking the southern Pennine passes.

The Allied commanders, as shown in Chapter Five, reacted to the news of Rupert's arrival by breaking up the Siege of York and moving to Hessay Moor. Rupert's obvious route from Knaresborough to York was via Wetherby. With this in mind the Allied forces set up a blocking position on this route. On 1 July the Prince again outwitted his opponents. Marching via Boroughbridge, he crossed to the north bank of the River Ouse, putting the river between the two armies. To pin the enemy in position he had sent a body of cavalry along the main Wetherby–York road. Later in the day this body disappeared to the west. By nightfall Rupert was encamped in the Forest of Galtres. His men had captured a bridge of boats across the Ouse, which would be put to use on the following morning. The two armies lay close to one another, separated by the Ouse. York had been relieved.

Chapter 7

The Approach to Battle

In Marston corn feilds falls to singing psalms . . .

As both the Allied and Royalist armies settled into their quarters for the night, their respective commanders had a number of difficult decisions to make. How should they proceed with the campaign? Should they fight? What was the enemy's next move going to be? The only certainty was that York had been relieved. The Allied generals – Leven, Manchester and Lord Fairfax – met their senior commanders during the night to discuss what Prince Rupert's next move might be. Several options were apparent. First, the Prince could throw reinforcements and supplies into York and withdraw into Lancashire, and once there, continue to recruit his army. Second, he could march southwards and threaten the Eastern Association, which was the heartland of the Parliamentarian cause and a rich source of men, money and supplies. Any threat to it had to be prevented. Finally, he could force the Allied Army into a battle, although at the time, this seemed unlikely. Thomas Stockdale sums up the council of war's decision in a letter to John Rushworth, which was read to the House of Commons on 8 July by its recipient:

> Upon this the Generalls and principall feild Officers held another consultation upon Monday at night, wherein it was resolved the next morning to rise from thence, and march to Cawood, Tadcaster, and those parts, from whence they could not onely safe guard the forces from Chesshire &c., but also p'vent the marching of Prince Rupert Southwardes, and likewise (by the helpe of a bridge of botes then at Cawood) to stop all provisions going to Yorke either from the West or East Ryding, and soe in time necessitate him to draw out and fight.[1]

On 23 June Sir Henry Vane had written to the Committee of Both Kingdoms from the siege lines around York.[2] In his letter he reported 4,000 horse and 4,000 foot ready to march into Yorkshire under Sir John Meldrum, plus a force of an unspecified size under the Earl of Denbigh, although it is very unlikely that Denbigh actually marched into Yorkshire. By the end of June Meldrum had gathered a sizeable force at Manchester and was ready to march into Yorkshire. It is not clear which pass, or passes, Meldrum's force used to cross the Pennines. One strong possibility is the Woodhead Pass, which emerges west of Barnsley. As Meldrum debouched into Yorkshire close to Wakefield he must have used one of the southern passes, of which the Woodhead Pass was, and still is, the main one (if Meldrum's men had crossed further north they would have continued their march through Halifax or Bradford).

The Allied commanders had received news of the approach of this large body of reinforcements.[3] Unfortunately, Meldrum was still some distance away and would not arrive at Wakefield until 3 July. If a battle was to take place, then the arrival of his reinforcements could have proved decisive. As Prince Rupert's army had won success after success in Lancashire, so its size had become exaggerated. By the time Rupert had relieved York the Allied commanders believed his force to be of an equivalent strength to their own, as is reported by one Parliamentarian correspondent: 'We understanding, that Prince Rupert was drawing towards York, with (as common fame gave him) twenty five thousand horse and foot.'[4]

The same correspondent also reports 8,000 troops leaving York on the morning of the battle. It is quite clear from such reports that the Allied commanders believed that the combined forces of Rupert and Newcastle at least equalled, if not exceeded, their own. With this in mind a decision was taken to move southwards to the area of Cawood. There were several other reasons for a move to the south, as mentioned by Thomas Stockdale in his letter quoted previously. The Allies had built a bridge of boats across the Ouse at Cawood, which would enable them to block Rupert's march south along either bank of the river. It would also enable their horse to prevent supplies from reaching York from the East or West Ridings. While at Cawood they could cover Meldrum's approach and by marching south had enabled these reinforcements to reach them a day earlier, probably on the 4th or 5th.

With the prevailing situation the march to Cawood made sound strategic sense. That said, the decision does not seem to have been reached without some argument. Sir Thomas Fairfax wrote that: 'We were divided in or opinions wt to do. The English were for fighting ym; the Scotts, for Retreating, to gaine (as they alledged) both time & place of Advantage.'[5] These disagreements may have gone deeper than Sir Thomas's statement implies. Thomas Fuller, in his *Worthies of England*, writes:

> Such were the present Animosities in the Parliaments Army, and so great their Mutuall Dissatisfactions when they drew off from York, that (as a prime Person since freely confest) if let alone, they would have fallen foul

amongst themselves, had not the Prince preparing to fight them, Cemented their Differences to agree against a Generall Enemy.[6]

However deeply the disagreements between the Scots and Parliamentarian commanders ran, it would not be given time to show. The decision had been made to march south but subsequent events would change the resolve of the Allied commanders.

As Leven and his commanders discussed their options at Long Marston no such debates were taking place in the Royalist camp. Rupert spent the night with his men in their bivouac in Galtres Forest, north-west of York. Instead of entering York and discussing his plans with the Marquis of Newcastle, he simply sent a message to the Marquis, ordering him to march with his infantry at first light and rendezvous with the Prince's army on Marston Moor.[7] Although Prince Rupert was the senior commander and quite within his rights to send Newcastle such a peremptory order, a little more tact may have been diplomatic. As a sop to Newcastle's sensibilities the order was carried by George Goring, who had been the commander of Newcastle's horse during the early part of 1643. The Marquis of Newcastle sent 'some persons of quality to attend his Highness'[8] and to invite him into the city to discuss the situation. The Prince declined to enter York and met Newcastle early the following morning as the Prince's troops began deploying on Marston Moor. The Duchess of Newcastle writes of their discussions:

> After some conferences, he declared his mind to the Prince, desiring his Highness not to attempt anything as yet upon the enemy; for he had intelligence that there was some discontent between them, and that they were resolved to divide themselves, and so to raise the siege without fighting: besides my Lord expected within two days Colonel Cleavering [Sir Robert Clavering], with above three thousand men out of the North, and two thousand drawn out of several garrisons (who also came at the same time, though it was then too late). But his Highness answered my Lord, that he had a letter from his Majesty (then at Oxford), with a positive and absolute command to fight the enemy; which in obedience, and according to his duty he was bound to perform. Whereupon my Lord replied, That he was ready and willing, for his part, to obey his Highness in all things no otherwise than if his Majesty was there in person himself; and though several of my Lord's friends advised him not to engage in battle, because the command (as they said) was taken from him: yet my Lord answered them, that happen what would, he would not shun to fight, for he had no other ambition but to live and die a loyal subject to his Majesty.[9]

Once again the subject of the disagreements among the Allies raised its head. Sir Robert Clavering had been operating in County Durham, along with the Marquis of Montrose, and had had some success against isolated Scots garrisons. He was moving south to support the Marquis of Newcastle with a force raised in County Durham, Northumberland, Westmoreland and Cumberland. Both of these were good reasons to pause before offering battle. Hindsight is a wonderful thing and it is easy to say that Rupert should not have fought, but Rupert believed he was doing the right thing, as well as obeying a direct order from his uncle, the King, to fight the Scots as soon as possible. This command, contained in a letter from the King to Rupert, is discussed in Appendix IV. Whether or not the King had intended his letter to be a peremptory command to fight or not, Rupert believed it was and acted on it. Thus both sides had made their decisions, and early on the morning of Tuesday 2 July 1644, began to carry them out.

The Approach to the Field

Early on the morning of the 2nd the Allied Army began its southward march towards Tadcaster and Cawood. A body of Scots foot formed the vanguard, while Manchester's foot, or part of it, formed the rear. A body of 3,000 horse and dragoons[10] remained near Long Marston to form a rearguard, commanded by the three lieutenant generals: Oliver Cromwell, Sir Thomas Fairfax, and David Leslie.[11] The early start of the Allied march may have been prompted by the movements of a body of Royalist horse:

> Upon Tuesday morning, a partie of the enemies horse, having faced us awhile, wheeled back out of sight, which gave us cause to suspect that the maine body was marched towards Tadcaster (having relieved Yorke), where he might cut off the River, and so both scant us of provisions and get down suddainly into the South.[12]

As already mentioned, one of the Allies' great fears was the breakout of Prince Rupert's army into the Eastern Association. They did not know Rupert's exact whereabouts on the night of the 1st. He may well have entered York with his whole army. By using the bridges in the city to cross to the south bank of the Ouse, he would have been able to march south. If he had done this he would have gained a march on his opponents and could have blocked their southward move at Tadcaster. Such a move would also have put the Royalist Army between the main Allied Army and Sir John Meldrum's approaching Lancashire and Cheshire force, which was just debouching into the south of the county. With hindsight it is clear that no such plan had occurred to

Prince Rupert, and his sole intention was to fight the enemy wherever he found them.

With this in mind the Prince had his army on the move by four in the morning.[13] As the Allied rearguard waited on the ridge above Long Marston village, large bodies of enemy horse began appearing on the moor below. These were followed by bodies of foot and the whole mass began to form for battle. By nine o'clock the commanders of the Allied rearguard were convinced that the enemy was intent on fighting, and with this in mind, a message was sent to their superiors, recommending an immediate return to the vicinity of Long Marston:

> Where about 9 a clock in the morning they discovered that the enemy had drawne over a great part of their Army by the bridge they surprised the night before, and by a foord neare to it. Whereupon the Generalls gave present order to call back the foote with the Ordinance, ammunition, and carriages.[14]

Leonard Watson also states that it was about nine o'clock when the Allied Army was recalled.[15] By this time the vanguard of Scots foot had almost reached Tadcaster and the rear of foot, Manchester's brigades, were several miles from the field. It would take some time for them to return.

Prince Rupert had a similar problem. By nine o'clock his army was beginning to deploy onto Marston Moor, having crossed the Ouse by a pontoon bridge built by the Allies and captured by the Prince the previous evening. One contemporary correspondent, Thomas Stockdale, also mentions the use of a ford close to the site of the bridge.[16] It is possible that Rupert's horse used the ford while his foot and ordinance used the bridge. Although enough of Rupert's forces had deployed onto the moor by nine o'clock to prompt the Allied lieutenant generals to recall their army, it would still be some time before the bulk of his forces were deployed in battle formation. Despite the fact that he had sent orders to the Marquis of Newcastle to come to the field with his foot by four in the morning, there was still no sign of them.

While Rupert awaited the arrival of the remainder of his army, and Newcastle's forces from York, he decided to attempt to gain an advantage over his opponents by seizing the western end of the ridge, upon which their 3,000 horse were positioned. Captain William Stewart wrote an account of this incident:

> In the mean while, the Enemy perceiving that our Cavalry had possessed themselves of a corn hill, and having discovered neer unto that hill a place of great advantage, where they might have both Sun and Winde of us,

advanced thither with a Regiment of Redcoats and a party of Horse; but we understanding well their intentions, and how prejudiciall it would be unto us if they should keep that ground, we sent out a party which beat them off, and planted our left wing of Horse.[17]

There is a strong possibility that the 'party which beat them off' was part of the Earl of Manchester's horse, perhaps led by Oliver Cromwell himself. This fight took place on, or near, the area known as Bilton Bream, which now overlooks Tockwith village. The same area was later occupied by Cromwell and David Leslie with the left wing of the Allied horse.

At about nine o'clock the Marquis of Newcastle arrived on the field with his newly raised bodyguard troop, formed from a body of 'gentlemen of quality which were in York (who cast themselves into a troop commanded by Sir Thomas Mettam)'.[18] The Prince stated his regret that the Marquis and his troops had not arrived earlier and Newcastle replied that his men had been pillaging the Allied siege lines and he had been unable to gather them at the time required. His lieutenant general, James King (Lord Eythin), was gathering them together and would arrive as soon as he could. This could not have been very reassuring to Prince Rupert, as he had no liking for James King, whom he blamed for his imprisonment following the Battle of Vlotho during the Thirty Years War in Germany. Sir Hugh Cholmley also states that the Prince was all for attacking the Allies with only his own army once he realised Newcastle's infantry would not arrive for some time, but was restrained by the Marquis, who told him that 'he had 4,000 good foot as were in the world'.[19]

After the fight for Bilton Bream the two armies continued deploying and by two o'clock the armies were in position:

About two of the clock we had indifferently well formed our Army, as also the enemy theirs, part of their foot being beyond Owse, that morning, which made them as late as wee in drawing up.[20]

This is supported by Thomas Stockdale, who also states that: 'by 2 a clocke afternoon they were all disposed of in their orders.'[21] It is possible that the York foot did not arrive until after this time. Sir Hugh Cholmley states that they did not arrive until four o'clock.[22] Notwithstanding the possible late arrival of the York foot, by two o'clock the two armies were well enough deployed for the first shots to be fired by the Allied artillery.

The Field of Marston Moor
Unlike many battlefields, the field of Marston Moor is clearly delineated by geographical features. To either side of the field lie two villages: Long Marston

to the east, and Tockwith to the west. To the south a ridge runs between the two villages, and it was on this ridge that the Allied Army formed its line of battle. To the north lies Wilstrop Wood, and this marks the northern extremity of the field. Although the enclosing of the moor in the late eighteenth century has changed the character of the terrain considerably, the battlefield still remains a peaceful rural setting for what was a far from peaceful event. Little building has taken place on the battlefield. The two villages have encroached onto the flanks of the battlefield, as they have expanded over the years, but not enough to mar the field, as has happened at other sites. There are no large housing developments covering the area, as at Wakefield, for example. A row of cottages and a manor house are all that have been built on the battlefield itself.

There are no major roads running through the area. A country road connects Tockwith and Long Marston, and another road runs northwards from Long Marston, approximately along the course of Atterwith Lane. Neither of these roads is heavily used. Several dirt tracks leave the Long Marston–Tockwith road. One of these, Moor Lane, leads north through the Royalist lines towards Wilstrop Wood. Walk several hundred yards along this lane and – with the exception of the occasional aircraft – the noises of the modern world disappear, and the walker is left listening to the sounds of insects and the song of birds. On 2 July 1644 the noise would have been somewhat louder and more threatening.

How did the field differ in July 1644 from that which the modern visitor finds today? In some respects very little, and in others quite a lot. The under-lying shape of the land has changed very little. The ridge upon which the Allied Army deployed rises to a height of about 38 metres. Along much of its length it drops to 30 metres within 100 metres of its crest. By the time the Long Marston–Tockwith road is reached 300 metres further north, the ridge has dropped to the 23-metre contour line. After this the slope becomes barely perceptible and the 15-metre contour line is not reached for another 1,000 metres, making a gradient of less than 1 metre per 100 metres covered. The ground continues towards Wilstrop Wood on a virtually level plain.[23]

The bulk of the fighting took place to the north of the Long Marston–Tockwith road, so the Allied ridge line had little bearing on events until late in the day. Looking at the ridge from the road, or from further north towards the Royalist lines, it seems to be a continuous unbroken line. In fact, for much of its length, it is two ridge lines with a pronounced valley in between, although this is not apparent from the Ordnance Survey map. Some authors have placed much relevance on this hidden valley, but it is hard to see why, when most of the fighting took place 500–600 metres further north along the line of the ditch, which will be discussed shortly. There are, and were, no natural water features on the field, the nearest being the River Nidd, which lies over 1,000 metres to the north-east.

It is the man-made features on the battlefield that have changed considerably over the last 350 years. These take three forms: buildings, field systems, and communications. As mentioned previously, little building has been done on the battlefield. Obviously, as the population of Tockwith and Long Marston has grown the villages have begun to spread along the road towards one another. Fortunately, this growth is still limited and does not encroach too far onto the field. At the time of the battle the villages would have been immediately surrounded by small enclosures. As was common in most of England at the time, both villages had three large open fields surrounding them and the names of several of these fields are given on the OS map. At Tockwith the fields were known as: West Field, East Field, and Mill Field. At Long Marston two fields are shown to the west and south-west of the village and are called Marston Field and Church Field. Marston Field is actually mentioned by Sir Thomas Fairfax: 'The place was Marston Feilds (wch afterwards gave ye name of this battle).'[24] Sir Thomas is not quite correct in this, as it was the moorland to the north of the cultivated land that gave the battle its name. By the time of the battle the cultivated land between Tockwith and Long Marston had joined into one large field, which had begun to encroach onto the moorland north of the road. This cultivated area is variously described as 'a Corne-field close to the Moore',[25] 'a large field of Rie'[26] and 'a corn hill'.[27] To the north of this large corn field was the moor from which the battle takes its name. This is described by Thomas Stockdale as: 'a large plaine common lying betwixt Marston, Torwith [Tockwith], and Wilstrop.'[28] The area of the moor was enclosed towards the end of the eighteenth century and instead of being a 'large plaine' it is now broken up into numerous fields.

Between the cultivated land and the moor lay a man-made obstacle. This is described variously as: 'a small dich and a bank',[29] 'the hedge and ditch'[30] and 'ye hedges of ye Cornfields'.[31] This was almost certainly not a continuous ditch and hedge but a series, or a combination of both, which delineated the cultivated land from the moorland to the north. There is also evidence for a number of small enclosures forming part of the obstacle. Towards Tockwith, in front of the Allies' left wing of horse, the obstacle does not seem to have been as great as it was towards Long Marston. Leonard Watson describes it as 'a small ditch and bank'.[32] Next in line came the Earl of Manchester's infantry, and to their front the obstacle was negligible, if it existed at all. William Stewart writes that: 'only between the Earl of Manchesters foot and the enemy there was a plain'.[33] This gap in the obstacle was covered by two bodies of Royalist foot, including Prince Rupert's own regiment, which were placed well in advance of the Royalist first line. To the right of Manchester's infantry the obstacle resumed and is described as a hedge in front of Lord Fairfax's foot[34] and a ditch in front of the Scots foot to his right.[35] In neither case does it seem to have formed a major obstacle to their advance, as will be seen. Only in front of Sir Thomas Fairfax did the obstacle become a major problem. Close to Atterwith Lane the cultivated land ended in an abrupt 6-foot-high bank, dropping down onto the moor.[36] The moor also seems to have been more rugged here than it was further to the west. Sir Thomas Fairfax describes the ground to his front as being full of 'Whins and Diches wch we were to pass over before we could get to ye enemy, wch put us into great disorder'.[37] As can be seen the hedge/ditch line was not a complete continuous line and varied considerably in the severity of its effect on troops trying to cross it.

In addition to the Tockwith–Long Marston Road several tracks ran across the moor. To the west of Long Marston, Atterwith Lane ran north onto the moor. A few hundred metres up the lane were several enclosures. About 400 metres further west is Moor Lane. After 1,200 metres Moor Lane reaches a crossroads, where it turns sharp right and heads off towards the village of Hessay and then on towards York. It was along this lane that Newcastle's infantry marched onto the field. At the crossroads they continued west along Sugar Hill Lane for almost 600 metres, until they debouched onto the moor in the area of White Syke Close, although the close itself postdates the battle. Running north from the crossroads was another track, which joined the York–Boroughbridge road north-east of Wilstrop Wood. Sugar Hill Lane also turned north and continued on to join the York–Boroughbridge road, having passed to the west of Wilstrop Wood. These tracks had existed for a long time before the battle and should not be thought of as the farm tracks they are today, but as major thoroughfares crossing the moor from York towards Boroughbridge and Wetherby.[38]

One final piece of terrain that existed at the time of the battle is the rabbit warren on Bilton Bream, which is at the western end of the Allied ridge, to the east of Tockwith village. Cromwell deployed his horse in this area. Although it had little bearing on the fighting, as Cromwell descended from the ridge towards the ditch, it caused problems for Manchester's Lieutenant General of Horse as he tried to deploy his men. Wild rabbits have not always been the pests they are today and formed an integral part of the village economy, providing a ready supply of fresh meat during the winter months. They were such a valuable part of the village's food supply that they were often hedged or walled in and provided with a keeper. Leonard Watson writes of pioneers having to clear the ground to allow the wings of the army to deploy.[39] It is suggested that these pioneers were used to clear the hedge surrounding the rabbit warren, which allowed Cromwell's troopers to fully deploy.

The Long Wait

About two o'clock the first shots of the battle were fired. Leonard Watson writes:

> About two of the clock, the great Ordnance of both sides began to play, but with small success to either; about five of the clock wee had a generall silence on both sides, each expecting who should begin the charge.[40]

Other contemporary writers agree with Watson as to the start of the bombardment and its general lack of effect.[41] The bombardment continued until about five o'clock, when quiet descended upon the field. Few casualties are reported, but one or two individuals are named. Sir Henry Slingsby tells of the death of a Captain Haughton, son of Sir Gilbert Haughton, but then goes on to say that the Allied guns fired only four shots before ceasing their fire.[42] This seems a very slow rate of fire for a three-hour bombardment and Sir Henry is almost certainly in error. Another named casualty was Captain Valentine Walton, Cromwell's nephew. This is reported by Oliver Cromwell himself in a letter to his brother-in-law, Colonel Walton: 'Sir, God hath taken away your eldest Son by a cannon-shot. It brake his leg. We were necessitated to have it cut off, whereof he died.'[43]

This blunt statement bears witness to the problems in treating wounds that existed until the end of nineteenth century. Simeon Ash reports an incident related by Lord Grandison, a Royalist officer, which took place during the bombardment:

> Before the fight, while the Canon was playing on both sides, a Trooper hearing the singing of Psalms in our severall Regiments, came three times to his Lordship with bloody oaths and fearfull execrations in his mouth, telling him, That the Round-heads were singing Psalms, and therefore, they should be routed that day, and that himself should be slain: His Lordship did reprove him, and cane him for his swearing and cursing, but he proceeded in his wickednesse: and as these words, God damn me, God sink me, were in his mouth, a Drake bullet killed him.[44]

As stated, about five o'clock the bombardment ceased and a general silence covered the field. Both sides awaited the advance of the other, but neither seemed keen to do so. If the Allied troops commenced an attack they would have to fight their way over the ditch, while the Royalists would have to attack uphill. As both sides waited the Allied soldiers fell to singing psalms, as reported by Simeon Ash above, and by Sir Henry Slingsby, who writes that the Allied troops: 'in Marston feilds falls to singing psalms.'[45]

While the Allied Army sang, the Royalist commanders were in deep discussion. James King, Lord Eythin, had arrived on the field with the York infantry. Sir Hugh Cholmley reports a discussion between Prince Rupert and Eythin:

> The Prince demanded of King how he liked the marshalling of his Army, who replied he did not approve of it being drawn too near the enemy, and in a place of disadvantage, then said the Prince 'they may be drawn to a further distance.' 'No Sir' said King 'it is too late;' It is so, King dissuaded the Prince from fighting, saying 'Sir your forwardness lost us the day in Germany, where yourself was taken prisoner,' upon the dissuasions of the Marquess and King and that it was near night, the Prince was resolved not to join battle that day, and therefore gave order to have provisions for his Army brought from York, and did not imagine the enemy durst make any attempt; so that when the alarum was given, he was set upon the earth at meat a pretty distance from his troops, and many of the horsemen were dismounted and laid on the ground with their horses in their hands.[46]

The Duchess of Newcastle also reports these discussions and writes that her husband was in his coach when the action began.[47] Some time between five and seven o'clock the Allied Army had advanced a couple of hundred yards towards the Tockwith–Long Marston road, in an attempt to draw the Royalists into an attack, but Prince Rupert was not drawn. By seven o'clock the Royalist commanders had decided that no fighting would take place that day and had retired to feed and refresh themselves. They would be proved to be wrong.

Several reasons are given by contemporary authors for the Allies' decision to advance around half-past seven. Arthur Trevor, in a letter to the Marquis of Ormonde, states that the cause of the Allied advance was the arrival of the York infantry and the Allies' wish to attack before these reinforcements had been incorporated into the Royalist line.[48] Sir Hugh Cholmley gives the precipitating factor for the Allied advance a much more sinister tone:

> The reason why they fell thus suddenly upon the Prince, as many conjecture, is that a Scottish officer amongst the Prince his horse, whilst the armies faced one another, fled to the Parliament Army and gave them intelligence; and it was further observed that Hurry a Scotchman having the marshalling of the horse in the Princes right wing, his own troop were the first that turned their backs; yet I have heard the Prince in his own private opinion did not think Hurry culpable of infidelity.[49]

There seems to be little evidence to support this claim, as Sir Hugh writes, Prince Rupert did not believe Urry capable of such treachery. A much more convincing reason is that given by Edmund Ludlow, who writes that Cromwell:

> Engaged the right wing of the enemy commanded by Prince Rupert, who had gained an advantageous piece of ground upon Marston Moor, and caused a battery to be erected upon it, from which Capt. Walton, Cromwell's sister's son, was wounded by a shot in the knee. Whereupon Col. Cromwell commanded two field-pieces to be brought in order to annoy the enemy, appointing two regiments of foot to guard them; who marching to that purpose, were attacked by the foot of the enemy's right wing, that fired thick upon them from the ditches. Upon this both parties seconding their foot, were wholly engaged, who before had stood only facing each other.[50]

It is a fairly common occurrence in military history that a battle is brought on against the wishes of the opposing commanders by an over-active subordinate. The Royalists had placed several guns in an advantageous position and had opened fire on Cromwell's horsemen. Cavalry is hard pushed to stand under artillery fire, and as previously mentioned, the Royalist horse had made a short withdrawal under similar circumstances. Cromwell ordered two guns forward to bring counter-battery fire down upon the enemy's battery. He supported this with two regiments of foot. These would have been part of the Earl of Manchester's foot and their commander, Lawrence Crawford, must have agreed to this. These regiments were engaged by Royalist infantry along the line of the ditch, most likely Rupert's own Bluecoats and Byron's regiment. More troops would have been drawn into contact, in support of the troops already engaged. At this point it is often easier to order a full-blown attack than to disengage, and this is the decision Leven took. At about half-past seven the whole Allied Army began its advance towards the ditch.[51] Simeon Ash describes this advance: 'Our Army in its severall parts moving down the Hill, was like unto so many thicke clouds.'[52]

As late as it was in the day, both armies prepared to lay on. With the advance of the Allied Army the Battle of Marston Moor had begun.

Chapter 8

The Armies Deployed

Did with flying colours looke each other in the face . . .

Before discussing the deployment of the two armies at the Battle of Marston Moor it would be worth looking at the theoretical organisation of the armies and how their soldiers were equipped. As was the norm throughout Western Europe at this time, the Civil War Armies were divided into three parts: foot, horse and dragoons. Each had its own battlefield role, which was greatly affected by the terrain on the battlefield. Each will be discussed it turn.[1]

The foot regiments of all the armies at Marston Moor – Royalist, Parliamentarian and Scots – were organised and equipped in very similar manner. In theory a regiment of foot comprised 1,200 men divided into ten companies, but not all companies were the same size. The first three companies – Colonel's, Lieutenant Colonel's and Major's – were the largest: the higher the rank, the larger the company. The remaining seven companies were commanded by captains. Each company also had a lieutenant and an ensign. The chain of command was completed by the non-commissioned officers – sergeants, corporals, etc. It is usual in contemporary documents not to number the officers and NCOs in the strength of the unit, and as these men could make up a decent proportion of a unit's strength, numbers given can be somewhat misleading. Herein lies one of the problems with the armies during the Civil Wars. As the strength of units decreased – due to sickness, desertion and battle casualties, and so on – the number of officers did not. This meant that regiments retained their ten-company organisation although each company may have only contained twenty or thirty other ranks. This led to a very top-heavy organisation. When the New Model Army was raised in early 1645 it was short of foot, so thousands of conscripts had to be found to bring the regiments up to strength. At the same time, it was found that the number of officers available greatly exceeded the number required, so the surplus were forced to resign their commissions or fight on as volunteers. As will be seen in due course, many regiments were well below their paper strength. One of the main reasons for this was the number of regiments raised: there were only so many recruits to go round, and obviously, the more regiments raised, the fewer troops were available to each. On occasion smaller regiments were absorbed into larger ones to bring them nearer to their paper strengths, but the usual ploy was to combine several small regiments into one body on the battlefield.

Having briefly discussed the organisation of the foot regiments it is worth looking at how they were armed and equipped. Once again there was little difference between any of the regiments of foot at Marston Moor: be they Royalist, Parliamentarian or Scots. A normal foot regiment was divided into two parts: shot and pike. In theory there should have been two musketeers for each pikeman, although in practice this was not always realised. At the beginning of the Civil War the main bases of arms production, and the main armouries, were firmly in Parliament's hands. The King had to rely on arms being provided by three limited sources: private individuals, local Trained Band armouries, and foreign imports. The first two were very limited. Private individuals and Trained Bands held limited supplies of weapons. In theory, the third source, foreign imports, had the potential to provide a virtually boundless supply of arms and armour, but in practice this was far from the case. The first limiting factor on foreign imports was, quite simply, money. Continental arms manufacturers were not going to supply weapons for nothing: hence the Queen's departure to the Continent with a substantial portion of the royal jewels. A second, and very important, limiting factor was Parliament's control of the Navy. With control of the Fleet came control of the seaborne approaches. Once money had been found to purchase the arms a ship had to be found to carry them across the North Sea and penetrate the Parliamentarian blockade. These factors meant that during the early months of the Civil War, while many of Parliament's regiments achieved the desired 2:1 ratio between shot and pike, few of the King's regiments did so, many only achieving parity between the two.

With the capture of Bristol in 1643 the Royalists gained a major arms manufacturing centre and a large port. This went a long way towards alleviating the Royalists' supply problem. The Oxford Army, and to a lesser degree the Western Army, began to build up the number of musketeers in their regiments, until the desired ratio was achieved in many units. Unfortunately, the further from the main arms centres, the fewer weapons filtered down to the armies. The two main Northern armies, Newcastle's and Lord Fairfax's, never seem to have achieved this 2:1 ratio. That said, on a number of occasions Lord Fairfax's foot comprised musketeers with few, if any, supporting pikemen: for example, at Seacroft Moor and Adwalton Moor; but this was caused by a lack of men, not a surfeit of muskets.

As the war progressed the ratio of shot-to-pike grew. Although the pike was still considered the more honourable weapon, tactical experience had shown that muskets were more effective. While the New Model Army seems to have retained its 2:1 ratio, the King's Oxford Army had a number of 'musket only' regiments during the Naseby campaign of 1645. But, as with Lord Fairfax's army, this was probably due to a lack of men. As the seventeenth century neared its close the ratio of shot-to-pike increased, until early in the eighteenth century, the pike disappeared altogether.

Each company in a foot regiment contained the appropriate ratio of shot-to-pike, in essence being a miniature version of the whole regiment. Tactically, all the pikemen in the regiment formed a block in the centre of the unit. The musketeers were divided into two blocks, one either side of the pikes. This meant that the company was actually an administrative unit not a tactical one. In theory both pike and shot formed six ranks deep, but in practice regiments might have formed with fewer ranks, in order to maintain a larger frontage, and this may have been the case with some Royalist units at Marston Moor. Sometimes the pike and shot formed separate units, but this was unusual and was dictated by the tactical situation. Two examples of this are Lansdown Hill and Adwalton Moor, both fought during the summer of 1643. Much of the fighting at both battles was between bodies of musketeers engaged in enclosed terrain. Both were decided by an attack launched by a body of pikemen. Although bodies of pike fighting as independent units were fairly rare, this was not the case with musketeers. In enclosed terrain horse and pike were of limited use, but musketeers came into their own. Such was the situation at the Battle of Bolden Hill, near Sunderland, during the Scots march south. These bodies of musketeers were often referred to as 'commanded musketeers'. These 'commanded' men had other uses. Very often they led the assault on defended works and were also used to support the horse on occasion, small bodies of shot being placed between the units of cavalry.

In the main, the musketeers were equipped with the matchlock musket. This type of musket gets its name from the lighted match that fired the charge. Initially a long, heavy, weapon, which had a rest to help support it, as the war progressed it became shorter and more manageable. Looking at contemporary drill books has led some historians to conclude that it would have taken several minutes for each round to be loaded and fired. This was far from the case. In the hands of trained men two or three rounds a minute could be fired. Ammunition was carried in several different ways. The first was the 'twelve apostles'. This was a bandolier with a number of wooden containers suspended from it, very often twelve, although more (or less) could be carried. Another was the cartridge box or bag. This contained a number of ready-made cartridges similar to those used in later periods. Finally, the cartridges could simply be carried in the pockets of a soldier's jacket. In action soldiers often carried a number of musket balls in their mouths, for ready use. When surrendering garrisons were granted the honours of war they were often allowed to march out with 'Matches lighted on both ends' and with 'Bullets in their mouths'.[2] Many musketeers were also equipped with a cheap, crude sword. These seem to have been mainly used for chopping firewood or threatening frightened civilians. In action most musketeers preferred to use their muskets as crude but effective clubs.

As already mentioned, the pike was considered the more honourable weapon. The strongest men in a unit were used to carry pikes. In theory the pike was 16 feet in length with a steel point at its business end, but it was a regular occurrence for pikes to be shortened by hacking several feet off the bottom. Although this was frowned upon by the powers that be, it provided a ready source of firewood and made the pike considerably easier to handle. As with the musketeers, the pikemen were equipped with a cheap sword, which proved more ornamental than useful in action. One major difference between the musketeer and the pikeman was the amount of armour that, in theory, was worn by the latter. The pikeman should have been equipped with a breast- and back-plate, tassets to protect his thighs, a gorget to cover his throat, and a steel pot for his head, as shown in the drill books of the time. In practice, armour for pikemen was difficult to come by – more so for the Royalists than the Parliamentarians. It was also heavy and cumbersome to wear and must have been a nightmare to march in, especially on a hot summer's day. As the war progressed fewer and fewer pikemen wore armour, and with the exception of the odd helmet, little infantry armour would have been worn by either side at Marston Moor.

At the start of the Civil War the horse was divided into two types: Cuirassiers and Arquebusiers. The two types were differentiated by the amount of armour they wore not by the tactics they used, as had been the case in the past. The Cuirassier was fully armoured from his head to his knees and his legs were protected by high leather boots. Only a few units were equipped in this manner, mainly bodyguards, although individuals who could afford such armour may have worn it. This type of armour was very constrictive and consequently unpopular. One unit that is known to have been equipped in this manner was Sir Arthur Haselrig's regiment of horse, known as the 'Lobsters'. Even this regiment seems to have converted to normal Arquebusier equipment after its defeat at Roundway Down.

The Arquebusier was the standard Civil War cavalryman and when contemporary accounts speak of 'horse' this is usually what they mean, so

Arquebusiers will be referred to as horse from now on. Ideally, a horseman would be defensively arrayed with a stout buff coat, over which was worn a breast- and back-plate. To finish off his armour he would wear a steel helmet, usually of the 'lobster pot' style, while thigh-length boots would protect his legs and buff leather gauntlets his hands. The rider's left or 'rein' hand might also have an armoured gauntlet. Ideally, the horseman carried a variety of weapons: a sword, suspended on a baldric over his right shoulder, plus a pair of pistols and a carbine for firepower. Occasionally, the cavalryman's armoury might include a pole axe – an effective anti-armour weapon. In reality, how-ever, equipment varied greatly from man to man. Meanwhile, the Scots horse added another weapon to the list. Although the majority of Scots troopers were equipped in a similar manner to their English counterparts, two regiments each had a squadron of lancers. Only one of these regiments, Balgonie's, fought at Marston Moor.

Regiments of horse varied in size and strength. In theory regiments were made up of a certain number of troops. These troops could vary greatly in size. Scots troops had a paper strength of sixty, and eight troops formed a regiment. Two Eastern Association regiments, Manchester's and Cromwell's, were very large units, having eleven and fourteen troops respectively. When the New Model Army was raised, an attempt was made to standardise the size of cavalry regiments into six troops of 100 men each.

Cavalry troops were tactical units, unlike the companies in regiments of foot. In theory troops formed three deep, but as with the foot, shallower formations were occasionally used to maintain a wider frontage. At the start of the Civil War two tactical systems held sway. The Parliamentarian horse attempted to halt and disorganise their opponents by the use of firepower. In the early battles this proved a disastrous tactic and the Parliamentarian horse was regularly beaten by their Royalist opponents. One exception to this was the horse of Lord Fairfax's army, which seem to have used similar tactics to their Royalist enemies. Whether this was brought about by a distinct tactical decision or by a lack of firearms is open to debate. On the other hand, the Royalist horse used the full-blooded charge from the very start, reserving their pistols for the hand-to-hand fight or the pursuit of their enemies. One problem caused by this break-neck charge was a lack of control once the enemy had been beaten. Time after time victorious Royalist horse would disappear from the field in pursuit of their opponents, leaving their infantry to fend for them-selves, and return to the field after some considerable time with their horses blown. This almost led to defeat at Edgehill and was a major factor in the defeats at Marston Moor and Naseby.

The regular defeat of the Parliamentarian horse brought a change of tactics. With the exception of Lord Fairfax's horse, the Parliamentarian cavalry does not seem to have used the charge at the gallop, as did their Royalist opponents. Parliamentarian regiments were trained to charge knee-to-knee at the trot. When used by disciplined, well-trained troops this was a very successful tactic. This was shown by the success of the Eastern Association horse, under its Lieutenant General, Oliver Cromwell. This success would be carried forward into the New Model Army, whose regiments of horse were raised mainly from Eastern Association troops. The charge at the trot, and the discipline of the troops, allowed victorious regiments to rally and continue the fight. This was to prove decisive at both Marston Moor and Naseby.

The other type of soldier contained in most Civil War armies was the dragoon. Basically, the dragoon was a musketeer who rode to battle. In this respect he was similarly equipped to a musketeer. There is a definite blurring in contemporary accounts between true dragoons and mounted musketeers. True dragoons were used for scouting and raiding, while mounted musketeers carried out the same tasks as their dismounted compatriots but were able to move more rapidly. The main tactical use of dragoons on the battlefield was to protect the flanks of the army or to harass the flanks of the enemy.

The final element of a typical Civil War army was the artillery. Guns came in a variety of shapes and sizes. The main types of guns were:[3]

Weapon	Calibre of piece (inch)	Weight of piece (lb)	Length of piece (feet)	Weight of shot (lb)
Cannon Royal	8	8,000	8	63
Cannon	7	7,000	10	47
Demi–cannon	6	6,000	12	27
Culverin	5	4,000	11	15
Demi–culverin	4½	3,600	10	9
Saker	3½	2,500	9½	5¼
Minion	3	1,500	8	4
Falcon	2¾	700	6	2¼
Falconet	2	210	4	1¼
Robinet	1¼	120	3	¾

The heaviest of these pieces were of little use on the battlefield. The Cannon Royal, Cannon, Demi-cannon and Culverin were all siege pieces. Some of the heavier field pieces would not have been very mobile and once emplaced would have remained where they stood on the field. The lighter pieces were more than capable of being moved around the field, and examples of the redeployment of guns have already been mentioned in the previous chapter.

Having discussed the disparate elements of an English Civil War army it is now time to put those pieces together to form an army on the battlefield. The deployment of an army obviously depended on the terrain and the tactical situation it faced. What follows is a theoretical deployment in a face-to-face confrontation on an open field, as at Edgehill, Marston Moor and Naseby.

The foot formed the centre of the battle line. Two or more regiments formed a brigade and several brigades formed a line, although, on occasion (the Royalist Army at Naseby for example), regiments from a brigade could form in two lines. Usually an army formed in two lines, with the second providing support for the first. Small groups of guns might be placed between the regiments of the front line or formed into larger batteries placed on a prominent feature. On either flank of the foot would be the horse, formed into brigades and deployed in two lines. On the far wings of the army would be the dragoons. Finally, a reserve of horse, foot or both might be deployed behind the centre of the line ready to reinforce any threatened area. If Allied forces were involved the line was usually divided in two. The foot of one army formed the right wing of the centre, with its horse forming the right wing of horse. The other force would form the left side of the army.

This is the theory. It is now time to examine the deployment of the armies at Marston Moor. Although two battle plans and a wealth of contemporary accounts exist, there is still plenty of room for debate. This debate has raged for well over 150 years and continues today, as will be seen.

The Royalist Army
The main source for the deployment of the Royalist Army at Marston Moor is Sir Bernard de Gomme's plan.[4] Few other details are available from other contemporary sources. There are a few errors in de Gomme's plan, usually omissions, but it is the main source of what follows.

The Royalist right wing was commanded by Lord Byron and comprised mainly horse. Its front line, commanded by Byron himself, was formed of four regiments of horse divided into eleven bodies and totalling about 1,100 men. From right to left this line was formed by the following regiments: Lord Byron (three bodies), Sir John Urry (two bodies), Sir William Vaughan (three bodies) and Colonel Marcus Trevor (three bodies). Supporting this front line were 500 musketeers divided into eleven small bodies. Protecting the right flank of Byron's front line, and slightly set back from it, was the regiment of Colonel Samuel Tuke. Tuke's 200 men were divided into four small bodies. Byron's second line was commanded by Lord Molyneux and was formed of four regiments. Molyneux's own regiment was formed in two bodies on the right. Then came Sir Thomas Tyldesley's regiment, once again in two bodies. The

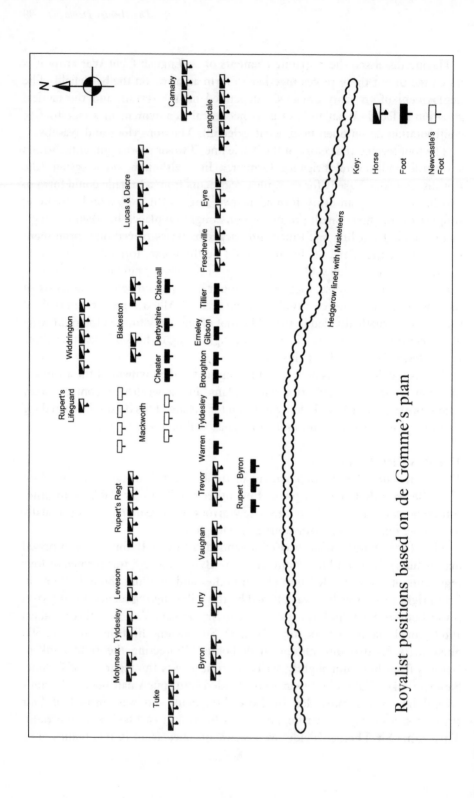

Royalist positions based on de Gomme's plan

line continued with two bodies formed from Colonel Thomas Leveson's regiment. De Gomme gives these three regiments a total strength of 800 men. The final regiment in Byron's second line was Prince Rupert's own regiment. De Gomme gives no figures for this regiment, but a rough total of 400–500 men is probably close. This gives a total of 2,600 horse and 500 musketeers for Byron's wing.

In front of Trevor's regiment of horse was a brigade of foot, formed in three bodies: two from Prince Rupert's Bluecoats and one from Colonel Robert Byron's regiment, although de Gomme states that this third body was from Lord Byron's regiment. This brigade was commanded by Colonel Thomas Napier and seems to have been somewhat of an orphan, belonging neither to the centre or the right wing of horse and, as it transpired, supported by neither during the battle.

The Royalist centre was formed into several lines of foot with horse in reserve. Due to the late arrival of the York infantry, Rupert had formed his front line and the left half of his second line from his own regiments of foot. As the York infantry had arrived they had formed the right side of the second line and a short third line. Supporting these infantry lines were several bodies of horse. Rupert's infantry was commanded by Henry Tillier, a veteran of the Irish Wars. Newcastle's foot was commanded by Sir Francis Mackworth. The front line was made up of eight bodies from six regiments. On the right of the line was Colonel Henry Warren's regiment forming a single body. Next came two bodies from Sir Thomas Tyldesley's regiment. Colonel Robert Broughton's Greencoats formed the next two bodies and to their left was a combined body formed from the two weak regiments of Sir Michael Earnley and Colonel Richard Gibson. Completing the line was Tillier's own regiment of Greencoats, formed into two bodies. With the exception of Tyldesley's regiment all the front line regiments were veterans of the Irish Wars. Several of them, particularly Earnley's and Gibson's, had suffered heavy casualties at Nantwich earlier in the year. Tyldesley's regiment had been raised early in the war but contained many recruits gathered during Prince Rupert's march through Lancashire.

The second line of foot was formed of seven bodies. De Gomme shows them covering the gaps between the units of the first line. On the left came the regiment of Colonel Edward Chisenhall in a single body. Next in line came a body to which de Gomme gives no name. Peter Young ascribed the Derbyshire foot to this body, some 220 strong, and gives its commander as Colonel John Millward. Most modern historians concur with this. There is little evidence to support this theory other than the absence of the Derbyshire foot from de Gomme's plan. This small body was reported by Sir John Gell to be marching from Derbyshire to join Prince Rupert in Lancashire (see Chapter Five for details). The final two bodies of Prince Rupert's foot were provided by Colonel Henry Cheater's regiment. Completing the second line were three bodies of Newcastle's foot. Behind these three bodies a further four formed the right hand of the third line. De Gomme gives little information about Newcastle's infantry.[5] Other sources give a strength of between 3,000 and 4,000 men, commanded by Sir Francis Mackworth. Lord Eythin had left three regiments in York when he marched out on the morning of the 2nd: Sir Thomas Glemham's, Sir John Belasyse's, and Sir Henry Slingsby's. Elements of eighteen other regiments may have been present on the field:[6]

Sir Phillip Byron's	Sir Richard Tempest's
Colonel Conyer's	Lord Eythin's
Colonel Kirkebride's	Sir Timothy Featherstonhaugh's
Sir William Lambton's	Colonel Floyd's
Colonel Lamplugh's	Colonel Foster's
Sir Francis Mackworth's	Sir John Girlington's
Lord Mansfield's	Colonel Hilton's
Marquis of Newcastle's	Sir Richard Huddleston's
Sir Charles Slingsby's	Sir Richard Hutton's

Using a mid-range figure of 3,500 for the Northern Foot, and assuming all eighteen regiments listed were present, this gives a strength of 500 to each body with two or three regiments in each. This gives an average strength of less than 200 men per regiment! De Gomme gives a total of 11,000 foot. Taking away 3,500 for the Northern Foot and another 1,000 for the commanded muskets, 500 on each wing, this leaves 6,500 men for Rupert's regiments. Millward's regiment may have only been a couple of hundred men strong, so this gives a strength of just over 400 men per body. Several of Rupert's regiments formed two bodies, and so may have been as large as 800 men each – four times the average strength of Newcastle's regiments. That said de Gomme states that the ditch was 'lined with musquetiers' and these would have been provided by the regiments of foot, thus reducing the strength of individual bodies even further.

Completing the third line was a brigade of horse, divided into two bodies, and commanded by Sir William Blakiston. De Gomme provides no details of the strength of this brigade but about 500 troopers would be close. Behind this third line was a reserve formed of several bodies of horse. On the left was Sir Edward Widdrington's brigade, assigned a strength of 400 by de Gomme and formed in five bodies. On the right was Prince Rupert's Lifeguard, 150 strong. De Gomme misses off two other lifeguard troops known to have been on the field: those of Commisary General George Porter and the Marquis of

Newcastle, commanded by Sir Thomas Metham. De Gomme lists Porter's troop but fails to assign it a position on his plan. Both these troops had a strength of about fifty men.

The Royalist left wing was commanded by George Goring. Once again it was formed into two lines, with a regiment of the first line refused to protect its flank. De Gomme totals the first line at 1,100 horse and 500 musketeers. The horse was divided into eleven bodies. The right-hand three were provided by Colonel John Frescheville's regiment. This regiment and the one to its immediate left, Colonel Rowland Eyre's, were part of Prince Rupert's horse. The remaining six bodies are assigned to Sir Charles Lucas's brigade, which was part of the Northern Horse. Completing the first line was Colonel Francis Carnaby's regiment of 200 men. As mentioned above, this regiment was set back a short distance to protect the first line's left flank. Sir Charles Lucas commanded the second line, formed by six divisions of Sir Richard Dacre's brigade, which was 800-strong according to de Gomme.

Once again Sir Bernard gives few details as to the regiments comprising the Northern Horse. Several officers and units are not mentioned at all. Sir Marmaduke Langdale was certainly present and may have commanded a brigade in the first line. Sir John Mayney and his brigade were also present. This brigade comprised five regiments belonging to Sir John Mayney, Sir William Pelham, Sir John Preston, Sir Robert Dallison, and Sir William Eure. It had gathered at Newark before marching into Lancashire in the wake of the Northern Horse. Up to twenty-one regiments of horse may have been present on the field.[7] Only one of these regiments is mentioned in a contemporary source, that of Sir Philip Monckton.[8]

De Gomme gives a total strength of 6,500 to the Royalist horse. The strengths listed on his plan come to a total of 4,600, but several bodies of horse have no strength assigned. These are: Prince Rupert's regiment, Prince Rupert's Lifeguard, Blakiston's brigade and the lifeguard troops of Newcastle and Porter. These have been assigned an approximate strength of 1,250 by modern authors, giving a total of 5,850. This is still almost 700 less than de Gomme's total. It is suggested that the bulk of these missing troopers belonged to the Northern Horse and the Newark contingent and were under Goring's command. In this instance de Gomme's plan is much too tidy. Both wings of horse are assigned identical numbers of men, 1,100 in the front line, 800 in the second line, and a refused regiment of 200. The chances of both wings having identical numbers is very remote and the left wing may have been quite a bit stronger than the right, perhaps even 1,000 men stronger.

The final element of the Royalist Army was its artillery. In his plan de Gomme states that they had sixteen guns. Contemporary accounts of the battle disagree with this. Several figures are given by Parliamentarian and Scots correspondents. Robert Douglas[9] and Sir James Lumsden[10] state that twenty guns were captured, while Leonard Watson,[11] Thomas Stockdale[12] and Captain Stewart[13] give a figure of twenty-five. To confuse matters further, two other correspondents report different figures. Robert White gives a total of '18 Peeces, and five Drakes'[14] being captured. Simeon Ash only gives the number of guns captured by the Earl of Manchester's army, which was 'ten pieces of Ordinance' and 'one case of Drakes'.[15] As can be seen from the figures quoted above, de Gomme's total of sixteen guns is too low. It is likely that the figure given by de Gomme only includes the ordinance brought to the field by Prince Rupert. The remaining guns reported as captured were brought to the field from York with the Marquis of Newcastle's infantry.

The Allied Army

As with the Royalist Army a contemporary plan of the Allied deployment exists. This was part of a letter sent by Sir James Lumsden to the Earl of Loudon[16] and will be used as one of the main sources for what follows. Contemporary writers gave much more information about the Allied deployment than they did about the Royalist order of battle. Unfortunately, some of this information is contradictory and has led to a debate that has fizzed for well over 100 years; it will be discussed in due course. Because of this discussion the two wings of horse will be described first and then the two variations of the centre will be examined.

The right wing of horse was commanded by Sir Thomas Fairfax, seconded by Colonel John Lambert. It comprised the whole of Lord Fairfax's horse, deployed in two lines and supported by three regiments of Scots horse. Sir Thomas commanded the first line, which is shown on Lumsden's plan as comprising five bodies. Unfortunately, part of the right-hand side of the page is missing and other bodies may have been shown there. In the gaps between three of the four bodies small units of commanded musketeers are shown. Beneath the right wing of horse Sir James wrote the following:

> Upon the richt of horss 500 draguners, betwixt everie squadron of horss 50 musqueteirs marked with the letter P. The Lord Fairfax had on his wing 3000 horss under the command of his sone Sir Thomas generall major and with them on the same hand we had 1000 horss commandit by the Lord Eglintoun.

This is quite an informative paragraph. First, 500 dragoons formed the right hand of the line. These are not shown on the diagram but may well have been drawn onto the missing section. His next statement, when combined with his

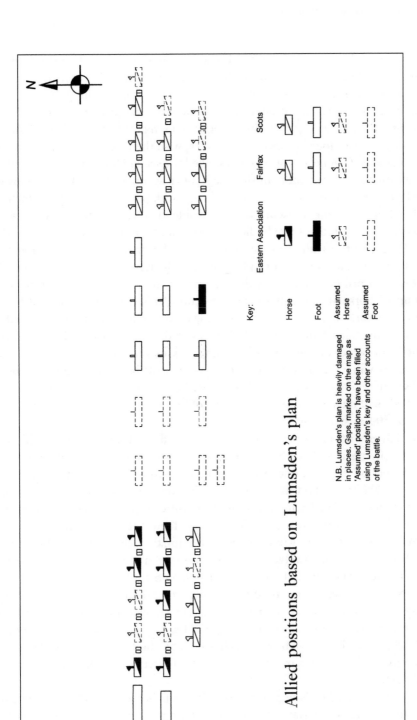

Allied positions based on Lumsden's plan

Key:

Eastern Association | Fairfax | Scots

Horse

Foot

Assumed Horse

Assumed Foot

N.B. Lumsden's plan is heavily damaged in places. Gaps, marked on the map as 'Assumed' positions, have been filled using Lumsden's key and other accounts of the battle.

plan, gives a clue to the number of bodies on the right wing. The front line is shown with five bodies, but only three of the four gaps between the bodies contain musketeers. This is obviously an omission, as Sir James writes: 'betwixt everie squadron of horss 50 musqueteirs marked with the letter P.' It is suggested, therefore, that Sir Thomas commanded five bodies of horse interspersed with four bodies of musketeers, with their right flank protected by 500 dragoons. Colonel Lambert commanded the second line. Only three bodies are shown but the remainder of the line is, once again, missing. A third body of musketeers is shown to the right of the line, which points to at least one further body of horse being present. It is probable that two further bodies were present, giving a total of five bodies of horse and four of musket, similar to the first line. The third line was formed by three Scots regiments, from right to left: Earl of Dalhousie, Earl of Eglington, and the Earl of Leven's, commanded by his son Lord Balgonie. This third regiment comprised two squadrons: one of normal horse and one of lancers. In Lumsden's plan two bodies of Scots horse are clearly shown. The left-hand side of a third body is shown at the edge of a continuation of the damaged area. Some distance to the right, the lower right-hand corner of another body is shown. This gives a possible total of four bodies. As will be seen in the next chapter the Scots horse seem to have fought as discrete regiments, and should therefore be in three bodies, interspersed by two bodies of muskets. This gives a total of ten bodies of fifty musketeers for a total of 500 as stated by Lumsden.

Sir James writes that there were 3,000 of Lord Fairfax's horse under his son and this figure is well within the bounds of possibility. As has already been mentioned in Chapter Four, Sir Thomas returned to Yorkshire with approximately 2,000 horse. To this can be added between six and eight troops, which returned with Colonel Lambert to hold Bradford while awaiting Sir Thomas's arrival. Earlier in the year Sir William Constable had led a number of raids from Hull into the East Riding with a substantial force of cavalry. This force was between ten and twelve troops in strength. At fifty men per troop this gives between 800 and 1,000 troopers to add to Sir Thomas's 2,000. There is evidence that some troops could have had a strength of 60 to 70 men,[17] which brings these strengths up somewhat. As can be seen from this, Lumsden's figure of 3,000 could be close to the truth. This would give each line a strength of 1,500, divided into five bodies, each averaging about 300 troopers. Added to this were the 1,000 Scots troopers, divided into three regiments of just over 300 men each.

As with the Earl of Newcastle's army few details are given of the regiments that formed Lord Fairfax's horse. Only four regiments are named in contemporary accounts: Sir Thomas Fairfax's, Colonel John Lambert's, Colonel

Charles Fairfax's, and Colonel Hugh Bethell's. It is likely that Lord Fairfax's own regiment was present and there is a strong possibility that Sir William Constable's, Sir William Fairfax's, and Sir Thomas Norcliffe's regiments were also on the field, as all three officers had been present at the Siege of York. It is a fair assumption that Sir Thomas's regiment was in the front line with their commander, while Colonel Lambert's probably fought in the second line. Sir Hugh Bethell's was definitely part of the first line as its presence, and its defeat, is reported by Sir Philip Monckton.[18] There were many raw Lancashire recruits in Sir Thomas's first line, as is reported by Captain Stewart.[19] There were almost certainly other regiments present, but whose they were has not come down through the years.

Having discussed the right wing of the Allied Army, it is now time to turn to the left wing. Once again Lumsden gives details of this portion of the Allied line. Unfortunately, there is damage, a hole, in the plan at this point. Fortunately, the text underneath this section of Sir James's plan is still intact:

Upon the left their was 3000 horss of the erle of Manchesters commandit by his Livetennant generall Cromwell and we had 1000 horss commandit by generall major Leslie with the intervall of musqueteirs. The enemies strength as their awin Livetennant generall affirms was 7000 Horss and 12000 foot.

Sir James provides some interesting details and his figure for the enemy army was quite close. The Allied left wing was commanded by Oliver Cromwell. It was divided into a number of bodies split into three lines. Cromwell commanded the first line, Colonel Vermuyden commanded the second line, and David Leslie led the Scots horse of the third line. Lumsden's plan shows five bodies in the first line. The left-hand body is labelled as 'dragoons', leaving four bodies of horse. Between the third and fourth bodies, from the right, is a large hole. In all probability this gap contained a fifth division of horse. The fact that Cromwell had five divisions of horse in his line is supported by Sir Henry Slingsby, who writes: 'Cromwell having ye left wing drawn into 5 bodys of horse.'[20] Between each division was a small body of fifty musketeers – four in total. Colonel Bartholomew Vermuyden commanded Cromwell's second line. Lumsden assigns six divisions to this line. This gives the second line one more division of horse than the first. If all the divisions were of a similar size this would mean that the second line was stronger than the first, which is unlikely. This leaves two possibilities: first, that the divisions of the second line were not as strong as those of the first line; or second, there should only be five divisions not six. It is suggested that the latter is the case. Once again the divisions of horse were interspersed with musketeers. The third line was made up of three regiments of Scots horse under the command of David Leslie. From right to left these were the regiments of Lord Balcarres, Lord Kirkcudbright, and David Leslie. As with the right wing, Lumsden shows four bodies forming this line. The same arguments apply here as put forward while discussing the right wing: the Scots horse fought as regiments, therefore the third line should have only three bodies, with two bodies of musketeers between them. This gives a total of ten bodies of musketeers. It is safe to assume that they were of a similar size to the bodies of shot on the right wing, and this gives a total of 500 musketeers.

Lumsden gives a total of 3,000 horse for the Earl of Manchester's army. Divided into ten divisions this gives an average of 300 men to each division. Interestingly, this is exactly the figure given by Leonard Watson for Cromwell's own division.[21] Few details are given as to which regiments were present, but it is safe to assume that the regiments of the Earl of Manchester, Lieutenant General Oliver Cromwell, Colonel Charles Fleetwood, and Colonel Bartholomew Vermuyden were there. Few details are given as to which regiments comprised each line. It is almost certain that Cromwell's regiment was in the first line, commanded by Cromwell himself. Using the same logic, Vermuyden's regiment formed part of the second line. How the other two regiments were deployed is not known, other than both lines had a similar number of men. The Earl of Manchester's army also contained a regiment of dragoons, five companies strong, commanded by Colonel John Lilburne. No mention is made in contemporary accounts of the presence of this regiment, but it is very likely that it formed part of the left wing. This may account for the sixth division shown by Lumsden in the second line, and the regiment may have operated in support of Colonel Fraser's Scots dragoons. This gives a total of 4,000 horse, 500 muskets and 500 plus dragoons.

In general, most historians have agreed as to the disposition of the Allied horse, only differing in details. This is certainly not the case with the Allied foot. There is a major difference of opinion about the deployment of the Allied front line, particularly with regard to the location of Lord Fairfax's men. There are two schools of thought. First, that Fairfax's men were deployed in the centre of the first line, and second, they were deployed on the right.[22] This may seem to be picking at details, but the matter is crucial to understanding the course of the battle. Before discussing the Allied centre's deployment in detail, a brief history of the debate, and the evidence for both sides, will be presented.

From the time of the battle until 1898 it was assumed that Lord Fairfax's foot formed the right of the Allied first line with the Scots forming the centre and the Earl of Manchester's foot forming the left. In 1898 Charles Firth published an article in the *Transactions of the Royal Historical Society*,[23] which challenged this theory and presented a convincing case for Lord Fairfax forming the centre of the line. In his introduction Firth writes:

> This investigation has led me to reject a view which is adopted in all modern accounts of the battle, and had been hitherto accepted by myself. The received view is that the infantry of the Parliamentarian right wing was entirely routed, while a portion of the centre stood firm. The conclusion which a reconsideration of the evidence obliges me to adopt in this paper is exactly the opposite. The Parliamentarian centre was entirely routed, but a portion of the infantry of the right wing held their ground until the cavalry and infantry of the left wing came to their relief, and turned a defeat into a victory.

This then became the 'received view' of the battle and was followed by Peter Young[24] and Peter Newman[25] in their works on the battle. Then in 1994 David Evans[26] threw down the gauntlet by putting forward the 'Fairfax on the right' theory again. Surely he must have got it wrong if such luminaries as Firth, Young and Newman subscribed to the opposite theory? In fact there is contemporary evidence to support both schools of thought, both in discussions on the deployments of both sides and in the story of the battle presented by witnesses. The evidence for the deployment of the Allied Army will be presented here, while the evidence in the battle accounts will be given in the next chapter. Although this author subscribes to the 'centre school', evidence for both sides will be presented.

What evidence brought pre-Firth authors to their conclusion that Lord Fairfax's men were deployed on the right? There seem to be two accounts that state this. First is the account of Captain Stewart:

> Next unto them was drawn up the right wing of the Foot, consisting of the Lord Fairfax his Foot, and two Brigades of the Scottish Foot for a Reserve. In the main Battell was the Regiments of the Earl of Lindsey, Lord Maitland, Earl of Cassilis, and Kelheads, and two Brigades of the Earl of Manchesters.[27]

Stewart is quite clear that Fairfax formed the right and the Scots the 'main battle', although he also states that Manchester's two brigades were with the Scots. The use of the term 'main Battell' is a throwback to medieval times, when armies were split into three 'battles', or 'wards', known as the 'van', 'main', and 'rear'. In this case the term means the centre. The second account is that of Captain W.H., who writes:

Our Army consisting of three Generalls, had a Generall for every part to conduct it: the main body was the Scots led on by General Leslie, the right by the Lord Fairfax, and the left wing by the Earl of Manchester.[28]

So here are two accounts that clearly state Fairfax was on the right. What are the sources that led Charles Firth to come to the opposite conclusion? He quotes two sources: Thomas Stockdale and Simeon Ash. Stockdale writes:

The Yorkshire forces strengthened with a great party of the Scotts Army having the maine battle, the E. of Manchesters forces the left wing, and the Scotts the right wing.[29]

Once again this is clear as to the positions of the various contingents. Simeon Ash adds to this:

Generall Leslies Foot were on the right hand, the Earle of Manchesters Foot were the left hand of the Lord Fairfax his foot who were the body.[30]

So far there are two accounts supporting each school, so what made Firth plump for the second? One of the main reasons was the situation of the correspondents. Captain Stewart was a troop commander in David Leslie's regiment of horse and as such was situated on the far left of the Allied third line. This was definitely not a good position from which to view the centre of the Allied line. Also, as a troop commander deployed in line of battle, he would have had little opportunity to view the disposition of other parts of the line. Captain W.H., whose full name is not known, is thought to have been a member of the Earl of Manchester's army, possibly a cavalryman. Once again he would have been some distance from the centre, commanding his own troop, and would have had little opportunity to view the Allied deployment, other than in his own immediate area. On the other hand Stockdale and Ash had better opportunities to view the centre. Stockdale was attached to Lord Fairfax's staff, and as such, would have been close to Lord Fairfax. This would have given him ample opportunity to view the Allied deployment. Simeon Ash was in a similar position as one of the Earl of Manchester's chaplains. This, and the course of the battle, led Firth to his conclusion.

By the time Peter Young wrote his book in the late 1960s another source had come to light. This was Sir James Lumsden's letter to Lord Loudon, which was discovered by a Mr H.L. Verry in a London antiquarian bookshop and subsequently sold to Peter Young. This reinforced Firth's conclusions and has already been used to discuss the deployment of the Allied left and right wings. It will be used further while examining the deployment of the Allied centre. All that need be said at the moment is that the plan, although damaged, clearly shows that the two right-hand brigades of the Allied front line were made up of Scots troops. Having discussed the credentials of the other authors quoted it is worth looking at Sir James's situation. Would he have had a good view of the area under discussion? Sir James commanded the part of the Allied second line directly behind the debated area, and as such, was well placed to see who was deployed directly to his front, and can therefore be regarded as a lead witness.

Having discussed the evidence for the whereabouts of Lord Fairfax's infantry and, hopefully, having come to the firm conclusion that they were in the centre, it is now time to look more closely at the deployment of the Allied foot. Further evidence both for and against the centre option will be presented in the next chapter.

Lumsden's plan has been badly damaged, particularly in the area covering the deployment of the Allied foot, but enough information remains to allow an accurate recreation of the Allied centre. First of all Lumsden shows three lines of foot and this is supported by Robert Douglas, who writes: 'In the battell we had our foot with some of Fairfax foot, and so in the reserve and rear.'[31] In Lumsden's plan three bodies are clearly shown in the Allied front line: a.a., b.b., and c.c. As the second line begins with f.f. it is a safe assumption that two further bodies completed the front line: d.d. and e.e. Each of these bodies represents a brigade. In the case of the Scots these brigades had two regiments, while in the case of the Parliamentarian troops they comprised varying numbers of regiments, although each brigade formed in two blocks. Lumsden provides a key to identify these bodies but, unfortunately, this too has suffered much damage. The right of the Allied front line, a.a., is labelled as '... Maitland their reg ...' ('...' represents holes in the plan). It is clear from this that the right-hand brigade was formed from the regiments of Crawford-Lindsey and Maitland, two Scots regiments. The next brigade, b.b., is labelled as '... artilearie and ...'. Once again this block represents a Scots brigade, formed by the regiments of Rae and Hamilton. So, although Sir James's plan is badly damaged, it still shows very clearly that the two right-hand brigades of the Allied front line were formed by four Scots regiments. The third brigade shown, c.c., is listed as '... rfax'. What else could this be but 'Fairfax'? Clearly a brigade of Lord Fairfax's foot formed the centre of the line. The final two brigades, d.d. and e.e., are listed together as 'Belonging to M ...'. Although 'M' is open to debate, other sources are all in agreement that the left of the Allied first line was formed by part of the Earl of Manchester's foot. This gives a front line of, from right to left, two brigades of Scots, one brigade of Lord Fairfax, and two brigades of the Earl of Manchester.

Continuing with the Allied second line, two bodies are clearly shown on Lumsden's plan: f.f. and e.e. As the third line starts with k.k., it is clear that the second line continues with three other brigades: h.h., i.i., and j.j. But Lumsden's list does not include an entry for i.i., so the second line comprised only four brigades. The first, f.f., is labelled 'To Lord Chancellor & Bu ...'. This brigade was formed by the regiments of Loudon and Buccleuch. Next in line, g.g., is marked as '... ssillis and Ke ...'. Once again this brigade was formed from two Scots regiments, those of Cassillis and Kilhead. The third brigade, h.h., is listed as '... mfermling and Co ...'. This third brigade comprised two Scots regiments, those of Dunfermline and Coupar. The final brigade in the second line, j.j., can also be identified as a Scots brigade. It is listed as '... Levingstoun and Y ... ster', or the regiments of Livingstone and Yester. It is clear, then, that the Allied second line was formed from four Scots brigades, eight regiments in total.

Lumsden's plan shows only two bodies – k.k. and l.l. – in the third line. It is obvious from Lumsden's attached list that there were three other brigades: m.m. to o.o. To conform to the alignment on Lumsden's plan, Peter Young[32] placed four brigades in the third line – k.k. to n.n. – and formed the final brigade, o.o., in a fourth line. There is no evidence to support the existence of this fourth line. Where was the final brigade on Lumsden's list if this fourth line did not exist? As has already been discussed, brigades of foot in second and subsequent lines were deployed to cover the gaps between brigades in the preceding line. This is clearly shown in de Gomme's plan. There is no reason to doubt that an old, experienced, soldier like the Earl of Leven did not follow this standard practice. If this was the case then the four brigades in the second line would have covered the gaps in the front line. The remaining five brigades would have formed a third line, lining up with the brigades of the front line and covering the gaps in the second. This is not shown on Lumsden's plan but is suggested as a probable solution to the mystery of brigade 'o.o.' and Peter Young's fourth line.

Having decided that the Allied third line was composed of five brigades, what were these brigades made up of? The right-hand brigade, k.k., is labelled 'Lord M ...'. This was the third of the Earl of Manchester's brigades of foot. Next, l.l., came a brigade listed as 'Lord Dudhope and ... rskyne'. This was another Scots brigade formed by the regiments of Dudhope and Erskine. The next two brigades, m.m. and n.n., are listed together as 'Lord ... x both ...'. These were the other two brigades of Lord Fairfax. The final brigade, o.o., is labelled as '... anchtoun ...'. It is difficult to identify this body, but Peter Young suggests it was another brigade of Scots.[33] This third line, therefore,

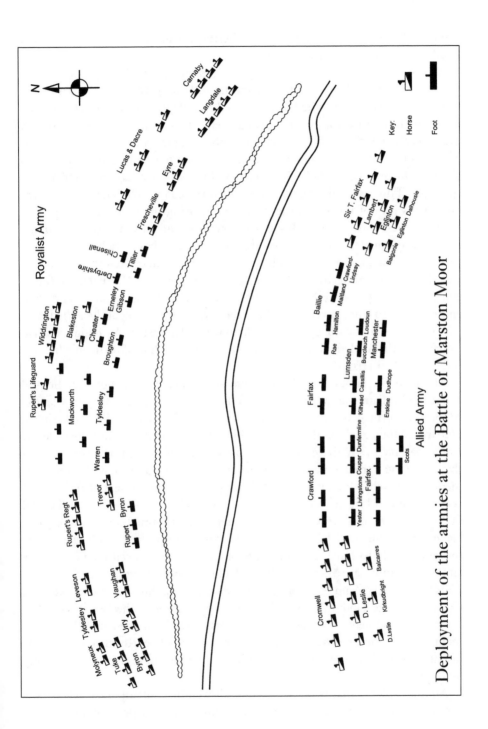

Deployment of the armies at the Battle of Marston Moor

comprised a brigade of the Earl of Manchester, a Scots brigade, two brigades of Lord Fairfax, and a final Scots brigade.

As can be seen from Lumsden's plan, and the above description, the deployment of the Allied foot flew in the face of the perceived wisdom of the time, which stated that allied armies should be deployed as distinct, separate bodies with their own horse supporting them. This strategy has been used by the 'Fairfax on the right' school to support their case. The theory goes: Manchester's infantry formed the left and were supported by their horse. Lord Fairfax's horse formed the right, therefore his foot must have also formed on the right. This leaves the Scots foot to form the centre. Obviously there were only two wings of horse and the Scots horse, being the weakest, was divided between these two wings. This is all very neat and tidy but there is much evidence to prove that this was not the case, and this has already been shown.

There is one final piece of evidence to show how intermixed the Allied foot was. Sir Henry Slingsby, a Royalist eyewitness, writes: 'Ye enemy's forces consisting of 3 parts, ye Scots, Manchester & Fairfax, were one mix'd with another.'[34] Sir Henry is very clear here about the intermixing of the Allied foot, which had been caused by the march towards Tadcaster. As regiments had returned to the battlefield they had been formed into a line of battle in whatever order they had arrived.

Although Sir James lists Scots regiments by name, he is not very helpful about the Parliamentarian infantry. The Earl of Manchester's foot at Marston Moor was formed of six regiments: Manchester's, Crawford's, Pickering's, Hobart's, Montague's, and Russell's, which were divided into three brigades. It would be easy to say these brigades had two regiments each, but this was not the case. One Parliamentarian source writes of a brigade formed by the regiments of Russell, Montague, and Pickering.[35] From the context of the letter it is clear that this brigade was one of Manchester's front-line brigades. The Earl of Manchester's own very large regiment probably formed an entire brigade, leaving the regiments of Crawford and Hobart to form the third brigade. The formation of Lord Fairfax's foot is even more obscure. Seven regiments were almost certainly at Marston Moor: Colonel John Bright's, Sir William Fairfax's, Sir William Constable's, Lord Fairfax's, Sir Alexander Rigby's, Colonel George Doding's, and Colonel Ralph Ashton's, the last three being Lancashire regiments.[36] Other regiments may have been present. Which regiments formed individual brigades is not known. The Royalist centre was heavily outnumbered by the Allied centre, which may have numbered as many as 18,000–19,000 men.

Another subject that is not covered at all well by contemporary accounts is the size of the Allied artillery train, as little information is provided. It is a safe assumption that the Allied train was considerably larger than that of the Royalists. Scots armies had had a fascination with artillery from its introduction during the Medieval period, and usually marched with large numbers of guns. The Earl of Leven's army was no exception to this. That said, artillery played a relatively small part in the ensuing battle, as will be seen in the next chapter.

Chapter 9

The Battle of Marston Moor

The bravest fight in the world.

At about 7.30pm the Allied Army began its march towards the ditch. Leonard Watson, the Earl of Manchester's scoutmaster, describes the initial Allied advance:

> About half an houre after seven a clock at night, we seeing the enemy would not charge us, we resolved by the help of God, to charge them, and so the signe being given, we marched down to the charge. In which you might have seen the bravest fight in the world; Two such disciplin'd Armies marching to a charge. Wee came down the Hill in the bravest order, and with the greatest resolution that was ever seen.[1]

Two other Allied officers write of their army's advance and the first contact in similar terms. Captain W.H., an officer with the Earl of Manchester's army whose full name is not known, writes:

> Which continued till between 7 and 8 with equall success, then the main bodies joyning, made such a noise with shot and clamour of shouts that we lost our eares, and the smoke of powder was so thick that we saw no light but what proceeded from the mouth of gunnes.[2]

What a wonderful description of the fog of war! Reading W.H.'s account it is hardly surprising that eyewitnesses have given differing versions of the same event. Anyone who has seen an English Civil War re-enactment will know how much smoke and noise is created by a few guns and a few hundred black powder muskets. At Marston Moor there was upwards of fifty guns and 15,000 musketeers, not taking into account the pistols and carbines of the horse. Anyone who has taken part in a re-enactment where black powder weapons are used will know how disorientating it is, and how limited one's view of events is. Sir James Lumsden, in his letter to Lord Loudon, says:

> This continued no long when it was resolved we should advance down the hill throch ane great feild of corne to ane ditch which they had in

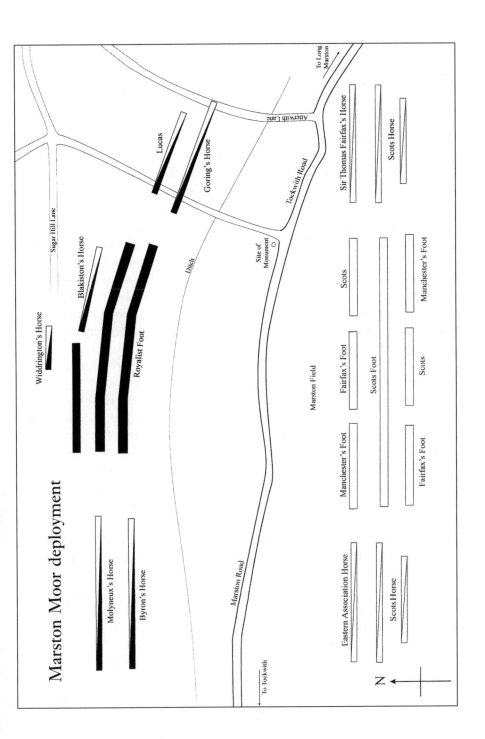

Marston Moor deployment

possession, which it pleased God so to prosper that they wer put from it, so that the service went on verie hot on all sydes.[3]

Sir James's description of the fighting as 'verie hot' is an apt one, as will be seen in due course.

Many Civil War battles followed a similar course. With the textbook deployment of the armies – that is, the foot in the centre and the horse on the wings – battles initially split into three parts. On both wings the horse of each side attempted to defeat their opponents or to keep the enemy horse clear of the foot's flanks. In the centre, the foot would advance to 'push of pike', hoping that their own horse would intervene on their behalf, as opposed to the enemy's horse crashing into their flank or rear. Obviously, this is a generalisation. There are as many variations on battlefield formations and types of battle in the Civil War as in any other war. It really depended on the terrain and the situation as to whether or not an army was able to deploy and fight in the textbook fashion. Three of the most important battles of the First Civil War were fought in this manner: Edgehill, Marston Moor, and Naseby. It is a real boon to authors that the initial fighting can be separated into three distinct sections and this is the course that the following description will follow.

The Defeat of Sir Thomas Fairfax

As Sir Thomas Fairfax and his troopers descended from the ridge they faced a formidable obstacle. To their right was Long Marston and its surrounding enclosures. This severely limited their scope for manoeuvre. To their front lay a ditch and hedge either side of Atterwith Lane. Captain William Stewart writes that Sir Thomas had: 'no passage but a narrow Lane, where they could not march above 3 or 4 in front, upon the one side of the Lane was a Ditch, and on the other an Hedge, both whereof were lined with Musketiers.'[4] This is a slightly confusing statement. It has been taken to mean that the lane had a ditch along one side and a hedge along the other. Both the ditch and the hedge were lined with musketeers and Sir Thomas's advance takes on the form of an ambush with his men, four wide, running the gauntlet of the Royalist fire as they charged down the lane. But this is not what Captain Stewart was describing. Firing across the width of a lane, only wide enough to take four horsemen, the Royalist musketeers would have caused as many casualties on each other as on the enemy horsemen. Stewart is describing the obstacle that ran across the front of the Royalist Army, running east to west with the lane crossing it. To one side of the lane the obstacle took the form of a ditch, to the other it took the form of a hedge. In places the obstacle was reinforced by a 6-foot bank, dropping from the cultivated land onto the moor.

The problem with terrain is also described by Sir Thomas himself, who writes that the lack of success on his flank was caused: 'by Reason of ye Whins and Diches wch we were to pass over before we could get to ye enemy, wch put us into great disorder.'[5]

As can be seen, Sir Thomas faced a formidable problem. How did he try to overcome it? It would seem that Sir Thomas expected his first line to be defeated, and with this in mind placed his recently raised Lancashire regiments in it. A couple of contemporary writers tell of this. Captain Robert Clarke, a Parliamentarian supporter, wrote to a friend, Captain Bartlett, who was a Royalist, to tell him of Prince Rupert's defeat, and to try to persuade him of the error of his ways. He reports Sir Thomas Fairfax's wing as being made up of 'Scottish horse and some raw souldiers of Lancashire'.[6] Captain Stewart seems to have thought that Sir Thomas was in error by placing his raw Lancashire troopers in the front line. He writes: 'and (by what mistake I know not) Sir Thomas Fairfax his new leavied regiment being in the Van.'[7] Not all Sir Thomas's first line troops were inexperienced, however, for his own regiment and that of Sir Hugh Bethell seem to have formed part of this line. Once his first line had absorbed the counter-attack by Goring's troopers, Sir Thomas's second and third lines would be able to defeat them.

Both sides had a large body of commanded musketeers attached to them. Goring deployed his forward of his first line, with the intent of causing heavy casualties on his opponents as they attempted to cross the obstacle. On the other hand, Sir Thomas had nullified the effect of his attached shot by advancing and outpacing them. As will be seen, on the Allied left flank Fraser's regiment of dragoons was used to clear the Royalist musketeers from the ditch, thus facilitating its crossing by Cromwell and David Leslie. Although Sir Thomas had both dragoons and musketeers under his command, there is no evidence that he made a similar attempt to use them to clear the enemy musketeers from the obstacle.

As Fairfax's men advanced they were met by heavy fire from the Royalist musketeers. A large concentration of musket balls have been found in this area and provide evidence for the weight of fire put down on Fairfax's troopers.[8] The Royalist musketeers would have been aided by the slowing effect of the obstacle, which allowed them to fire for longer than would have been the case had the field been more open. Having crossed the obstacle the Allied horse were unable to reform and went straight into the attack. To have halted to reform would have enabled the Royalist shot to continue firing at them, causing more casualties and further disorganisation. Sir Thomas himself takes up the story at this point:

Notwthstanding, I drew up a Body of 400 Horse. But bec: ye Intervalls of Horse in this wing onely, was lined with Musketteers (wch did much hurt wth their shott) I was necessitated to Charge ym. We were a long time engaged one with another till, at last, we routed yt part of their wing. We charged and pursued ym a good way towards Yorke. Myselfe onely, returned prsently, to get ye men I left behind me; but yt part of the enemy wch stood (pceiving ye disorder they were in) had charged ym, and routed ym before I could get to ym; so yt ye good successe, we had at first, was ecclipsed much by this bad conclusion.[9]

The success of the body under Sir Thomas's command is also reported by Captain Stewart, who writes that: 'Sir Thomas Fairfax, Colonell Lambert, and Sir Thomas his brother with five or six Troopes charged through the enemy and went to the left wing of Horse.'[10] Why had Sir Thomas's men been successful while the rest of his wing, with the exception of the Scots, had been put to flight?

Although no contemporary author states as much, Sir Thomas may have used the lane to cross the obstacle and thus began his charge in a more ordered state than the remainder of his wing. There is at least one more example of such a charge in the Civil Wars, where a column of horse charged along a narrow lane into the face of a deployed enemy and, after a hard fight, beat them. At the Battle of Langport, Major Bethell carried out a similar feat. Captain Stewart writes that Colonel Lambert was part of the body with Sir Thomas Fairfax, but Sir Thomas clearly states that this was not the case: 'But Coll. Lambert who should have seconded us, but could not get to us charged in another place.'[11] Stewart also reports five or six troops under Fairfax and Lambert arriving at the left wing. Once again this is contradicted by Sir Thomas, who states that he returned to the field alone, and goes on to describe his adventures in reaching the left wing of the army:

But I must not forget to remember wth thankfulnesse God's goodnesse to me this day, For having charged through ye enemy, and my men going after ye pursuit, returning back to goe to my other Troops, I was gotten in among ye enemy, wch stood up and downe ye Feild in severall bodys of Horse: so, taking ye signall out of my hat, I passed through ym for one of their owne Commanders, and so got to my Ld Manchesters Horse, in ye other Wing; onely with a Cutt in my cheeke, wch was given me in ye First charge; and a shot wch my horse received.[12]

Sir Thomas writes of removing 'ye signall' out of his hat. This was a field sign carried to differentiate one side from the other. The Allied Army carried a

Ousegate, Selby. Parliamentarian troops broke into the town along this street.

(Author's collection)

Selby Market Place and Abbey. Parliamentarian troops attacked this area from three directions. The Royalist horse fled down Finkle Street on the left and into Millgate.

(Author's collection)

York – St Mary's Tower. The tower and adjacent wall were demolished by an Allied mine. Lawrence Crawford's troops attacked through the breech.

(Author's collection)

4. King's Manor, York. Lawrence Crawford's men attacked into this area and were rep
by a Royalist counter-attack. *(Author's colle*

5. Bootham Bar, York. A musketeer's view down Bootham towards St Mary's Tower.
(Author's collec

6. King's Manor, York. *(Author's collec*

Marston Moor – looking from the ditch towards the initial positions of Goring's horse. Sir Charles Lucas led the Royalist second line in an attack on the Scots foot across the ground illustrated towards the camera.

Marston Moor – looking from White Syke Close towards the initial position of Oliver Cromwell's and David Leslie's horse.

Marston Moor – looking from White Syke Close towards the initial positions of the Royalist right wing horse.

10. Above: Marston Moor – looking through the Royalist lines towards the ridge.

(Author's c

12. Marston Moor – the Monument.

ow: Marston Moor – looking from the ridge towards the Royalist lines.

(Author's collection

arston Moor –
ing from the
outskirts of
with towards
Royalist right
wing horse.

r's collection)

14. Marston Moor – the ditch looking from Moor Lane towards Tockwith. Close to thi spot two Scots foot regiments held their position against several attacks by horse a foot.

15. Marston Moor – Four Lanes Meet looking towards York. Many Royalist troops trie escape the field along the lane in the centre of the photograph. It is still known loc as Bloody Lane.

16. Marston Moor – looking from White Syke Close towards Wilstrop Wood. When th Royalist right wing horse broke, it fled from left to right across the front of the wo

17. Marston Moor – White Syke Close. This is the traditional site of the Whitecoats' last stand. The close did not exist at the time of the battle.

18. Marston Moor – the pond close to the ditch and Moor Lane. This is an alternative site for the Whitecoats' last stand.

19. Sir Thomas Fairfax.

20. Lord Ferdinando Fairfax.

21. William Cavendish, Marquis of
    Newcastle.

22. Prince Rupert.

23. Oliver Cromwell.

24. George Goring.

piece of white paper or a handkerchief in their hat band, the Royalists did not. Each side also had a watch word, neither of which will come as a surprise. The Allies used 'God with us', while the Royalists used 'God and the King'.[13] One possible explanation for these contradictory statements is that two bodies of Parliamentarian horse managed to break through the Royalist line. The first, under Fairfax, continued pursuing the enemy horse towards York, leaving Sir Thomas to return to the field alone. The second, commanded by Lambert, seeing the collapse of their first line, charged into the gap created by Fairfax and continued through the Royalist lines to the left flank of the army. As will shortly be seen, some of the Scots horse attached to the right wing also managed to break through and reach Cromwell on the left wing. No details are given as to what part these survivors of the disaster on the right wing took in the remainder of the battle, although there is evidence that Sir Thomas may have withdrawn from the field due to his wound. Simeon Ash, commending Sir Thomas's courage, writes: 'For he stayed in the Field until being dismounted and wounded, hee was brought off by a Souldier. The hurt which Sir Thomas Fairfax received is in his face, but (God bee thanked) wee feare no danger.'[14]

While Fairfax and Lambert had been fighting their way through the Royalist lines what had been happening to the remainder of their wing? George Goring had bided his time well. Waiting until the enemy horse had been disordered by crossing the obstacle, and by the fire of his musketeers, he delivered a shattering counter-charge. Although Sir Thomas reports heavy fighting in his sector the remainder of the Parliamentarian first and second lines seem to have been swept away in very short order. Sir Philip Monckton, a regimental commander in Goring's first line, describes the short fight that took place:

> At the Battle of Hessy Moor I had my horse shot under me as I caracoled at the head of the body I commanded, and so near the enemy that I could not be mounted again, but charged on foot, and beat Sir Hugh Bethell's regiment of horse, who was wounded and dismounted, and my servant brought me his horse. When I was mounted upon him the wind driving the smoke so as I could not see what was become of the body I commanded, which went in pursuit of the enemy.[15]

It is interesting that Sir Philip speaks of charging the enemy on foot as his horse had been shot. This was either very brave or very foolhardy! In the time it took him to gain a new mount his regiment had disappeared into the distance in pursuit of the enemy. Robert Douglas also writes of the brevity of the fight saying: 'in the same instant, all Fairfax 3 thousand horse fled at once, our horsemen upon that hand stood till they were disordered.'[16] Douglas gives another possible reason for Sir Thomas's success, as opposed to the disaster that overtook the rest of his wing: Sir Thomas did not wait to reform his men but met the enemy at the charge, the remainder of his wing may not have done so. That said, Douglas is the only correspondent to report this.

One dissenting voice to the speed of the Parliamentarian rout is the Duchess of Newcastle, who speaks of 'Lord Goring and Sir Charles Lucas, having the better of the enemy's right wing, which they beat back most valiantly three times, and made their general retreat'.[17] The Duchess was writing many years after the battle. Interestingly, she writes of Sir Charles Lucas's involvement in the rout of Fairfax's horse. In fact Sir Charles commanded Goring's second line and led them against the Scots foot, taking little part in the fighting against the Allied right wing horse. The Duchess was Sir Charles's sister and speaks glowingly of him throughout the Duke of Newcastle's memoirs. Sir Charles was involved in three charges against the Scots foot before he was unhorsed and captured, and the Duchess may be getting muddled with this. All other accounts speak of a short, sharp, fight in which, with the exception of Sir Thomas Fairfax and Colonel Lambert's immediate commands, the Parliamentarian horse was put to flight.

As the two lines of horse to their front were being routed, what had happened to the Scots horse? Captain Stewart gives some details of their fate:

> The two Squadrons of Balgonies regiment being divided by the enemy each from the other, one of them being Lanciers charged a regiment of the enemies foot, and put them wholly to rout, and after joyned with the left wing of Horse, the other by another way went also to the left wing, The Earle of Eglingtons regiment maintained their ground (most of the enemies going on in the pursuit of the Horse and Foote that fled) but with the losse of four Lieutenants, the Lieut. Colonell, the Major, and Eglingtons Sonne being deadly wounded.[18]

From Captain Stewart's account it would seem that Dalhousie's regiment was caught up in the general rout and followed the Parliamentarian horse off the field. Balgonie's regiment managed to fight its way clear of the routing mob, and in two separate bodies, made it to the left flank. One of these bodies, armed with lances, attacked and routed a body of enemy foot. Stewart says it was a regiment of foot but this is unlikely. The flank of the Royalist foot was covered by the charges of Sir Charles Lucas's brigade. In all probability it was a body of Goring's commanded musketeers. Eglington's regiment stood its ground in very hard fighting. Stewart's account of this is supported by Sir James Lumsden, who writes: 'My Lord Eglintoun commandit our horss there who shew himself weill, his son releiving his father who was far engagded is evill wounded.'[19]

Goring had completely shattered the Allied right wing of horse. Most of his front line was off in pursuit of them and would play little further part in the battle. His second line was preparing to fall onto the flank of the Scots foot. With the exception of a few small bodies, which were trying to fight their way through to the left wing, the Allied horse had been swept away at first contact – those that stood long enough to come to contact. Amongst the Allied horse the few units that had not been routed had fought hard and received heavy casualties. The losses amongst the officers of Eglinton's regiment have already been discussed. Sir Thomas Fairfax gives details of the wounds received by some of his officers, as well as the cut he received to his cheek:

In wch charge also many of my officers and soldiers were slaine, and hurt. The Capt: of my owne Troop was shot in ye Arme. My Cornet had both his hands cut, wch rendred him ever after unserviceable. Capt. Micklethwayt, an honest stout man, was slaine; and scarce any officer, wch was in this charge, wch did not receive hurt. But Coll. Lambert who should have seconded us, but could not get to us charged in another place. Major Fairfax who was major to his Regiment had at least 30 wounds, whereof he died, after he was abroad, agn, & good hopes of his recovery. But yt wch nearest of all concerned me, was ye Losse of my Brother, who being desserted of his men, was sore wounded, of wch, in 3 or 4 days he died. So as, in this charge, as many were hurt, & killed, as in ye whole Army besides.[20]

Once again the horrors of war are brought home. With the defeat of the Allied right wing it is now time to turn to the infantry fight in the centre.

To Push of Pike

As the Allied foot advanced towards the ditch the Earl of Manchester's regiments, led on by Lawrence Crawford, were the first to make contact. To their front, covering a gap in the ditch, were three bodies of enemy foot. Two of these were from Prince Rupert's regiment and the other from the regiment of Sir Robert Byron.[21] Leonard Watson describes Manchester's men as 'going in a running march'.[22] The obstacle between the two forces was negligible or non-existent. Watson states that 'in a moment we were passed the ditch',[23] while Stewart writes that: 'between the Earl of Manchester's foot and the enemy there was a plain.'[24] Simeon Ash describes the clash between the two forces:

> Upon the advancing of the Earle of Manchester's Foote, after short firings
> on both sides, wee caused the enemy to quit the hedge in a disorderly
> manner, where they left behind them four Drakes.[25]

The Royalist foot were out on a limb, outnumbered by Crawford's men and, as
Thomas Fuller puts it, 'impressed with unequall numbers, and distanced from
seasonable succour, became a Prey to their Enemy'.[26] Their only support was
Colonel Marcus Trevor's regiment of horse, which seems to have got caught
up in the cavalry fight and was unable to support the infantry to their front.
Once Napier's men had been driven back, Crawford was able to bring pressure
to bear upon the Royalist foot defending the ditch to his right, which in turn
enabled the remainder of the Allied first line foot to cross the ditch.

It is now time to return once again to the debate as to the location of Lord
Fairfax's foot. This topic has already been discussed at length in the preceding
chapter. Further evidence will be presented for Fairfax's infantry forming
the centre of the first line as opposed to the right wing. Returning to Simeon
Ash's account of the battle, he states that: 'the Lord Fairfax his Briggade on
our right hand did also beat off the Enemy from the hedges before them,
driving them from their Canon, being two Drakes and one Demi-culvering.'[27]
Ash was one of Manchester's chaplains and his statement is very clear as to the
location of Fairfax's foot: that is, to the right of Manchester's. Ash goes on to
say that, after their initial success, Fairfax's men were: 'received by Marquesse
New-castles Regiment of Foot, and by them furiously assaulted, did make a
retreat in some disorder.'[28] The reference to a body of Newcastle's infantry
repulsing Fairfax's foot is interesting. Having defeated the enemy's first line
the Parliamentarian northern foot were repulsed by Newcastle's foot. One only
has to look at de Gomme's plan[29] to realise that this could only have been the
case if Fairfax was in the centre. If his men had formed the right flank of the
Allied first line, he would have been facing infantry from Prince Rupert's army
in both the Royalist first and second lines.

At the same time as Manchester and Fairfax's foot had fought their way
across the ditch, so had the Scots on the right of the line. Captain Stewart
describes the advance of the Scots foot:

> In this Ditch the enemy had placed foure Brigades of their best Foot,
> which upon the advance of our Battell were forced to give ground, being
> gallantly assaulted by the E. of Lindsies regiment, the Lord Maitlands,
> Cassilis, and Kelheads. Generall Major Crawford having overwinged the
> enemy set upon their flank, and did good execution upon the enemy,
> which gave occassion to the Scottish Foote to advance and passe the
> Ditch.[30]

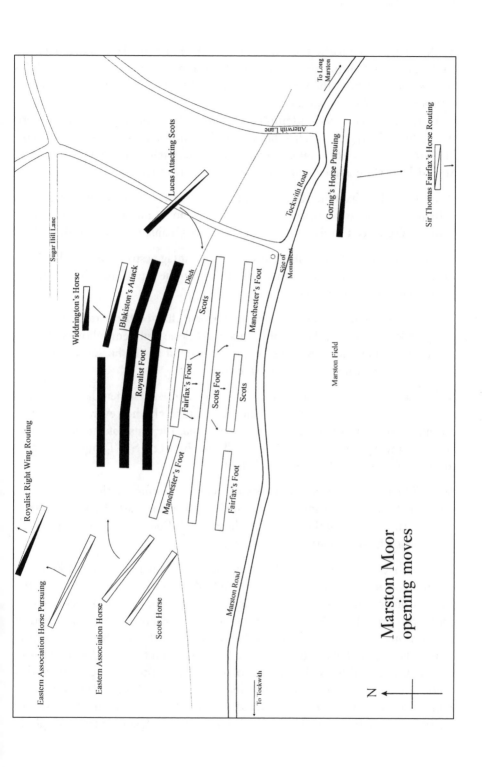

Marston Moor
opening moves

By this stage of the battle the whole of the Allied first line had passed over the ditch and were fighting the enemy on equal terms on the moor beyond. The only setback had been the repulse of Fairfax's foot by the Whitecoats. It was at this point that disaster struck.

As Lord Fairfax's foot attempted to reform from their repulse they were struck by a body of Royalist horse, in all probability part of Sir William Blakiston's brigade. Several contemporary writers tell of this attack. Thomas Stockdale, a close associate of Lord Fairfax, states that:

> the Lord Fairfax foote & Scotts that were joyned with them pursuing their advantage were charged by the enemyes horse and so disordered that they were forced to flye backe and leave our Ordinance behinde them.[31]

In a similar vein Simeon Ash writes: 'This advantage espyed by a body of the Enemies Horse, they charged through them unto the top of the hill.'[32] Finally, Robert Douglas reports that:

> In this mean tyme, some of the enemies horse charged the battell, Fairfax briggade of foot fled, the Edinburgh and artillerie regiment followed, first the Chancellor and Maclaines fled, some levie of all the horsemen of the enemy charged up where they were fleeing.[33]

So here are three reports that it was a body of enemy horsemen that caused the collapse of part of the Allied first line. Unfortunately, however, there is one dissenting voice: Captain Stewart. He writes that the cause of the disaster was not a charge by enemy horse but a collision between Sir Thomas Fairfax's routing troopers and Lord Fairfax's foot:

> Sir Thomas Fairfax his new leavied regiment being in the Van, they wheeled about, and being hotly pursued by the enemy came back upon the L. Fairfax Foot, and the reserve of the Scottish Foot, broke them wholly, and trod the most part of them under foot.[34]

This has been used as one of the main pieces of evidence for Lord Fairfax's infantry forming the right of the line: indeed Stewart is the mainstay of the 'Fairfax on the right' school. The relative positions of the various correspondents who provide evidence to fuel the debate have already been discussed in the previous chapter. It is highly unlikely that Stewart saw the demise of the Allied centre from his position with the Scots horse on the left. One only has to look at Captain W.H.'s description of the field, quoted at the start of this chapter, to realise how restricted visibility must have been. Even if Stewart could have seen the events described he would have been too far away to recognise friend from foe. All the English troops of both sides were so similarly dressed as to require the wearing of a field sign to distinguish them. Obviously, the above is the opinion of this author and others will differ, but there is one piece of evidence that could disprove Stewart's story. Continuing Robert Douglas's account he states that, after the rout of the Allied foot by a body of enemy horse:

> Generall Lesly [Earl of Leven] came up for horse to beat them in, and went towards the rescue of horse; in that same instant, all Fairfax 3 thousand horse fled at once, our horsemen upon that hand stood till they were disordered.[35]

It is very difficult to gauge in what order events took place in the battle, but here Douglas is clearly stating that Leven was riding towards the horse of the right wing to bring some of them up to counter-attack the Royalist horse, which had broken Lord Fairfax's men and part of the Scots reserve. It was only at this point that the Allied horse on the right wing broke and fled. So, quite clearly, the infantry of the centre broke before Sir Thomas Fairfax's troopers did. In that case a body of Allied horse could not have been the cause of the collapse of the Allied centre, so it must have been the enemy horse, as stated by Stockdale, Ash, and Douglas. Who were these enemy horsemen? They were almost certainly part of Sir William Blakiston's brigade, which had been deployed to support the foot of the Royalist centre. There is also some evidence to support the Marquis of Newcastle, and his bodyguard troop, taking part in this attack. His wife gives a colourful account of the Marquis' adventures:

> In this confusion my Lord (accompanied only with his brother Sir Charles Cavendish, Major Scot, Captain Mazine, and his page), hastening to see in what posture his own regiment was, met with a troop of gentlemen volunteers, who formerly had chosen him their captain, notwithstanding he was general of an Army; to whom my Lord spake after this manner. 'Gentlemen,' said he, 'you have done me the honour to choose me your captain, and now is the fittest time that I may do you service; wherefore if you will follow me, I shall lead you on the best I can, and show you the way to your own honour.' They being as glad of my Lord's proffer as my Lord was of their readiness, went on with the greatest courage; and passing through two bodies of foot, engaged with each other not at 40 yards' distance, received not the least hurt, although they fired quick upon each other; but marched towards a Scots regiment of foot, which they charged and routed; in which encounter my Lord himself killed three with his page's half-leaden sword, for he had no other left him; and

though all the gentlemen in particular offered him their swords, yet my Lord refused to take a sword of any of them. At last, after they had passed through this regiment of foot, a pikeman made a stand to the whole troop; and though my Lord charged him twice or thrice, yet he could not enter him; but the troops despatched him soon.[36]

Here is a description of one small part of the Royalist attack. Although it was written many years after the battle, and there is certainly an inherent element of hero worship, it is quite informative. The supporters of the 'Fairfax on the right' school state that it was not possible for Blakiston's brigade to have penetrated the Royalist infantry lines to get at the enemy foot and, therefore, it must have been an attack from their right flank. Here is an account describing exactly such a 'passage of lines'.

The Duchess of Newcastle speaks of the Marquis' bodyguard troop passing between two regiments, one Royalist and one Allied, which were actively engaging one another. It is well within the bounds of possibility that if Newcastle's troop carried out such an attack other bodies of Royalist horse could well have done the same. As Blakiston's men continued to pursue the broken Allied foot towards their baggage they were supported by a body, or bodies, of foot. As the Royalist horse and foot attempted to pursue their advantage one of the Earl of Manchester's regiments of foot 'did wheel on the right hand, upon their Flanck, and gave them so hot a charge, that they were forced to flie back disbanded into the Moore'.[37] This action by one of Manchester's regiments also points to the Royalist attack being against the centre of the Allied line and not the right.

At this stage of the battle the Allies were in trouble. The bulk of their right-hand wing of horse had been swept away. The survivors of Sir Thomas Fairfax's men were either pursuing the enemy towards York or trying to fight their way to the left flank. The Allied infantry front line was also in disarray. At the left-hand end of the line Manchester's men, under Crawford, were still making headway against the Royalist foot. To their right Lord Fairfax's infantry had broken and were fleeing southwards. Next in line came the Scots regiments of Rae and Hamilton: these had also turned on their heels and ran. It was probably one of these two regiments that the Duchess of Newcastle mentioned in her account, quoted above. The departure of these two regiments caused the rout of their immediate supports in the second line, the regiments of Buccleugh and Loudon. In a letter to the Earl of Loudon, Sir James Lumsden, describes the flight of these two regiments:

I commanding the battel was on the heid of your Lordship's regiment and Buccleuches but they carryed not themselffs as I would have wissed, nather could I prevail with them. For these that fled never came to chairge with the enemies, but wer so possessed with ane pannick fear that they ran for example to others and no enemie following, which gave the enemie occasioun to chairge them, they intendit not, and they had only the loss.[38]

Thousands of Allied soldiers, both horse and foot, were fleeing the field, pursued by the victorious Royalist horse. At this time Arthur Trevor, a Royalist supporter, was approaching the battlefield from the south and described this human flotsam in a letter to the Earl of Ormonde:

In this horrible distraction did I coast the country; here meeting with a shoal of Scots crying Weys us, we are all undone; and so full of lamentation and mourning, as if their day of doom had overtaken them, and from which they knew not whither to fly: and anon I met with a ragged troop reduced to four and a Cornet; by and by with a little foot officer without hat, band, sword, or indeed any thing but feet and so much tongue as would serve to enquire the way to the next garrisons, which (to say the truth) were well filled with the stragglers on both sides within a few hours, though they lay distant from the place of the fight 20 or 30 miles.[39]

Thomas Stockdale states that some of these fugitives reached Lincoln, Hull, Halifax and Wakefield before they ceased their flight.[40]

Returning to the plight of the Allied front line, on the extreme right a single brigade of Scots foot stood its ground. This was formed from the regiments of Maitland and Crawford-Lindsey. With the flight of the Allied horse to their right, the flank of this brigade was left open to an attack by Royalist horse. Although Goring's first line was rapidly disappearing into the distance in its pursuit of the Allied horse, Sir Charles Lucas, who commanded Goring's second line, still had his men in hand. With the demise of the troops to their left, the Scots foot had withdrawn to the south of the ditch. The Royalist infantry, which they had initially pushed back, commenced a counter-attack. Then Lucas led his troopers forward in an attack against their right flank. The two Scots regiments were in a terrible predicament, but faced it with courage and resolution. Sir James Lumsden writes: 'They that faucht stood extraordinarie weill to it; whereof my Lord Lyndsay, his brigad commandit by himself, was one.'[41] Captain Stewart also describes the attacks upon Lindsey's brigade:

Sir Charles Lucas and General Major Porter having thus divided all our Horse on that wing, assaulted the Scottish Foot upon their Flanks, so that they had the Foot upon their front, and the whole Cavalry of the enemies left wing to fight with, whom they encountered with so much courage and resolution, that having enterlined their Musquetiers with Pikemen they made the enemies Horse, notwithstanding for all the assistance they had of their foot, at two severall assaults to give ground; and in this hot dispute with both they continued almost an houre, still maintaining their ground; Lieut. Generall Baily, and General Major Lumsdain (who both gave good evidence of their courage and skill) perceiving the greatest weight of the battell to lye sore upon the Earl of Linsies, and Lord Maitelands regiment, sent up a reserve for their assistance, after which the enemies Horse having made a third assault upon them, had almost put them in some disorder; but the E. of Lindsey, and Lieut. Colonell Pitscotti, Lieut. Col. to the Lord Maitlands Regiment, behaved themselves so gallantly, that they quickly made the enemies Horse to retreat, killed Sir Charles Lucas his Horse, tooke him Prisoner and gained ground upon the foote.[42]

The stand of Lindsey's brigade is one of the pivotal points of the battle. If these regiments had followed their comrades in their flight south, Lucas would have been able to bring his men to bear against the open flank of the Allied infantry, many of whom were already shaken by the flight of the bulk of their front line. Meeting successive attacks by horse and foot Lindsey's men held their ground. Baillie and Lumsden led forward part of the reserve to Lindsey's relief. Lumsden names four regiments – Cassillis, Kelhead, Coupar and Dumfermline – as forming this relief force.[43] Interestingly, he also mentions 'part of Cliddisdaills regiment' as also being present. It is difficult to identify this regiment other than as the General of Artillery's regiment, which was raised in Clydesdale. This regiment is listed as one of those that broke during the Royalist horse's attack. Possibly, part of the regiment did not break and rallied on the reserve. With the arrival of these reserves the situation on the right and in the centre was stabilised. Sir Charles Lucas led his men forward for a third time but was unhorsed and captured.

At this stage of the fight the Royalists had definitely gained the upper hand. With the rout of their horse and foot, Leven and Lord Fairfax had both left the field. James Somerville reported Leven as fleeing to Leeds at the behest of his staff:

As for General Lesslie, in the beginning of this fight having that part of the Army quite broken where he had placed himself by the valour of this prince, he imagined, and was confirmed by the opinion of others then upon the place with him, that the battle was irrecoverably lost, seeing they were fleeing upon all hands, therefore they humbly entreated his excellence to retire, and wait his better fortune, which without farther advising he did, and never drew bridle untile he came the length of Leads.[44]

Robert Douglas also writes of Leven's precipitate withdrawal from the field, although he states that Leven withdrew to Bradford not Leeds.[45] He also mentions Lord Fairfax's withdrawal to Cawood. Finally, he reports the Earl of Manchester's withdrawal and subsequent return to the field:

> My Lord Manchester was fleing with a number of Scots officers. God used me as ane instrument to move him to come back againe; for I was gathering men a mile from the place, and having some there he drew that way, and having a purpose to goe away, and some of our officers, as Collonell Liell, was persuading him to goe away, but I exhorted him before many witnesses to goe back to the field, and he was induced; we came back about 5 or 600 horse; he only of all the Generalls was on the field.

All three of the Allied senior commanders had left the field. Manchester did return and would be the only commander of either side to be on the field at the close of the day. As for the Royalist commanders, Newcastle was riding the field, operating as a troop commander, and Rupert would be caught up with the rout of the Royalist right. The final phases of the battle would be led by lieutenant generals and junior commanders. Fortunately for the Allies, the lieutenant generals commanding their left flank, Oliver Cromwell and David Leslie, were up to the task. As the Allied right fled the field, followed by the three commanders, and Lindsey's men tried to hold their ground against the attacks of the Royalist horse, it was left to Cromwell and Leslie to attempt to pull victory from the jaws of defeat.

The Ironsides Victorious

As Cromwell and David Leslie descended from Bilton Bream towards the ditch, they faced a similar problem to Sir Thomas Fairfax over a mile to their east. To their front lay a ditch, behind which the enemy horse awaited them. This horse was interspersed with small bodies of commanded musketeers, and further bodies of shot lined the obstacle. The ditch does not seem to have been anywhere near as serious an obstacle in front of Cromwell as that faced by Sir Thomas Fairfax. That said, it would still pose a major problem. The Allied horse would have to cross it in the face of the Royalist musketeers, becoming disordered in the process. Then they would have to face the charges of formed bodies of Royalist horse while trying to recover their own order. Fairfax had faced exactly the same tactical scenario and failed. Could Cromwell and Leslie succeed?

Forming the extreme left of the Allied line was a regiment of Scots dragoons, commanded by Colonel Fraser. Unlike Fairfax, who did not use his dragoons to assist him in crossing the ditch, Cromwell and Leslie did. Captain Stewart reports the actions of Colonel Fraser and his men:

> The Scottish Dragoons that were placed upon the left wing, by the good managing of Colonel Frizell acted their part so well, that at the first assault they beate the enemy from the ditch, and shortly after killed a great many, and put the rest to the rout.[46]

Fraser led his men forward and drove the Royalist musketeers from the ditch. This would then allow Cromwell's men to cross the ditch without having to face the Royalist firepower. Here fate, and Lord Byron, took a hand. Instead of waiting for the Eastern Association horse to cross the ditch, then charging them while they were disordered, Lord Byron led his front line into the attack, crossing the ditch himself. This is reported by Thomas Fuller, who writes:

> besides a right valiant Lord, severed (and in some sort secured) with a Ditch from the Enemy, did not attend till the foe forced their way unto him, but gave his men the trouble to pass over that Ditch: the occasion of much disorder.[47]

Although Fuller was not an eyewitness he continually asserts that he got his information from 'a prime person' who 'since freely confest'.

Although no other source mentions the crossing of the ditch by Byron's first line, it could easily account for their rapid defeat. By crossing the ditch Byron had foregone two advantages. First, although his musketeers lining the ditch had been beaten back by Fraser's dragoons, the remainder of his commanded shot were still in position. By advancing he had masked their fire, thus nullifying any effect they may have had on the battle. Second, it would now be his men who would face a charge by formed enemy while trying to regain their own formation. But was Byron's attack simply caused by his rashness, or is there another possible explanation?

There is another possible cause for Byron's advance. It has already been mentioned in Chapter Seven that Byron's horse had been under artillery fire during the afternoon and evening, and had, at one point, made a short withdrawal. With the opening of the action the fire against Byron's wing would have intensified. It is very difficult for horse to stand under artillery fire and they must either withdraw or advance. The first option was not feasible. Cromwell's cavalry were advancing from the hill and any withdrawal would have opened the flank of the infantry to attack by Cromwell or Leslie's horse.

Taking casualties from the artillery fire, and unable to withdraw, Byron may have had no choice but to advance.

Meanwhile, the defeat of the Royalist first line seems to have been fairly quick. Sir Henry Slingsby writes:

> Cromwell having ye left wing drawn into 5 bodys of horse, came off the Cony Warren, by Bilton bream, to charge our horse, & upon their first charge rout'd ym; they fly along by Wilstrop woodside, as fast & as thick could be.[48]

Oliver Cromwell himself wrote in his letter to Colonel Walton, informing him of the death of his son: 'we never charged but we routed the enemy.'[49] At least one body of Royalist horse seems to have put up a hard fight. Leonard Watson reports Cromwell's own division having:

> a hard pull of it: for they were charged by Ruperts bravest men, both in Front and Flank: they stood at the swords point a pretty while, hacking one another: but at last (it so pleased God) he brake through them, scattering them before him like a little dust.[50]

In this 'hard pull' Cromwell received a wound and is reported by Robert Douglas as leaving the field for a short time to have it dressed.[51] Following up their initial success the Parliamentarian troopers ran into the Royalist second line being led forward by Lord Molyneux. Thomas Stockdale writes: 'yet after a little time the E. of Manchesters horse were repulsed by fresh supplyes of the enemyes, and forced to retreate in some disorder.'[52]

In Cromwell's absence, David Leslie stabilised the position and by the time of Cromwell's return, shortly afterwards, the Allied horse were ready for a second attack.

Before discussing Cromwell's second advance it would be worthwhile putting the events on the Allied left wing in context with those on the remainder of the field. Although the fighting along the line has been split into three parts, events were taking place simultaneously. The defeat of Byron's first line took place early in the evening's proceedings. This is evidenced by the account of the Duchess of Newcastle, who writes:

> Where upon he immediately put on his arms, and was no sooner got on horseback, but he beheld a dismal sight of the horse of his Majesty's right wing, which out of a panic fear had left the field, and run away with all the speed they could; and though my Lord made them stand once, yet they immediately betook themselves to their heels again, and killed even those of their own party that endeavoured to stop them.[53]

The Marquis of Newcastle had not even had time to put on his armour and return to the field by the time the first of the Royalist fugitives were passing him. As has already been described, the Duchess describes her husband's participation in the rout of the Allied foot during Blakiston's attack. It has also been described how the Earl of Leven attempted to bring a body of horse from the right flank to counter-attack Blakiston's men, but Sir Thomas Fairfax's horse routed before he had chance to do so. With this in mind, one probable course of events is that as Cromwell defeated the first line of Byron's horse the Allied centre was successfully crossing the ditch with the aid of Manchester's foot, which had already beaten Napier's brigade from the gap in the ditch. In the meantime, Sir Thomas Fairfax was leading his men over the ditch to attack Goring's horse. Blakiston's attack against the Allied centre roughly coincided with the repulse of Cromwell's first attack. Shortly after this Sir Thomas Fairfax's wing, with a few exceptions, routed.

At this point the Allied right and much of their centre was in broken flight. Lindsey's brigade was under attack by Sir Charles Lucas, and Cromwell's wing was attempting to reform, its commander having left the field to have a wound dressed. The only part of the Allied Army that was winning its fight was the Earl of Manchester's foot. In due course General Baillie and Sir James Lumsden would lead forward part of the reserve to the relief of Lindsey's brigade, while Cromwell and Leslie were preparing to lead a second attack against Byron's remaining horsemen.

Leading his men forward, Cromwell was once again heavily engaged. This time Leslie's Scots horsemen were to take an active role in the defeat of the Royalist second line. Captain Stewart, a member of David Leslie's own regiment of horse, describes Leslie's attack against the flank of the Royalist horse:

> he charged the enemies horse (with whom L. Generall Cromwell was engaged) upon the flanke, and in a very short space the enemies whole Cavalry was routed, on whom our fore-troopes did execution to the very walls of Yorke; but our body of Horse kept their ground.[54]

Herein lies the turning point of the battle. Having defeated the enemy horse, Cromwell and Leslie sent only a portion of their troops to pursue them, keeping the majority in hand to continue the fight. The decisive nature of this decision will be seen shortly. It could be argued that, although Goring's first line was off in pursuit of the Allied right wing horse, Sir Charles Lucas's brigade was in a position to fall upon the Allied flank. This was quite so. Unfortunately for the Royalist cause, Lucas struck Lindsey's brigade, which gallantly held its ground and negated the Royalists' advantage. With one exception, late in the day, no such stand would occur on the Royalist right.

As yet, one of the major players in the story of the campaign for York had taken no part in the battle. While his army was fighting hard where was Prince Rupert? The Prince, usually the most active of commanders, had been caught by the suddenness of the Allied attack. When the Allies began their march towards the ditch he was off the field taking refreshment. Returning to the field, at the gallop, Rupert met his right wing in flight. Sir Hugh Cholmley reports the events which followed:

> Upon the alarum the Prince mounted to horse and galloping up to the right wing, met his own regiment turning their backs to the enemy which was a thing so strange and unusual he said 'swounds, do you run, follow me,' so they facing about, he led them to a charge, but fruitlessly, the enemy having before broken the force of that wing, and without any great difficulty, for these troops which formerly had been thought unconquerable, now upon a panic fear, or I know not by what fate, took scare and fled, most of them without striking a stroke, or having the enemy come near them, made as fast as they could to York.[55]

Rupert's regiment formed part of Byron's second line and, therefore, Rupert must have arrived on the field after the defeat of this second line. Cholmley expresses his surprise at the defeat of Rupert's right flank, which contained some very experienced regiments, Prince Rupert's included. It is difficult to judge why regiments with such a good record should perform so badly. Their subsequent military records continued to be honourable. Was it just an off day? Thomas Fuller puts forward one possible explanation, and once again treachery raises its head, as does the name of Colonel Urry. He writes:

> Some suspected Colonel Hurry (lately converted to the Kings party) for foul play herein, for he divided the Kings Old Horse (so valiant and victorious in former fights) into small Bodies, alledging this was the best way to break the Scottish Lanciers. But those Horse, always used to charge together in whole Regiments or greater Bodies, were much discomposed with this new Mode, so that they could not find themselves in themselves.[56]

Although there is little to support Fuller's allegations of treachery, the dividing of the King's horse into smaller bodies than usual may have had some effect on them. The battlefield is the last place to try new tactics and formations. Add to this Byron's advance across the ditch, David Leslie's flank attack, and their being outnumbered by the Allied horse, and it is not difficult to see why Rupert's right flank was beaten. Rupert was caught up in the rout.

Parliamentarian propagandists have him hiding in a bean field to avoid Allied troopers, while a Royalist source, Mr Ogden, reports him killing '4 or 5 with his owne hands' before leaving the field and returning to York at eleven o'clock at night.[57]

The Fall of the Whitecoats

With the demise of the Royalist right wing the climax of the battle had been reached. Several modern historians – Firth, Young and Newman among others – have asserted that at this point Cromwell and Leslie led the Allied left wing around the rear of the Royalist Army and attacked Goring and Lucas's remaining troopers before closing in to finish off the Royalist foot. This seems highly unlikely. A more probable course of events is that Cromwell and Leslie turned into the flank of the Royalist foot in support of Manchester's victorious infantry. Several contemporary writers report exactly this action. James Somerville writes:

> These two commanders of the horse upon that wing, Leslie and Cromwell wisely restrained the great bodies of their horse from pursuing these broken troops, but wheeling to the left [right] hand, falls in upon the naked flanks of the prince's main battalion of foot, carrying them down with great violence.[58]

Sir Hugh Cholmley writes in a very similar vein:

> Those that gave this defeat were most of them Crumwell's horse to whom before the battle were joined David Leslie, and half the Scottich horse; and who kept close together in firm bodies, still falling upon that quarter of the Prince's forces which seemed to make most resistance, which were the foot who fought most gallantly and maintained the field three hours after the horse had left them.[59]

Sir Hugh comes out with one very telling phrase: 'that quarter of the Prince's forces which seemed to make most resistance.' Why would Cromwell have ridden around the rear of the Royalist Army to attack Goring's returning troopers when he had a mass of Royalist foot still fighting much closer to hand? Did Cromwell carry out such a ride at Naseby in the following year? No, he turned and attacked the flank of the Royalist foot, and this is also what he did at Marston Moor. Cromwell himself sums it up:

> The Left Wing, which I commanded, being our own horse, saving a few Scots in our rear, beat all the Prince's horse. God made them as stubble to our swords. We charged their regiments of foot with our horse, and routed all we charged.[60]

This attack into their open flank, by Cromwell and Leslie's horsemen and Crawford's infantry, marked the beginning of the end for the Royalist foot. Leonard Watson, fighting with Cromwell's men writes that Cromwell's horse and Crawford's foot attacked the Royalists: 'dispersing the enemies Foot almost as fast as they charged them, still going by our side, cutting them down that we carried the whole Field before us.'[61] With one exception, the destruction of the Royalist infantry takes little telling, and few details are provided by contemporary writers. The one exception was a body of Newcastle's Whitecoats, who made a stand against the advancing Allied horse. It is difficult to ascertain whether the Whitecoats' stand was a deliberate attempt to slow the Allied advance and protect the flank of the remaining Royalist infantry, or the end of an attempt to retreat from the moor in some semblance of order.

Most authors have placed the stand at the end of Sugar Hill Lane, where White Syke Close, which postdates the battle by more than 100 years, now stands. This is the traditional site of the Whitecoats' stand, and their subsequent burial. This area was close to where Newcastle's men had deployed onto the moor and was their obvious line of retreat. However, recent artefact evidence seems to disprove this.[62] The artefacts found in White Syke Close show little evidence of infantry fighting but are mainly the detritus of a cavalry rout, probably from the Royalist right wing. If the last stand did not take place at White Syke Close, where did it take place?

One possible alternative site is close to the junction of Moor Lane and the ditch. This area has revealed a mass of finds, particularly musket balls. The western side of the lane has a large concentration of finds in a fairly small area. Interestingly, a nineteenth-century map shows a small wood covering this ground, called White Syke Whin. Could this be local tradition getting muddled between the grave pits being in White Syke Whin, which no longer exists, and White Syke Close, which does?

A further intriguing piece of evidence comes from a newspaper article published in 1859. A party of workmen were building an underground drain across the moor when they cut into a massive grave pit. The article goes on to say that they uncovered an area 12 yards long by 8 wide and had still not found the edge of this 'vast sepulchre'. Unfortunately, the article does not give any further clues as to where the grave pit was situated, although an underground drain does run close to the junction of Moor Lane and the ditch. Another site close to Atterwith Lane has also been put forward but the artefact evidence also seems to discount this. It is probable that the exact site of the Whitecoats' stand will never be known for certain, unless their grave pits are found.

Although the exact site of the stand is not known, the subsequent course of events is. Before the Whitecoats had chance to leave the moor Cromwell's

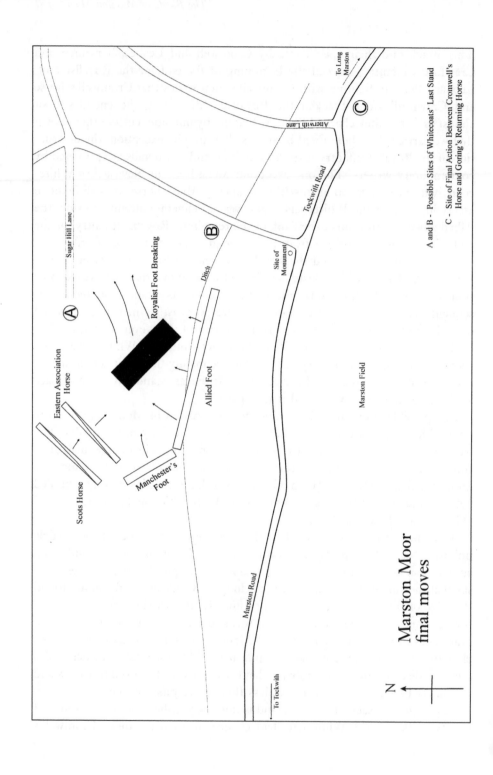

Marston Moor
final moves

N

To Tockwith

Marston Road

Scots Horse

Eastern Association Horse

Manchester's Foot

Allied Foot

Ⓐ

Royalist Foot Breaking

Ditch

Ⓑ

Site of Monument

Marston Field

Sugar Hill Lane

Tockwith Road

Atterwith Lane

Ⓒ

To Long Marston

A and B - Possible Sites of Whitecoats' Last Stand

C - Site of Final Action Between Cromwell's Horse and Goring's Returning Horse troopers had caught up with them. James Somerville describes the action which then ensued:

> Neither met they with any great resistance, until they came to the Marquis of Newcastle his battalion of White Coats, who first peppering them soundly with their shot when they came to the charge stoutly bore them up with their pikes, that they could not enter to break them. Here the parliament horse of that wing received their greatest loss, and a stop for some time to their hoped-for-victory, and that only by the stout resistance of this gallant battalion, which consisted near of four thousand foot, until at length a Scots regiment of dragoons, commanded by Colonel Frizeall, with other two, was brought to open them upon some hand, which at length they did; when all their ammunition was spent, having refused quarters, every man fell in the same order and rank wherein he had fought.[63]

Having been caught in the open field the Whitecoats formed a hedgehog with the pikes sheltering the muskets. It is doubtful that the Whitecoats amounted to the 4,000 men attributed to them by Somerville – it is unlikely that Newcastle had 4,000 infantry in the field. The fact that the Whitecoats fell in formation is also mentioned by the Duchess of Newcastle, who writes that they: 'showed such an extraordinary valour and courage in that action, that they were killed in rank and file.'[64] Sir Henry Slingsby, commander of one of Newcastle's foot regiments (although his regiment was not on the field as it formed part of the York garrison) also writes of the Whitecoats' stand.[65] Slingsby's account has a much more personal feel. In the stand he lost a nephew, Colonel John Fenwick, and a 'kinsman', Sir Charles Slingsby. Although Colonel Fenwick's body could not be identified and must have been buried with his men, Sir Charles's body was located and buried in York Minster. One other account of the end of the Whitecoats is worth recounting. Although written by William Lilly, who was not present at the battle, it was told to him by one Captain Camby, who had been a trooper under Cromwell's command and had taken part in the final attack on the Whitecoats. Lilly writes:

> A most memorable action happened on that day. There was one entire regiment of foot belonging to Newcastle, called the Lambs, because they were all new cloathed in white woollen cloth, two or three days before the fight. This sole regiment, after the day was lost, having got into a small parcell of ground ditched in, and not of easy access of horse, would take no quarter; and by mere valour, for one whole hour, kept the troops of horse from entering amongst them at near push of pike: when the horse

did enter, they would have no quarter, but fought it out till there was not thirty of them living; those whose hap it was to be beaten down upon the ground as the troopers came near them, though they could not rise for their wounds, yet were so desperate as to get either a pike or sword, or piece of them, and to gore the trooper's horses as they came over them, or passed by them. Captain Camby, then a trooper under Cromwell, and an actor, who was the third or fourth man that entered amongst them, protested, he never in all the fights he was in, met with such resolute brave fellows, or whom he pitied so much, and said, 'he saved two or three against their will.'[66]

This is the only account to mention a terrain feature. Lilly states that they were edged in by ditches. This is probably where the tradition of the last stand in White Syke Close originated. After causing some loss on the attacking Allied horse, the Whitecoats were subjected to heavy fire by Fraser's dragoons. This fire tore gaps in their previously impenetrable formation. Into these gaps charged Cromwell and Leslie's troopers. Only thirty of the Whitecoats survived. Thomas Fuller sums up the action nicely:

> The Marquess of New-castles White-coats (who were said to bring their Winding sheets about them into the field) after thrice firing fell to it with the But-ends of their Muskets, and were invincible; till mowed down by Cromwells Carasires, with Jobs Servants, they were all almost slain, few escaping to bring the Tidings of their overthrow.[67]

With the fall of the Whitecoats the Royalist Army began to disintegrate. The remainder of the Royalist foot broke ranks and fled along Moor Lane, back towards York. This lane is still known locally as 'Bloody Lane'. All that remained for the Allied forces was the pursuit of the Royalist Army, or so they thought. On the ground originally occupied by Sir Thomas Fairfax's horse, several large bodies of Royalist horse were seen. Turning from the destruction of the Royalist foot Cromwell turned his attention to these bodies. In a short, sharp, action the remainder of the Royalist horse broke and fled towards York. Simeon Ash reports this closing action:

> Yet their horse there still in full bodies; our left wing was neither wearyed by their former hot service, nor discouraged by the sight of that strength which yet the enemy had unshaken and intire, but continuing and renuing their valour, they charged every party remaining in the field, till all were fully routed and put to flight: our men pursued the Enemies about 3 miles, till they came neere unto Yorke.[68]

The victorious Allied Army had cleared the field. The Allied horse set off in pursuit. Leonard Watson states that the field was cleared by about nine o'clock.[69] With the battle commencing at between 7.00 and 7.30pm this seems a little early, although not by too much. Captain W.H. states that the pursuit was brought to a stop by nightfall, which means it must have commenced in daylight.[70] Some small bodies of Royalist horse and officers hung around the fringes of the battlefield until late at night. Sir Philip Monckton, who earlier in the day had charged a regiment of Fairfax's horse on foot after his horse had been shot, writes of remaining on the field with Sir Marmaduke Langdale until midnight, when Sir John Urry gave them an order from Prince Rupert to retire.[71] As the remnants of the Royalist Army straggled back to York during the night, the Allied Army settled down to sleep on the ground they had fought on. How great a victory had they won?

The Spoils of War

With the exception of the Earl of Manchester, the Allied commanders were unaware of their victory. Both the Earl of Leven and Lord Fairfax had fled the field along with their men. Lord Fairfax received news of the victory, at Cawood Castle, during the night and rising from his bed wrote a letter to the Mayor of Hull:

> After a dark Cloud, it hath pleased God to shew the Sun-shine of his glory, in Victory over his Enemies, who are driven into the walls of York; many of their chief Officers slain, and all their Ordnance and Ammunition taken, with small losse (I praise God) on our side. This is all I can now write.[72]

The Earl of Leven took longer to find and did not receive the news until noon on 3 July.

While messengers took news of the victory to their commanders, the Allied troops began to count their losses and what spoils they had gained. Contemporary accounts are very close in their summaries of casualties and prisoners. For example, Leonard Watson tells of 4,000 Royalist dead and 2,000 prisoners, including Sir Charles Lucas and Major General Porter.[73] He also states that twenty-five pieces of ordnance and 8,000 arms were captured and the whole of the Royalist baggage train. Thomas Stockdale gives very similar figures but also mentions 5,000 Royalist wounded in York, as persons fleeing from York to the Allied Army had reported.[74] Simeon Ash writes:

> wee judge that about three thousand of the Enemies were slaine; but the Countreymen (who were commanded to bury the Corpses) tell us they have buried foure thousand one hundred and fifty bodies.[75]

He also reports that Prince Rupert's dog had been found amongst the dead.

On the Allied side losses seem to have been light compared with those of the Royalists. Captain Stewart reports just over 300 dead.[76] Simeon Ash gives figures for the Earl of Manchester's foot as one officer, Captain Pugh, and six men killed and only twenty wounded.[77] He goes on to state that by far the heaviest loss to the Allies was amongst those who ran and the 'Carriage-keepers', the carriages having been pillaged by Goring's horse.

The Allied victory had been greater than they could have believed as night fell on 2 July. If the figures quoted above are to be believed the Royalists had suffered over 50 per cent losses in dead, wounded and prisoners. Although much of their horse had escaped from the field, their infantry had suffered horrendous losses, particularly amongst the Marquis of Newcastle's northern foot. With the exception of a few thousand horse, Newcastle's northern army had ceased to exist.

How would Rupert and Newcastle respond to their defeat? Would they rally their forces and fight again? With the magnitude of the Allied victory this was unlikely. Would they hold York against another siege? This was much more likely. With the return of Lord Fairfax and the Earl of Leven to the army, the Allies could turn their thoughts once more to the City of York.

Chapter 10

The Fall of York

To avoid the effusion of Christian blood ...

A defeated army is never a pretty sight. The roads between Marston Moor and York were thronged with the detritus of Rupert's and Newcastle's army. Bodies of Allied horse pursued the routed mass almost to the walls of the city. There was a danger that the Allied horse might have penetrated the city intermingled with the remnants of the Royalist forces. So concerned was York's governor, Sir Thomas Glemham, that he closed Micklegate Bar to the refugees. This was the situation when Sir Henry Slingsby approached the gate. He reports that: 'at ye barr none was suffer'd to come in but such as were of ye town, so yt ye whole street was throng'd up to ye barr with wound'd & lame people, wch made a pitiful cry among ym.'[1]

The governor's precautions may seem a little extreme but were eminently sensible. By far the bulk of the Prince's army were not known in York. As has already been mentioned, the armies were clothed and equipped so similarly that field signs had to be worn to differentiate the two sides. Sir Thomas Fairfax had ridden around the Royalist Army after the defeat of his horse by using the simple expedient of removing his field sign. How simple it would have been for an enterprising troop commander to use a similar ploy to gain access to York and even control of the gate. As it happened Sir Thomas Glemham's precautions prevented any possibility of this happening.

As the night deepened more and more survivors of the battle arrived at York. Eventually the Marquis of Newcastle, accompanied only by his brother and two servants, met Prince Rupert and Lord Eythin as he approached the city.[2] The three commanders had much to discuss. Other than a few thousand men, their army was either dead, prisoner or scattered. The bulk of the survivors were horsemen who would be much better employed outside a siege as part of a relief force. The discussions between the Prince and the Marquis went on far into the night. Several contemporary writers report the night's proceedings.[3] Allied accounts speak of a heated disagreement between the Prince and the Marquis but, hardly surprisingly, Royalist accounts speak of no such argument. Rupert was determined to have another attempt to defeat the Allied Army and thus relieve York. He would march into North Yorkshire and recruit his forces, while the Marquis would recruit in County Durham. This would provide rallying points for the survivors of the battle and allow reinforcements to reach Rupert from Lancashire, Westmorland and Cumberland. Sir Robert Clavering was already marching south with a force of several thousand men. If Sir Thomas Glemham could hold York for just a few weeks the situation in the north might be turned around.

Newcastle seems to have gone along with this plan initially, according to Sir Hugh Cholmley, but changed his mind during the night. Lord Eythin seems to have been the main cause for this change of heart as, Sir Hugh writes: 'but as is said General King considering the King's affairs absolutely destroyed by loss of this battle persuaded the Marquess (against all the power of his other friends) to quit the kingdome.'[4] Newcastle was very much under the influence of Eythin, as can be seen throughout the campaign in the north. It is understandable that Newcastle took the decision to go into voluntary exile. He had been a very wealthy man prior to the war but most of his fortune had been spent on his army. This army had virtually been destroyed at Marston Moor. Of the three options available to him – to go into voluntary exile, to raise another army, or to join the King's court at Oxford and face the ridicule of the courtiers – the first seemed by far the simplest. Once set upon this course the Marquis could not be deflected from it. Similarly, Prince Rupert was determined to follow through his plan to rebuild his army and try again. On Wednesday 3 July both commanders went their separate ways.

Newcastle and his entourage departed York for Scarborough, escorted by a troop of horse and another of dragoons, provided by Prince Rupert.[5] He seems to have had some doubt as to Sir Hugh Cholmley's reaction and thought Sir Hugh might have prevented him from departing.[6] Sir Hugh remained loyal and as he himself writes: 'but the Marquess soon found to the contrary, by the governor's usage, who knew his duty was to obey his general, and not to question his errors.'[7] In fact, Scarborough's governor was keen to expedite his commander's departure, in case his presence in the town attracted the attention of the Allied generals. On the second day after his arrival in Scarborough, probably 5 or 6 July, Newcastle boarded a ship and sailed for Hamburg – not Holland, as reported by several contemporary writers. He was accompanied by his two sons and a number of his close supporters. There is some evidence that Newcastle and Eythin had a disagreement before their departure, as they sailed in separate ships.[8] Having been informed of Newcastle's departure by Rupert, the King paused in his pursuit of the Earl of Essex into the West Country, to write the Marquis a touching letter:

Newcastle,

My nephew Rupert sends me word of that which troubles me, that you and General King are going or gone beyond sea. It is a resolution that looks like discontent, which you cannot have occasion for without blemish to that sense which I ought to have of your eminent services, and particularly in your late gallant defence of York; which I would not have you believe that any subsequent ill-fortune can lessen, but that I shall ever retain such a memory of that and your other actions of great merit as ought to be expected from a good master to so deserving a servant. If you persist in that resolution which I cannot but be sorry for, I shall commit the charge of those countries under your command to George Goring and Sir Thomas Glenham, in your absence, who I make no doubt will be the acceptablest persons to you, and who will be likely to give you the best account of their trust at your return, when you shall be sure to be received and ever entertained with that favour and estimation which you may expect. Your most assured constant friend,

Charles R.

Bath, July 17th, 1644.[9]

Newcastle would not return to England until after Charles II's restoration in 1660.

With the departure of the Marquis of Newcastle, Prince Rupert left York with a force reported as between 1,500 and 4,000 horse and less than 1,000 foot.[10] The lower number for this horse is probably too low and the higher figure, 4,000, may be nearer the truth. By the evening of the 3rd the Prince had reached Thirsk, where he was met by Sir Robert Clavering and his force. Once again numbers differ, varying between 1,300 and 2,000.[11] From there the combined force marched to Richmond, where it remained several days, awaiting the arrival of stragglers from the battle. The most promising area for recruiting lay to the west of the Pennines in Lancashire, Westmorland, and Cumberland. With this in mind the Prince began marching west. On 7 July he moved his army from Richmond to Bolton Castle. From there he wrote a letter to Sir Philip Musgrave, commander of the King's forces in Westmorland and Cumberland, requesting any forces Sir Philip had to join him.[12] By the 10th the Prince had crossed the Pennines and had reached Hornby.

Between the 10th and 18th Rupert marched to and fro in northern Lancashire, trying to gain recruits, with the intention of marching back into Yorkshire and relieving York. On the 18th he was at Kirkby Lonsdale when news reached him of York's surrender two days earlier. Although this is not implicitly stated it can be surmised from his subsequent movements.[13] On the

20th he returned to Garstang and then continued his southward movement through Lancashire. On the 21st he reached Preston and continued on to Lathom House on the following day. On the 23rd Rupert's army crossed the Mersey at Hale Ford near Liverpool. By the 25th the Prince was in Chester. Clearly news had reached him of York's demise while he was at Kirkby Lonsdale, and any further efforts to fight in the north would have been futile. The Allies had attempted to prevent Rupert's southward march but were unsuccessful. These attempts will be discussed in the next section.

The Northern Horse, under Langdale, moved much more slowly. On 20 August a Royalist force under Lord John Byron was defeated at Ormskirk by Sir John Meldrum. Langdale's men seem to have looked on as Byron's force was driven from the field. With their defeat at Ormskirk the Royalists withdrew into Cheshire on the 21st. Following this withdrawal, with the exception of a few garrisons, Yorkshire and Lancashire had been cleared of Royalist forces.

The Allied Reaction

As day broke on 3 July, the Allied Army remained on the field. It must have presented a terrible sight. Simeon Ash writes: 'That night we kept the field, when the Bodies of the dead were stripped. In the morning, there was a mortifying object to behold, when the naked bodies of thousands lay upon the ground, and many not altogether dead.'[14] The Allied Army spent the day reorganising, tending their wounded, and arranging for the burial of the dead by the local villagers.

On Thursday the 4th the Lancashire and Cheshire forces, under Sir John Meldrum and Sir William Brereton, arrived at Long Marston. The arrival of these reinforcements prompted the Allied commanders to return to their siege lines around York.[15] A Royalist correspondent reports the arrival of the Allied forces before the city:

> When the enemy heard that the Prince was gon they faced Yorke againe on Thursday, though farr off upon a hill: and Yorke salutes them with 3 peeces of ordnance wch they never heard before. They sumoned the City to yeeld within 6 houres, but they set them at defyance and Sr Tho. Glemham sent the Prince word that hee would keepe it to the last man.[16]

With Sir Thomas Glemham's refusal to surrender, the second Siege of York had begun.

News of Prince Rupert's departure and march towards the north had reached the Allied commanders and plans were put into effect to intercept him and prevent his return to York or his march into the south. Captain Stewart writes of the Allied commanders' efforts to intercept the Prince:

> Upon Thursday at night he [Prince Rupert] was at Richmond, so that it is yet doubtful whether he intends for the Bishoprick of Durham or Lancashire; if he shall goe to Durham and those parts, we hope Calendar [The Scots commander at Newcastle] (who for certaine is before New-Castle) will entertaine hime; however, we have sent after him all the Scottish Cavalry, all the Lord Manchesters, 1000 of the Lord Fairefax's, and one thousand Dragoons, in all seven thousand. While I was about to close my Letter we received information that the Lord Clavering with about 2000 foote and horse are joyned with the Prince, and that he is gone to Lancashire, whereupon Sir John Meldrum with the Lancashire and Scottish foot that were there formerly, and Sir William Brereton with 1500 horse are returned the nearest way to Lancashire to stop the Prince his passage into the South till our Horse be able to overtake him.[17]

Simeon Ash also writes of a large body of horse setting off in pursuit of Prince Rupert on Saturday 6 July, but states it was only 6,000 strong.[18] Both figures are reasonable. If the Prince marched into County Durham the Earl of Callendar would be able to face him with a second, smaller, Scots Army, which was blockading Newcastle. This army, combined with the pursuing Allied horse, should have been able to deal with the Prince. If he marched into Lancashire the Allied horse would continue to pursue him and any southward movement would be intercepted by Meldrum and Brereton. This was a sound plan but did not come to fruition. By 16 July the Earl of Manchester's horse, and its commander, were quartered close to York, so the pursuit by the Allied horse was not longlived. Meldrum and Brereton failed to intercept the Prince in Lancashire and prevent his crossing of the Mersey into Cheshire, although Meldrum did clash with Lord Byron and the Northern Horse as they followed in the Prince's wake.

It is interesting to look at two letters despatched by the Committee of Both Kingdoms as an example of political interference in military matters and as an illustration of the problems with communications during the seventeenth century. On 25 July two letters were despatched by the Committee to the Allied Generals and to Sir William Brereton.[19] Both letters tell their recipients of the situation in Lancashire and the danger of allowing Prince Rupert to remain there:

> By certain information we hear that Prince Rupert is in Lancashire with 8,000 or 9,000 horse and dragoons, which will enable him in a short time

to destroy those countries, and with the assistance of the Earl of Derby, who is very active and of great power, to raise such forces as may put things to a hazard which way soever he shall march, either to the northern or southern parts. He has the haven of Liverpool, and by that means is like to have an addition of much strength from Ireland.

This information must have come as a great surprise to the Allied commanders! The Committee then goes on to suggest a march into Lancashire by at least part of the Allied Army:

Yet we desire that your Lordships will appoint such a strength as, with the forces of Lancashire and those parts, which, as they represent, will be at least 1,000 horse and 4,000 foot, may be able to go up to him and fight with him or prevent any mischief which may otherwise fall upon his motion northward, southward, or towards the Earl of Manchester's Association. What ways to march, what number, and with what forces you, who are upon the place, can best judge, to whom we leave it.

At least the Committee had the grace to allow the local commanders to choose the strength of their force and its route into Lancashire. By the date of despatch of these two letters Prince Rupert was safely ensconced in Chester, York had fallen, and the Allied armies were about to go their separate ways.

The Second Siege of York
The story of the second siege of York is quickly told. The Royalist defenders were in no condition to hold the city for a prolonged period. Sir Henry Slingsby writes of the state of affairs in the city after the departure of Prince Rupert and the Marquis of Newcastle:

Thus were we left at York, out of all hope of releif, ye town much distract'd, & every one ready to abandon her: & to encourage ym yt were left in ye town, & to get ym to stay, they were fain to give out false reports, yt ye prince had fallen upon ye enemy suddenly & rout'd ym, & yt he was coming back again to ye Town; yet many left us, not liking to abide another seige; wch after began.[20]

The survivors of Marston Moor had been formed into several regiments to aid in quartering them. They were in no fit state to undergo another siege and desertions were rife.

The Allies' initial move was to raise several new batteries, one between Walmgate and Layerthorpe Postern and another on a hill in Bishopsfield.[21] Other preparations were apparent. A bridge of boats had been prepared to allow the Fosse to be crossed and many ladders had been built to aid in the assault. Sir Henry Slingsby believed that the assault would be close to Layerthorpe Postern, which was merely protected by a ditch that, due to the hot weather, was almost dry.[22] Simeon Ash also reports the Allied preparations and their intention to storm the town.[23] These preparations took seven days. On Thursday 11 July the Royalist commanders requested a parley and Simeon Ash goes on to report the ensuing negotiations:

> Hereupon a treaty being desired by the enemy, Sir William Constable and Colonell Lambert, were sent by the Lord Fairfax into the Citie, upon Hostages sent out for their securite and safe return. They went in on Saturday morning, and having spent that day in parley, they returned with this request to the three Generals, That there might be Commissioners authorized, to treat and conclude upon Articles for the peaceable surrender of the Citie. Our three Generalls having demanded the judgement of some Ministers, whether the work of the Treaty, might be approved on the Lords day, and receiving incouragement, they appointed the Lord Humby, Sir William Constable, and Colonell Mountague, to go the next day into the Town, three Hostages being sent out of the Town for their securitie: They continued their debate till Munday, about noon they returned, with Articles to be subscribed by the Generals.

The articles agreed upon by the two sides are shown in full in Appendix V. In brief, all officers and soldiers, and their families, would be allowed to march to the nearest garrison with full honours of war. They would march no more than 10 miles a day and would be protected from plundering. Any officer or soldier who wished to return to his home would be allowed to do so. Any sick or wounded soldier would be allowed to abide in York until he was well enough to travel and would then have the same rights as any other member of the garrison. The citizens of the city would be protected, the city would not be plundered or its churches damaged, and its new garrison would be two-thirds Yorkshiremen. Any citizens of the city absent at the time of the surrender would have the same privileges as those living in the city.

It is interesting to compare these propositions to those put forward by the Marquis of Newcastle on 15 June (shown in Chapter Five). They are very similar and differ only in details. For example, in Newcastle's propositions the army would march no more than 8 miles a day and York's new garrison would be solely of Yorkshiremen, while in the propositions agreed upon in July the army would march no more than 10 miles a day and the new garrison would be two-thirds Yorkshiremen. Comparing the July propositions to the demands of the Allied Generals in June it can be seen how lenient these articles of surrender were. Simeon Ash tries to explain the leniency of these terms:

> If any upon the perusall of those Articles do imagine too much favour was granted to the enemy, we desire that this may be considered for their satisfaction. That the benefit which could be expected for our Armies, or the Kingdom, by taking the Town by storm, could not possibly in any measure counterveil the miserable consequences thereof, to many thousands. Who knows how much precious blood might have been spilt upon so hot a service. How few in the Town could have preserved their houses and shops from spoyl, if more than 20 thousand Souldiers had broken in upon them, with heat and violence? How much would this County have suffered in the ruines of this Citie? And how many of our good friends in other places who drive Trades with Citizens, here, would have been pintched in their estates, by the impoverishing of their Debtors.[24]

These are very laudable sentiments but included in the reasons for giving such lenient terms to the garrison of York should be the shadow of Prince Rupert, lurking to the north and busily recruiting his army to attempt a second relief of the city. Whatever the reasons for granting such lenient terms, granted they were, and it was agreed that the garrison should march out on Tuesday 16 July.

The Fall of York

At eleven o'clock on the morning of 16 July the Royalist garrison began its march out of Micklegate Bar. The Allied Army lined the road for a mile from the gate and officers patrolled the line to ensure no looting ensued.[25] Earlier that morning the garrison of the Mount, a star fort on the road south from Micklegate Bar, had panicked and fled into the city leaving their arms behind them. Simeon Ash reports the state of the garrison as it filed through the gate:

> The fourth part of them, at least, who marched out of the Town were women, many very poor in their apparell, and others in better fashion. Most of the men had filled, and distempered themselves with drink; the number of the Souldiers, as we conjectured, was not above a thousand, besides the sick and wounded persons.[26]

Once the Royalist troops had left the town, the Allied generals, accompanied by many of their officers, attended a service in the Minster where a psalm was sung and, according to Simeon Ash, 'thanks given unto God by Master Robert Duglas, Chaplain to the Lord Leven'. The city was in a bad state. The suburbs had been burnt or demolished by the Royalist defenders and Simeon Ash reported that it would take more than £100,000 to repair the damage done during the siege.[27] There were many wounded in the city and many more sick of the 'spotted fever'. The care of the city was given over to Lord Fairfax and his army, and a plaque in the Chapter House at York Minster commemorates his good ministrations.

It must have been with heavy hearts that the garrison marched from the gates. That night they camped at the village of Hessay, east of the battlefield. Many of the Royalists were local men and would not see their homes for a long time. Sir Henry Slingsby wrote of his feelings that night:

> Upon these articles we march out, but find a failing in ye performance at ye very first, for ye soulgier was pilleg'd, our Wagons plunder'd, mine ye first day, & others ye next. Thus disconsolate we march, forc'd to leave our Country, unless we would apostate, not daring to see mine own house, nor take a farewell of my Children, altho' we lay ye first night at Hessey wthin 2 miles of my house.[28]

Sir Henry lived at the Red House at Moor Monkton only a few miles from where he lay. He is not the only one to mention the plundering of the Royalist wagons. Simeon Ash writes at length of the 'wrongs' committed against their enemies.[29] As the Royalists were passing through the quarters of the Earl of Manchester's horse the Parliamentarian troopers 'fell upon their Carts and Waggons, and pillaged them very deeply, taking away both cloathes, plate, and some moneys'.

Upon being informed of what was happening their officers rode from their quarters and restrained them. It is much to the credit of the Earl of Manchester that he immediately ordered his Lieutenant General, Oliver Cromwell, and a number of other officers to enquire into the circumstances of these offences. After an initial enquiry, during which a number of troopers were handed over to the Provost Marshal and others to their troop captains, a second enquiry took place. In their defence many of the accused pleaded ignorance of the contents of the agreement. This is quite feasible. The agreement had been signed at noon on the Monday and the Royalists had marched out of the town less than twenty-four hours later. The horse quarters were some distance from York and spread over a large area. Others said that Royalist soldiers had pointed out which wagons belonged to Catholics and encouraged the Parliamentarian troopers to pillage them, even helping them to do so. It was also stated that arms had been found in some of the wagons. Although each soldier could march with his own personal weapons all other arms were to be left in the town. This, the Parliamentarian troopers believed, was a breach of the articles of surrender and as such negated their adherence to the same articles. These enquiries were still continuing when the three armies went their separate ways.

The Generals Depart

By 22 July the three Allied armies had gone their separate ways. The area around York was short of supplies and it was deemed necessary to divide their army and move to areas where provisions could be more easily procured. The movements of each army will be dealt with in turn.

Initially the Scots moved into the West Riding, around Leeds and Wakefield. By the 30th a decision had been taken to march north to support the Earl of Callendar's army at Newcastle. In a letter to the Committee of Both Kingdoms, the Earl of Lindsey and Sir Thomas Fairfax give the reasons for this northward movement by the Scots Army:

> First, that the whole Scottish Army, horse and foot, shall presently march northward and be employed according to the tenor of this enclosed Act, being the result of our consultations concerning it; and that because the Earl of Callender's Army, which is now lying before Newcastle upon the south side, will not be able to deal with Goring, Montrose, Clavering, and the rest who are all marching towards him with a power of horse far greater than his, whereby in place of gaining Newcastle he will be necessitated with the hazard of his horsemen to betake himself with his foot into Sunderland or Hartlepool, now in his hands, for safety, and so be disenabled to do the kingdom service, the event whereof might prove no other than the loss or hazard of all that which with so much labour and expense has been gained in these counties. This was conceived an argument strong enough for that Army's march northwards, howbeit the reducing of Newcastle were a matter of small importance to the kingdom.[30]

Although Prince Rupert had crossed the Mersey into Cheshire, the Northern Horse, Sir Robert Clavering and the Marquis of Montrose were still at large. If their combined forces descended on County Durham, Callendar would have to withdraw into his base at Sunderland. With this in mind Leven led his army northwards. The expected threat did not transpire and the combined Scots Army lay down in front of Newcastle and dug its siege lines. Newcastle would not fall until 19 October.

It was decided that the Earl of Manchester would lead his army southwards, back into the Eastern Association, where it could recruit and re-equip its tired regiments. By 22 July it had reached Ferrybridge and then continued its march on the 23rd, arriving at Doncaster. From Doncaster the Earl despatched 200 dragoons, under Lieutenant Colonel Lilburne, to Tickhill to summon the castle.[31] Tickhill Castle was garrisoned by eighty musketeers and a troop of horse. These few troops had caused a major interruption to the cloth trade from Leeds and Halifax to Hull, Lincoln and Boston. On the 26th the garrison, commanded by Major Monckton, surrendered on terms. The garrison would be allowed to return to their homes but only the officers would be allowed their horses, swords and pistols. Welbeck House and Sheffield Castle were also summoned and surrendered on 2 and 11 August, respectively. The Army of the Eastern Association continued its slow march southwards, eventually taking part in the Second Battle of Newbury on 27 October 1644.

While the Scots marched north and the Earl of Manchester marched south, Lord Fairfax and his son began the reduction of the remaining garrisons in Yorkshire and Lancashire. One thousand horsemen were despatched to reinforce Sir John Meldrum in Lancashire. By the end of the year Sir John had cleared the county. Garrisons in Yorkshire, Nottinghamshire and Derbyshire fell in quick succession:

Tickhill Castle	26 July 1644
Welbeck	2 August 1644
Sheffield Castle	11 August 1644
Bolsover Castle	12 August 1644
Wingfield Manor	14 August 1644
Staveley House	21 August 1644
Bolingbroke Castle	3 November 1644
Helmsley Castle	22 November 1644
Scarborough Town	17 February 1645

By the beginning of the 1645 campaign season only Pontefract Castle, Scarborough Castle, Sandal Castle, Bolton Castle, Skipton Castle, Belvoir Castle and Newark remained in the King's hands. Active field operations were virtually at an end and the war in Yorkshire devolved into a series of sieges. The Northern Horse returned to the county twice, first in February/March 1645 to relieve Pontefract Castle and then later in the year, when they fought an unsuccessful action at Sherburn-in-Elmet (15 October 1645) before continuing north to surrender near Carlisle later in October.

The fall of York had cost the King dear. He had lost a fertile recruiting ground that he would never recover. One of the King's three main field armies had been destroyed at the Battle of Marston Moor. In the 1645 campaign season the King's other two armies were lost: the Oxford Army at Naseby (14 June 1645) and the Western Army at Langport (10 July 1645). At the start of the campaign season the Royalist command had two main strategic choices:

should it march into the south and face the New Model Army while it was still forming; or should it go north to defeat the Scots?

With the advantage of hindsight the first option would probably have been the better. The whole Oxford Army, including Goring's contingent, could have combined with the Western Army and fought the New Model Army with equality of numbers. George Goring pushed for this option. On the other hand, Prince Rupert pushed equally hard for a march into the north. Marston Moor had been his first real defeat and it stung him. It is not beyond the realms of possibility that a thirst for revenge led Rupert to support the northern option. As it happened, the King tried to adopt the best of both plans. The main army marched northwards, while Goring and a large detachment of horse headed for the West Country. The road north would lead to another meeting between Prince Rupert and Sir Thomas Fairfax and Oliver Cromwell – now the commanders of the New Model Army – at Naseby, where the King's Oxford Army met its end. The reputation gained by the two Parliamentarian commanders during the campaign for York led to their choice as general and lieutenant general of the New Model, respectively. They would prove to be King Charles's nemesis.

In his letter to Prince Rupert, the King had stated that: 'If York be lost I shall esteem my crown little else.' How prophetic his words would prove. Not only would the King lose his crown, but the head upon which it sat. Although fighting continued for several years after the Battle of Marston Moor, from 2 July 1644 the Royalist cause was on a slippery slope to defeat. The Marston Moor campaign would prove the decisive campaign of the First Civil War.

Appendix I

A List of the Severall Regiments and Chief Officers of the Scotish Army

His Excellency the Earl of Leven, General*
Treasurer and Commissary-General, Sir Adam Hepburne, Lord of Humbee*
Quarter-Master-General, Lodowicke Lesly*
General of the Artillery, Sir Alexander Hamilton*
Lieutenant-General of the Foot, John Bayly*
Major-General of the Horse, David Lesly*

Places where Levied	Colonels	Lieutenant-Colonels	Majors	Companies
Kyle and Carrick	Earl of Cassils	John Kennedy	Houghton*	10
Galloway	William Steuart*	Gordon	Agnew	10
Fyfe	Earl of Lindsey	Thomas Moffet*	Mungo Murray*	10
East-Louthian	Sir Patrick Hepburne	William Home*	Robert Hepburne*	10
Stratherne	Lord Cowper	John Browne*	Browne*	10
Loudon-Glasgow	Earl of Loudon	Robert Home*	John Haddon*	10
Middle-Louthian	Lord Maitland	Colm Piscotty*	John Hay*	10
The Mers	Sir David Home	George Home*	Lumbsdale*	10
Sterlingshire	Lord Levingston	Bruce*	Ja. Levinston*	10
Tweddale	Earl of Buccleugh	William Scot*	Tho. Moffat*	10
Edinburgh	James Rae	Andrew Melve*	David Logan*	10
Fyfe	Earl of Dumfermlyn	Robert Halsel*	David Fynne*	10
Clidsdale	Gen. of the Artillery	William Carmichael*	Lindsay	10
Perthshire	Lord Gask	Lachlane Rosse*	Campbel*	10
Tiviotdale	Earl of Lothian	Patrick Lesly*	Sir George Douglas*	10
Niddesdale, Annandale				
	Douglas of Kelhead	John Hog*	Macbray*	10
Angus	Lord Dudhope	Bonar*		10
Lithgow and Twedale				
	Master of Yester	Johnston*	Wiliam Hamilton	10
Mernes & Aberdeen	Earl Marshal	Wood*		3
Ministers Regiment	Arthur Erskin	Ja. Brison*	John Lesly	5
Levied Regiment	Lord Sinclair	James Somerville*		

Besides seven Companies of the Earl-Marshal's upon the March, and four Companies remaining in Berwick.

*Those men who had 'Served beyond the Sea before'.

[Source: Rushworth, Vol. V, pp. 604–605.]

Regiments of Horse of about Sixty in a Troop:

Colonels	Lieutenant-Colonels	Majors	Troops
His Excel. the Earl of Leven	James Ballantine*	Sir Robert Adair*	8
Major General, David Lesly	Sir John Browne*	Thomas Craig	8
Earl of Eglington	Hugh Montgomery*	Montgomery*	8
Lord Kirkudbright	James Mercer	Alexander Cruke	7
Earl of Dalhousy	Innis*	Blair*	6
Lord Balcarras	Strachan	Alexander Home*	6
Michael Welden	Alexander Home*		7
Lord Gordon			1
Marquess of Argyle			1

'Dragooners': Colonel Freiser,* Lieutenant-Colonel Crawford,* Sergeant-Major Monroe.*
* Those men who had 'Served beyond the Sea before'.
[Source: Rushworth, Vol. V, pp. 604–605.]

Articles and Ordinances of War

That no man pretend ignorance, and that everie one may know the dutie of his place, that he may do it; The Articles and Ordinances following, are to be published at the generall Rendezvous in everie Regiment apart, by the Majors of the severall Regiments, and in the presence of all the Officers. The same shall afterward be openly read to every Company of Horse and Foot, and at such times as shall be thought most convenient by the Lord Generall: and in like manner shall be made knowne to so many as joyne themselves to be professed Souldiers in the Army. For this end, everie Colonell and Captaine shall provide one of those Books, that hee may have it in readinesse at all occasions, and every Souldier shall solemnly sweare this following Oath:

I, N. N., promise and sweare to be true and faithfull in this Service, according to the heads sworn by me in the Solemn League and Covenant of the three Kingdomes: To honour and obey my Lord Generall, and all my superiour Officers and Commandrs, and by all meanes to hinder their dishonour and hurt: To observe carefully all the Articles of War and Camp-Discipline: never to leave the defence of this Cause, nor flee from my Colours so long as I can follow them: To be ready to watching, warding, and working, so farre as I have strength: To endure and suffer all distresses, and to fight manfully to the uttermost, as I shall answer to God, and as God shall help me.

I   Kirk Discipline shall be exercised, and the sick cared for in every Regiment, by the particular Eldership, or Kirk-Session to be appointed, even as useth to be done in every Parish in the time of Peace: And that there may be an uniformitie thorowout the whole Army in all matters Ecclesiasticall, there shall be a generall Eldership, or common Ecclesiastick Judicatory, made up of all the Ministers of the Camp, and of one Elder direct from every particular Regiment, who shall also judge of Appellations made unto them from the particular Sessions or Elderships.

II   For deciding of all questions, debates and quarrellings that shall arise betwixt Captains and their Souldiers, or any other of the Army, and for the better observing of Camp-Discipline, two Courts of justice, the one higher, and the other lower, are appoynted, wherein all Judges are sworne to do justice equally: The higher also to judge of Appellations to be made from the lower Court. And if any man shall by word or gesture shew his contempt or mis-regard, or shall fall out in boasting or braving, while Courts are sitting, hee shall be punished by death. And both these Judicatories, as well of the Kirk matters, as of War, shall be subject to the Generall Assembly, and Committee of Estates respective.

III   Whosoever shall wilfully or carelesly absent himselfe from morning and evening Prayers, or from preaching before and after-noon on the Lords Day, or other extra-ordinarie times appoynted for the worship of God, when the signe is given by sound of Trumpet or Drum, hee shall be censured and punished for his neglect or contempt, by penaltie, imprisonment, or other punishment, as his fault deserveth.

After the warning given, there shall be no Market, nor selling of Commodities whatsoever, till the Prayers or Preaching be ended, upon the paine of forfeiting the things so sold, and of the imprisoning of the offenders.

IV   Common and ordinary swearing and cursing, open prophaning of the Lords Day, wronging of his Ministers, and other Acts of that kind, shall not only be punished with losse of pay and imprisonemene [sic], but the Transgressors shall make their publike repentance in the midst of the Congregation, and if they will not be reclaimed, they shall with disgrace be openly casseered and discharged, as unworthy of the meanest place in the Army.

V   If any shall speak irreverently against the Kings Majestie & his authoritie, or shall presume to offer violence to his Majesties Person, he shall be punished as a Traytor. Hee that shall speak evill of the Cause which wee defend, or of the Kingdomes, the Parliaments, Convention of Estates, or their Committees in the defence thereof, or shall use any words to the dishonour of the Lord Generall, he shall be punished with death.

No man shall at his own hand, without warrant of the Committee, or of my Lord Generall, have, or keep intelligence with the enemy, by speech, letters, signes, or any other way, under the pain to be punished as a Traytour. No man shall give over any Strength, Magazin, Victuall, &c. Or make any such motion, but upon extremitie, under the same paine. No man shall give supply, or furnish money, victuall, or any com-modities to the enemy, upon pain of death.

Whosoever shall be found to do violence against the Lord Generall, his Safe-guard, or Safe-conduct, shall dye for it.

Whosoever shall be found guiltie of carelesnesse and negligence in his service, although he be free of treachery and double-dealing, shall beare his owne punishment.

VI All Commanders and Officers shall be carefull, both by their authority and example, that all under their charge, live in godlinesse, sobernesse, and righteousnesse: And if they themselves shall be common swearers, cursers, drunkards, or any of them at any time shall come drunke to his Guard, or by quarrelling, or any other way shall commit any notable disorder in this quarter, losse of place shall be his punishment; And further, according to the sentence of the Court of War.

The Captaines that shall be negligent in training their Companies, or that shall be found to withhold from their souldiers any part of their pay, shall be disgraced of their place, and further censured by the Court of War.

No Commander or Officer shall conceale dangerous and discontented humours, inclined to mutinies, or grudging at the orders given them, but shall make them knowne to the prime Leaders of the Army, upon the paine to be accounted guilty of mutiny.

No Commander or Officer shall authorize, or wittingly permit any Souldier to goe forth to a singular combate, under paine of death: But on the contrary, all Officers shall be carefull by all meanes to part quarrellings amongst Souldiers, although they be of other Regiments or Companies, and shall have the power to command them to prison, which if the Souldiers shall disobey or resist by using any weapon, they shall die for it.

No Captaine shall presume at his owne hand, without warrant of the Lord Generall, to casseer or give a Passe to any enrolled Souldier or Officer, who hath appeared at the place of the generall Rendezvous, nor shall any Commander, Officer, or Souldier depart without a Passe, or staye behind the time appointed him in his Passe; and whosoever transgresseth the one way or the other, shall be punished at the discretion of the Court of War.

VII All Souldiers shall remember that it is their part to honour and obey their Commanders, and therefore shall receive their commands with reverence, and shall make no noise, but be silent, when the Officers are commanded, or giving their directions, that they may be heard by all, and the better obeyed: he that faileth against this, shall be imprisoned.

No Souldier shall leave his Captaine, nor servant forsake his Master, whether he abide in the Army or not, but upon licence granted, and in an orderly way.

Whosoever shall presume to discredit any of the great Officers of the Army, by Writ, Word, or any other way, and be not able to make it good; & whosoever shall lift his weapon against any of them; shall be punished by death; and whosoever shall lift his hand against any of them, shall lose his hand.

No Souldier, nor inferiour Officer, shall quarrel with, or offer injury to his superior, nor refuse any duty commanded him, upon paine of casseering, and to be further censured by the Court of War. And if any shall presume to strike his Superiour, he shall be punished with death. But if it shall happen, that any Officer shall command any thing to the evident and knowne prejudice of the publicke, then shall he who is commanded, modestly refuse to obey, and presently give notice thereof to the Lord Generall.

If any man shall use any words or wayes, tending to mutiny or sedition, whether for demanding his pay, or upon any other cause; or if any man shall be privy to such mutinous speeches or wayes, & shall conceal them, both shall be punished with death.

All must shew their valour against the Enemy, and not by revenging their private injuries, which upon their complaints to their superiour Officers, shall be repaired to the full. And if any man presume to take his owne satisfaction, or challenge a combate, he shall be imprisoned, and have his punishment decerned by the Marshall Court.

The Provost-Marshall must not be resisted or hindered, in apprehending or putting Delinquents in prison, and all Officers must assist him to this end; and if any man shall resist or breake prison, he shall be censured by the Court of War.

VIII　Murther is no lesse unlawfull and intollerable in the time of War, then in the time of Peace, & is to be punished with death.

Whosoever shall be found to have forced any woman, whether he be Commander or Souldier, shall die for it without mercy. And whosoever shall be found guilty of adultery or fornication, shall be no lesse severely censured and punished then in the time of Peace.

If any common whores shall be found following the Army, if they be married women, and run away from their husbands, they shall be put to death without mercy; and if they be unmarried, they shall be first married by the hangman, and thereafter by him scourged out of the Army.

Theeves and Robbers shall be punished with the like severity. If any shall spoile or take any part of their goods that die in the Army, or are killed in service, he shall restore the double, and be further punished at discretion. It is provided, that all their goods be forth-comming, and be disposed of according to their Testament and Will, declared by word or writ before witnesses; or if they have made no Testament, to rheir [sic] Wives, Children, or nearest Kindred, according to the Lawes of the Kingdome.

All shall live together as friends and brethren, abstaining from words of disgrace, contempt, reproach, giving of lies, and all provocation by word or gesture: He that faileth, shall be imprisoned for the first fault; and if he be incorrigible, he shall be with shame punished, and put out of the Army.

IX   All Souldiers shall come to their Colours, to watch, to be exercised, or to muster, with their owne Armes: And if any Souldier shall come with another mans Armes, he shall be punished with rigour, and the lender shall lose his Armes. All shall come also with compleate and tight Armes in a decent manner, otherwise to be severely punished.

If any man shall sell or give in pawne his horse, his Armes, or any part of the Ammunition committed to him: or any Instruments; as Spades, Shovels, Pickes, used in the Field, he shall for the first and second time be beaten through the quarter, and for the third time be punished as for other theft: And he that buyeth them, or taketh them to pawne, be he Souldier or Victualler, shall pay the double of the Money, beside the want of the things bought or impawned, and be further punished at discretion.

Whosoever in a debawched and lewd manner by Cards or Dice, or by sloath and unexcusable neglect, shall lose his Horse and Armes, in whole, or in part, to the hinderance of the service; An whosoever shall wilfully spoile, or breake his Armes, or any Instrument of War committed to him, by cutting downe of Trees, or any other way, he shall serve as a Pioner, till the losse be made up, and he furnished upon his owne charges.

X   No man on his march, or at his lodging, within or without the Countrey upon whatsoever pretext, shall take by violence, either horse, cattell, goods, money, or any other thing lesse or more, but shall pay the usuall prices for his meat and drinke, or be furnished in an orderly way upon count, at the sight of the Commissar, according to the order given by the Committee upou [sic] paine of death, without mercy.

If any man shall presume to pull down, or set on fire any dwelling house, though a Cottage, or hew downe any Fruit-trees; or to waste or deface any part of the beauty of the Countrey, he shall be punished most severely, according to the importance of the fault.

In marching, no man shall stay behinde without leave: No man shall straggle from his Troop or Company: No man shall march out of his ranke, and put others out of order, under all highest paine.

XI   If any Colonell of Horse or Foot shall keep backe his Souldiers from the appointed musters, or shall lend his Souldiers to make a false muster, upon triall in the Court Marshall, he shall be punished as a deceiver. And if any Muster-master shall use any false Rols, shall have any hand in false Musters, or by connivance, or any other way be tryed to be accessary to them, he shall suffer the like punishment.

XII   No man shall presume to doe the smallest injury to any that bring necessaries to the Leaguer, whether by stealing from them, or deceiving them, or by violence in taking their Horse or goods, under the paine to be accounted and punished as enemies. No Victuallers shall sell rotten victuals, upon paine of imprisonment and confiscation, and further as they shall be judged to deserve.

No Souldier shall provide and sell Victuals, unlesse he be authorized, nor shall any that selleth Victuals, keep in his Tent or Hutte any Souldier at unseasonable houres, and forbidden times, under paine at discretion; Like as all the prices thereof shall be set downe by the generall Commisser, and be given to the Quarter-Master of the severall Regiments.

XIII   No man enrolled professing himselfe or pretending to be a Souldier, shall abide in the Army, unlesse hee enter in some Company, nor shall he that hath entred depart without licence, upon paine of death. No man having licence shall stay beyond the time appoynted him, upon paine of the losse of his pay during the time of his absence, and further punishment at discretion. If any man in a mutinous way, shew himselfe discontent with the quarter assigned him, hee shall be punished as a mutiner. And if any man shall stay out of his quarter, or go without shot of Cannon being intrenched, but one night, without leave of his superiour Office, he shall be casseered.

All that shall be absent from the watch after the signe is given for the setting thereof, shall be severely punished. Hee that revealeth, or falsifieth the watch-word given by the Office, within the Trenches, or before the Colours: He that is taken sleeping, or drunk upon his watch: Hee that commeth off the watch before the time, every one of those shall be punished with death.

Whosoever shall assemble themselves together for taking mutinous counsell, upon whatsoever pretext; they all, whether Officers or Souldiers, shall suffer death.

XIV Every man when the Alarme is given, shall repaire speedly to his Colours; no man shall forsake or flee from his Colours.

No man in the Countrey shall reset them that flee.

No man in the battell shall throw away his Musket, Pike, or Bandilier, all under the paine of death.

Whatsoever Regiment of Horse or Foot, having charged the enemy, shall draw back or flee before they come to stroke of sword, shall answer for it before a Councell of war; and whosoever Officer or Souldier shall be found to bee in the default, they shall be punished by death or some shamefull punishment, as the Council of war shall find their cowardise to deserve.

XV If it shall come to passe, that the enemy shall force us to battell, and the Lord shall give us victorie, none shall kill a yeelding enemy, nor save him that still pursueth upon paine of death. Neither shall there be any ransoming of persones, spoyling, pillaging, parting of the prey, or wasting and burning by fire, or disbanding from their charges; or Officers, but as the Lord Generall shall give order upon the same paine of death.

XVI Every mans carriage shall be diligently observed, and he according to his merit rewarded or punished: And whatsoever Officer or Souldier shall take Commanders, or the Colours of the enemy, or in the Siege of Townes shall first enter a breach, or scale the wals, and shall carry him-selfe dutifully in his station, and doth his part valiantly, in skirmish or battell, shall after the laudable example of the wisest, and worthiest Kingdomes and Estates, have his honour and reward according to his worth and deserving, whether hereafter we have peace or war.

Matters that are cleare by the light and lawe of nature are presup-posed: Things unnecessary, are past over in silence: and other things may be judged by the common customes and constitutions of war, or may upon new emergents, be expressed afterward.

[Source: Terry, C.S., *Papers Relating to the Army of the Solemn League and Covenant 1643–1647*, Edinburgh, 1917.]

Appendix III

A Declaration of the Committees for Billetting the Souldiers

Whereas the two Houses of the Parliament of England, considering the great and apparent danger of Religion and Liberty, in regard of the great Forces of Papists and others employed for the destruction thereof; have by their Commissioners desired the assistance of the Kingdom of Scotland to joyn with them in the just and honourable endeavours of preserving and reforming Religion, procuring the honour and happinesse of the King now engaged in Councell prejudiciall to himselfe and his Kingdomes, and of setling and maintaining the peace and liberty of his Dominions. And whereas the Kingdome of Scotland have readily yeelded thereunto, and raised an Army for the ends above expressed which is to be ordered by the Committees and Commissioners of both Kingdomes.

We the said Commissioners and Committees, being desirous to take the most orderly and reasonable way for the Provision of the said Army, have thought fit by this short Declaration to acquaint you with what is expected from you the Inhabitants of those parts through which this Army shall passe, that so you may not be oppressed with arbitrary Taxes and unreasonable spoyles, which you have suffered from those who have lived amongst you and upon you.

This is a cause and time wherein the endeavours of every one who loves his Religion, King or Countrey, ought to be exprest to the utmost, and that which is required at your hands, is to provide and furnish to your best ability, those Souldiers that shall be quartered with you with such provisions as shall bee necessary, not exceeding the allowances and rates mentioned in a schedule hereafter written, hereunto annexed.

And for the better keeping of accounts of what is delivered by you to the Officers and Souldiers according to the Rates of the said schedules; We desire that two sufficient men in every Town, Hamblet or Parish, the one for the horse, and the other for the foot, may exactly take and keep Notes of the Billities of every particular, and of what shall be delivered to every one of them, particular horsman and footman, that so allowance and satisfaction may bee made to every Inhabitant accordingly, which wee will take care shall bee speedily done either out of the Estates of Papists and other Delinquents against the Parliament, or otherwise as wee shall bee enabled thereunto.

Nor have you any reason to distrust us in this behalf, if you call to minde the equall proceedings you have heretofore found from the Scottish Army at their former entrance. And in so doing, you shall besides the service which you doe to the publike, free your selves from any irregular carriages of the Souldiers, and be the better enabled to require a just satisfaction for any injury done you against or beyond this Order, of which we hereby assure you.

A Schedule of Allowance to be made to Officers and Souldiers, horse and foot, in the Scottish Army for their entertainment in their march, or as they shall be quartered in England, not exceeding these Proportions and Rates here under mentioned, viz.

	L. S. D.
To a Major of the horse daily	00.06.00.
To a Root-master or Capt. of horse daily.	00.06.00.
To a Lieutenant of horse daily.	00.04.00.
To a Cornet	00.02.06.
To each Corporall, Quartermaster, and Trumpeter	00.01.06.
To every Trooper for his own diet daily	00.01.00.
For every horse Officer or Trooper, of straw five sheaves, or a stone of hay at 24 houres.	00.00.04.
And of Oates, the measure of three English Gallones at.	00.00.06.

If the Countrey people have no Oates they may have them at the Magazine at Barwick, and shall have allowance for the carrying of them.

The Lieutenant Colonell of foot daily	00.05.00.
The Major of foot daily	00.04.00.
The Captaine	00.03.00.
The Lieutenant	00.02.00.
The Ensigne	00.01.06.
The Quarter-master	00.02.00.
The Serjeant	00.01.00.
The Corporall and Drummers, each	00.00.08.
The common Souldiers daily	00.00.06.

To the Carriage-man, the like entertainment as on
   common foot Souldier; For the Carriage horse
   three penney-worth of straw or hay, and two penney-
   worth of Oates.

The Dragoner is to have for himselfe eight pence aday,
   and for his horse three penney-worth of straw or hay,
   and a groats-worth of Oates.

The Officers of Dragoners are to have entertainment
   at discretion, not exceeding the Rates following:

	L. S. D.
The Lieutenant Colonell daily	00.06.00.
The Major daily	00.05.00.
The Captaine daily	00.04.00.
The Lieutenant daily	00.03.00.
The Ensigne daily	00.02.06.
The Serjeant daily	00.01.04.
The Corporall and Drummer, each	00.00.10.

FINIS.

[Source: *The Scots Army Advanced into England Certified in a Letter*, reproduced in *Richardson's Reprints*.]

An Eyewitness Account of the Storming of Bolton

An Exact Relation of the Bloody and Barbarous Massacre at Bolton in the Moors in Lancashire, May 28, by Prince Rupert, Being Penned by an Eye-Witness Admirably Preserved by the Gracious and Mighty Hand of God in That Day of Trouble. Published according to order.

London: Printed by R.W. for Christopher Meredith, August 22, 1644. *An Exact Relation of the Bloody and Barbarous Massacre at Bolton in the Moors in Lancashire, May 28, by Prince Rupert, Being Penned by an Eye-Witnesse, Admirably Preserved by the Gracious and Mighty Hand of God in That Day of Trouble.*

After those two fatall and prodigious fountaines of our sad Counties misery, viz. ours in full security in too much resting upon our owne strength upon the one side, and our woefull and ruine-threatning divisions on the other, had long portended, and Gods Ministers had often warned us of that calamity which then we feared not, nor believed, but now smart under; it pleased the just and wise hand of Heaven, at last, to awake our dead spirits by that sad Alarme of War, and to cause that black cloud which hung over our heads to be dissolved, and first to be poured down in a bitter showre of blood, upon that Spectacle of sorrow and amazement, poor, sighing, and solitary Bolton; that England may see and be ashamed that she hath not long since spewed out such monsters as are bred in her owne bowels, and that all may take it to heart that there hath beene no more zeale in us for the Cause, Servants, Gospel, and glory of the Lord of Hosts, so much aimed at, and, by tongues set on fire of hell so vilified, as in this relation may further appeare.

On Tuesday, May 28, this sad towne being almost destitute of men, ammunition, or other means of defence, was in the morning relieved by that noble cordiall commander, Col. Rigbie; and certainly if some other aid designed for our helpe had come in time, there had been a good account rendered of that townes preservation, and the enemies discouragement; but that God, which intended not our deliverance, used not the meanes; yet in all there was about

2000 Souldiers and 500 Clubmen, a company sufficient if the securitye of the Inhabitants had not hindred their better fortifying of the same.

About two of the clocke in the afternoone the enemy was discovered about a mile off, and they made their approaches to the Town on the More south-west from the Town. Their number was guessed, and by themselves after confessed to be about 12000. They appeared at first like a wood or cloud, and presently were cast into severall bodies; divers scouts approached to discover the way for their entrance with most advantage. Our Commanders were very couragious, and our Souldiers very hardy, and both resolved to stand to it, and in the first encounter gave them about halfe an houres sharpe entertainment, were close in discharge, as the enemies confessed after, and repulsed them bravely to the enemies great losse and discouragement, and in their retreat cut them down before them in great abundance, and they fell like leaves from the tree in a winter morning.

Then was a breathing, or rather a new preparative for a fresh encounter, which was gallantly performed on both sides, wherein the worthy Colonell Rigby, and his Commanders, Captain Willougby, Captain Bootle, and the rest, did notable service. But, alas, what could naked men do against horse in an unfortified place: besides, it is conceived that a Townsman was their convoy to bring them on through a place called the Private Akers for a great reward; and when once the horse was got into the Town, there could be no resistance almost made, but every man left to shift for himself.

At their entrance, before, behinde, to the right, and left, nothing heard but kill dead, kill dead was the word in the Town, killing all before them without any respect, without the town by their Horsemen pursuing the poore amazed people, killing, stripping, and spoiling all they could meet with, nothing regarding the doleful cries of women and children, but some they slashed as they were calling for quarter, others when they had given quarter, many hailed out of their houses to have their brains dasht out in the streets, those that were not dead in the streets already pistoled, slashed, brained, or troden under their horses feet with many insolent blasphemous oathes, curses, and challenges to heaven itselfe, (no doubt) hastening the filling up of their cup, and bringing that swift destruction upon them, which they shortly after tasted of (and blessed, blessed ever be the great and just God for it) with many taunts and cruell mockings; as, 'See what your prayers are come to! Where is all your dayes of humiliation? O, that we had that old rogue Horrocks that preaches in his grey cloake!'

But I forbeare many sad things which might be inserted, the usage of children crying for their fathers, of women crying out for their husbands, some of them brought on purpose to be slaine before their wives faces; the rending, tearing, and turning of people naked, the robbing and spoiling of all the people of all things that they could carry: all which this Author being an eye witnesse, and a sharer in, who though quarter was given him by a Souldier that found him out in hopes of getting his money, yet had like to have been severall times killed after for his money, which others had gotten before, and doubtlesse had been slaine if a Commander had not appointed to carry him to the Prince, yet he that carried him forced him to go and borrow twenty shillings more, else he would leave him in the streets again, and that was present death.

The relator upon his own knowledge and good information further addes some particular instances of their then matchless cruelty, by which (as ex ungue leonem) you may judge and abhorre them, and their actions, and the Lord grant England at last an open eye and due sense of her owne misery, by this sad spectacle, and wofull example of Bolton.

First the massacring, dismembring, cutting of dying or dead bodies, and boasting, with all new coined oathes swearing how many Roundheads this sword or they had killed that day, some eight, some six, some more or lesse. Arms, legs, yea the braines themselves lying distant from their heads, bodies, and other parts.

Their treading under horse feet and prancing over halfe dying poore Christians, who were so besmeared and tumbled in dust and blood, that scarce anything of man remained in the cruell beastly actor or wofull sufferer, but onely proportion of men in both, the one being become so farr below the nature of a man in acting, the other cast below the condition of the most miserable of men, in suffering such unheard of things.

Their violent pursuit of their bloody victory in the Towne and 4 or 5 miles out of the Towne in outhouses, fields, highwayes and woods, killing, destroying and spoiling all they could reach, and crying out, 'Where is your Roundheads' God now? He was with you at Warrington, Wigan, Manchester, and other places, and hath he forsaken you Roundheads of Bolton now? Sure he is turned Cavalier,' &c.

Their bragginge how many wives they that day had made widowes and children fatherlesse, mercilessly casting off all pitty, insomuch as any if they were tumbling in the dirt or ditches, did but lift up their heads and cry 'Quarter, for the Lord Jesus' sake, quarter,' all the mercy they shewed them was to cry out to others, or to say, 'God damme, ile give this or that strong Roundheaded rogue one blow more to send him quickly to the Devill.'

William Boulton was fetcht out of his chamber with scorne, saying they had found a praying Saint, and fetcht him to kill him before his wives face, who being greate with childe and ready to be delivered, fell on him to have saved him, but they pulled her off without compassion, and bade him call on his God to save him, whilest they cut him to pieces.

James Syddal lying wounded and dying was heard by one of them to give a groan (after they had thought him long before to be dead) and presently one discharged his pistol at his heart, but it would not enter; the other he prepared after, and that tooke effect; and after boasted what an act he had done, saying, 'Yonder lies one of the strongest Roundheads that ever I met withall, for one of my pistols discharged at his heart would not enter, but I thinke I sent him to the Devill, with a vengeance, with the other.'

Katherine Saddon, an aged woman of 72 years old, run with a sword to the very heart, because she had no money to give, and some others killed outright after they were mortally wounded, because they stirred or answered not greedy unjust desires.

Elizabeth Horrocks, a woman of good qualitie, after that they had killed her husband, tooke her in a rope and dragged her up and down, after that they had robbed and spoiled her of all she had, and threatned to hang her unlesse she would tell them of her plate and money, who was yet wonderfully preserved.

Their inhuman usage of her and some other maids and wives in the town in private places, in fields and in woods, the trees, the timber, and the stones, we hope will one day be a witnesse against them, for some of them being destracted at the present day.

Alice Greg, the reverend late minister of Bolton's widow, stripped to her smocke – nay, she having two smockes on, they tooke one of them, and left her scarce old rags to cover her nakednesse.

But the principal stain of all this cruelty, as is reported, was set off by that Strange Earle, his ignoble, nay base killing of valiant Captain Bootle after quarter given, besides whom, and Captaine Horrocke, we lost no commander of note; but they lost, as is confessed, a Colonel, a Lieutenant Colonel, and divers other Commanders of good quality. Whether their losse or ours was greater for souldiers is somewhat questionable, so many of ours escaped, and so many of their were buried by them partly in obscure places, and a greate many of note by them lie buried in the chancell of the Church. Of their and oure side it is conceived there was slain about 1200 or 1500 in all.

Only this one thing may they boast of more in their bloody zeal for the worst of causes that ever was defended by English Spirits, that they left almost three score poor widows husbandlesse, and hundreds of poor children fatherlesse, and a sweet godly place a nest of owles and a den of dragons, almost without inhabitant: only a few women and children are the remnant left, without bit to eate, bed to lie on almost, or a cup to drink in, or any meanes of subsistence in the world. So that we may well conclude with Jeremiah (Lam. i. 12) 'Was ever sorrow like to my sorrow? Is it nothing to you, O yee that pass by?' &c.

Oh England! Oh Heaven! Oh Earth! &c. beare witnesse of our calamity. Oh London! and all ye places yet freed from our sorrows, think on the day of your peace with thankfulnesse, of our trembling and trouble with compassion. And oh, all ye Christians and people of the Land, let bleeding, dying, undone Bolton bespeake one thing at the hands of all sorts. Take heed of security and your own divisions, lay aside your own ends, spirits, interests, engagements, and distractions, and first labour to carry on God's work in the subduing of these cursed Edomites and Amalekites devoted unto destruction by the hand of heaven, or else look with Bolton to taste of the same cup of trembling which the Lord, the God of Hosts, in his due time, take out of all our hands, and fill up with the measure of our bloody enemies' sins, the measure of their plagues, which the just God will in due time return upon them for this and all their cruelty, that King, Parliament, and People may once more rejoyce in the due settlement of truth and peace in these our dayes, and Glory may still dwell in our land. Which God grant for Christ's sake. Amen.

FINIS

[Source: *An Exact Relation of the Bloody and Barbarous Massacre at Bolton in the Moors in Lancashire, May 28*, Bolton Library, B901.043PB EXA.]

Appendix V

King Charles's Letter to Prince Rupert

On 14 June 1644 King Charles wrote a letter to his nephew, Prince Rupert, which the Prince received on 19 June. This letter led directly to the Battle of Marston Moor and has been the subject of debate ever since. The main subject of discussion was whether the letter was, or was not, a direct order to fight the Scots. The text of the letter is shown below:

Nephew,

First I must congratulate with you for your good successes, assuring you that the things themselves are no more welcome to me than that you are the means. I know the importance of the supplying you with powder, for which I have taken all possible ways, having sent both to Ireland and Bristol. As from Oxford, this bearer is well satisfied that it is impossible to have at present; but if he tell you that I can spare them from hence, I leave you to judge, having but thirty-six left. But what I can get from Bristol (of which there is not much certainty, it being threatened to be besieged) you shall have.

But now I must give you the true state of my affairs, which if their condition be such as enforces me to give you more peremptory commands than I would willingly do, you must not take it ill. If York be lost I shall esteem my crown little less; unless supported by your sudden march to me; and a miraculous conquest in the South, before the effects of their Northern power can be found here. But if York be relieved, and you beat the rebels Army of both kingdoms, which are before it; then (but otherwise not) I may make a shift (upon the defensive) to spin out time until you come to assist me. Wherefore I command and conjure you, by the duty and affection which I know you bear me, that all new enterprises laid aside, you immediately march, according to your first intention, with all your force to the relief of York. But if that be either lost, or have freed themselves from the besiegers, or that, for want of powder, you cannot undertake that work, that you immediately march with your whole strength, directly to Worcester, to assist me and my Army; without which, or your having relieved York by beating the Scots, all the successes you can afterwards have must infallibly be useless unto me. You may believe that nothing but an extreme necessity could make me write thus unto you, wherefore, in this case, I can no ways doubt of your punctual compliance with

Your loving uncle and most faithful friend

CHARLES R.

P.S. I commanded this Bearer to speak to you concerning Vavasour.

Ticknell June 14th 1644

As can be seen, this letter is very confusing and open to several interpretations. Few historians agree as to the letter's exact meaning. It is worth breaking the letter down and looking at it more closely. The first paragraph is straight-forward. First the King congratulates Rupert on his successes to date at Stockport, Bolton and Liverpool. He then goes on to discuss supplying Rupert with powder from either Bristol or Ireland as the supply at Oxford was down to thirty-six barrels. It is the second paragraph which is confusing and this will be considered a sentence at a time. The first sentence goes:

> But now I must give you the true state of my affairs, which if their con-dition be such as enforces me to give you more peremptory commands than I would willingly do, you must not take it ill.

Here is the crux of the debate. Is what follows a series of 'peremptory com-mands'? If not why would the King have used the term? He then goes on to summarise his thoughts on his strategic situation:

> If York be lost I shall esteem my crown little less; unless supported by your sudden march to me; and a miraculous conquest in the South, before the effects of their Northern power can be found here.

If York was lost it would free an Allied Army of over 20,000 men to march into the south. The King was already faced by the combined armies of Essex and Waller. The addition of 20,000 Scots, Eastern Association and Northern Association troops against him would have been decisive, unless Rupert joined with the King and defeated Essex and Waller before the Allied Army could make its presence felt. The letter continues:

> But if York be relieved, and you beat the rebels Army of both kingdoms, which are before it; then (but not otherwise) I may make a shift (upon the defensive) to spin out time until you come to assist me.

If Rupert relieved York and beat the Allied Army the King believed he could remain on the defensive long enough for Rupert to come to his aid. So here is a mention of both York being relieved and the Allied Army being defeated. Now comes the crux of the matter:

> Wherefore I command and conjure you, by the duty and affection which I know you bear me, that all new enterprises laid aside, you immediately march, according to your first intention, with all your force to the relief of York.

Here is a direct order to march to the relief of York – 'I command and conjure you' as the King puts it. He continues in his next sentence:

> But if that be either lost, or have freed themselves from the besiegers, or that, for want of powder, you cannot undertake that work, that you immediately march with your whole strength, directly to Worcester, to assist me and my Army; without which, or your having relieved York by beating the Scots, all the successes you can afterwards have must infallibly be useless unto me.

Initially the King states that if York was lost, had already freed itself or Rupert did not have enough powder to effect a relief, then the Prince was to bring his whole Army to combine with the King's at Worcester. If Rupert did not do this or he failed to relieve York 'by beating the Scots' the King believed his cause was lost. In the last two sentences lie the grounds for Rupert claiming that the letter was a direct order to fight the Allied Army, as he ever after stated. First the King gives a direct order for Rupert to march to the relief of York and then he states that York will be relieved by beating the Scots. The letter finishes: 'You may believe that nothing but an extreme necessity could make me write thus unto you, wherefore, in this case, I can no ways doubt of your punctual compliance with ...'

This final sentence reiterates that it was extreme necessity that made the King write 'thus unto you' and that he doesn't doubt Rupert's 'punctual compliance'. It is very easy to see how the Prince took this to be a direct order to fight the Scots with statements such as 'peremptory commands', 'and you beat the rebels Army', 'command and conjure', 'relieved York by beating the Scots' and 'punctual compliance'. It is hardly surprising that Prince Rupert used this letter as vindication for fighting the Battle of Marston Moor. He is said to have carried the letter with him to the end of his life.

[Source: Warburton, Eliot, *Memoirs and Correspondence of Prince Rupert and the Cavaliers*, 1849, pp. 437–439.]

Appendix VI

Articles of Surrender of the City of York

The articles of the Surrender of the City of Yorke to the Earle of Leven ... on Tuesday July 16, 1644. Together with an explanation of some part of the Articles. London. Printed for Mathew Walbancke, July 23 1644.

Articles agreed upon betweene Alexander Earle of Leven, Generall of the Scottish Forces, Ferdinando Lord Fairfax, and the Earle of Manchester, Generalls of the English Forces about Yorke on the one part, and Sir Thomas Glenham Knight, Governour of the City of Yorke, and Colonell Generall of the Northerne Army, of the other part Anent the surrender and delivery of the said City, with the Forts, Townes, Cannon, Ammunition, and furniture of Warre belonging thereto, in manner after specified to the said Generalls, for the use of King and Parliament, the 15 day of July, 1644.

1. The said Sir Thomas, as Governour of the said Citie, shall surrender and deliver up the same, with the Forts, Tower, Cannon, Ammunition, and furniture of Warre, belonging thereunto, betweene this and the six-teenth of Iuly instant, at or about the 11 houre thereof in the forenoone, to the said Generals or any in their names for the use aforesaid, in manner, and upon the condition after written.
2. That the Governour, and all Officers and Souldiers, both Horse and Foot, the Governours, Officers, and Souldiers of Cliffords-Tower, the Officers and Souldiers of the Sconce, the Officers and Souldiers belonging to the traine and outworkes, shall march out of the City on Horse-back & with their Armes, flying Colours, Drums, beating Matches lighted on both ends, Bullets in their mouths, and withall their bag and baggage, that every souldier shall have 12 charges of Powder.
3. That Officers and souldiers shall not march above 10 miles a day, that they have accommodation of Quarter and convenience of carriages, that a Troope of Horse out of every of the three Armies, shall attend upon them for their convoy in their march, that no injurie or affront be offered them to Skipton, or the next Garrison Towne within 16 miles of the Princes Army.

4. That such Officers and souldiers as are sicke and hurt, and cannot march out of the Towne, shall have liberty to stay within untill they be recovered, and then shall have passage given them to goe into the Princes Army, where ever it shall be, or to their owne houses and estates, where they may rest quiet, or whither else they shall please, That it may be recommended to my Lord Fairfax for their subsistence during their cure or being ill.

5. All Officers and souldiers wives, children and servants, now in Towne, may have libertie to goe along with their husbands, or to them, or if they please to returne to their owne houses and estates, to enjoy them under such contributions as the rest of the Country payes, that they may have liberty to carrie with them their goods, and have a convenient time and carriages allowed to carrie them away.

6. That no Officer or souldier shall be stopt or plundered upon his march.

7. That no man shall intice any Officer or souldier as he marches out of the Towne with any promises of preferment or reward, or any other grounds whatsoever.

8. That the Citizens and Inhabitants may enjoy all their priviledges which formerly they did at the beginning of these troubles, and may have freedome of trade both by Land and Sea, paying such duties and customes as all other Cities and Towns under the obedience of King and Parliament.

9. That the Garrison that shall be placed here, shall be two parts of three at the least of Yorkshire men, and no free quarter shall be put upon any without his owne consent, and that the Armies shall not enter the City.

10. That in all charges, the Citizens resident and inhabitants shall bear such part with the County at large as war formerly used in all other Assessments.

11. That all Citizens, Gentlemen, and Residents, Sojourners, and every other person within the City, shall at any time when they please have free liberty to move themselves, their families, and goods, and to dispose thereof and of their Estate at their pleasure, according to the Law of the Land, either to live at their owne houses or elsewhere, and to enjoy their Goods and Estates without molestation, and to have protection and safeguard for that purpose, so that they may rest quietly at their aboad, and to travell freely and safely about their occasions, and for their better removall they shall be furnished with carriages, paying for their carriages reasonable rates.

12. That all those Gentlemen and others whatsoever that have Goods within the Citie, and are absent themselves, may have free liberty to take, carry away, and dispose of those Goods, as in the last Article.

13. That no building be defaced, nor any plundering, nor taking of any mans person, or of any part of his Estate, and that Iustice, according to Law,

within the Citie shall be administred in all cases by the Magistrates, and be assisted there if need be by the Garrison.

14. That all persons whose dwellings are in the City, though now absent, may have the benefit of these Articles, as if they were present in the City.

By the Articles of Agreement touching the Rendition of the City of York. The Generals of the Armies have treated as Generals in reference onely to themselves and their Souldiers, and it was not intended to intrench upon any Ordinances of Parliament, but all such persons and estates as were subject to Sequestrations, might still be liable and subject thereto, notwithstanding any generall words in the Articles.

And thus these Generals doe declare under their hands, and the Commissioners of the Treaty doe declare, That they did severall times during the Treaty expresse to the other Commissioners, that they had no order to meddle with any Ordinance of Parliament, or to goe further then the bounds of the Army. Subscribed by

The Lord Fairfax.   Sir Adam Hepborne.
The Earle of Manchester.   Lord Humby.
Sir William Constable.

Printed according to Order.

[Source: B.M., T.T. E3(5).]

List of Abbreviations Used for Contemporary Sources

Readers should note that titles of contemporary sources have been abbreviated in both the text and the endnotes. The following list gives both abbreviated and full forms for the reader's convenience (complete bibliographical data may also be found in the bibliography).

Anderson to Glenham: *Letter from Colonell Francis Anderson to Sir Thomas Glemham*, reproduced in *Richardson's Reprints*.

Articles of Surrender: *The Articles of the Surrender of the City of Yorke to the Earle of Leven on Tuesday July 16 1644, Together with an Explanation of Some Part of the Articles*, B.M., T.T. E3 (5).

Ash No. 2: *The Continuation of True Intelligence from the Right Honourable, the Earl of Manchester's Army, Since the Taking of Lincolne, May 6th, Until the First Day of This Instant Iune, 1644* (Number 2), B.M., T.T. E5 (33).

Ash No. 3: *A Particular Relation of the Most Remarkable Occurrences from the United Forces in the North, under the Command of Those Three Approved and Faithfull Friends Both unto the Church and Common-Wealth, Generall Lesly, the Lord Fairefax and the Earle of Manchester, from Saturday the 1st, Untill Munday the 10th, of This Instant Iune* (Number 3), B.M., T.T. E51 (3).

Ash No. 4: *A Continuation of True Intelligence from the English and Scottish Forces, in the North, for the Service of King and Parliament, and Now Beleaguring York, from the Eighth of This Instant June to the 17th Thereof* (Number 4), B.M., T.T. E51.

Ash No. 5: *A Continuation of True Intelligence from the English and Scottish Forces, in the North, for the Service of King and Parliament, and Now Beleaguring York, from the 16th of June, to Wednesday the 10th of July, 1644* (Number 5), B.M., T.T. E2 (1).

Ash No. 6: *A Continuation of True Intelligence from the Armies in the North, from the 10, Day, to the 27, of This Instant July, 1644, Wherein Is Given a Full and Particular Accompt of the Surrender of York, and of the Removes of the Armies Since* (Number 6), B.M., T.T. E4 (6).

Belasyse: Moone, J.A., *A Brief Relation of the Life and Memoirs of John Lord Belasyse*, HMC Ormonde MSS., New Series, 1903, Vol. II.

Capt. W.H.: *A Relation of the Good Successe of the Parliaments Forces under the Command of General Leslie, the Earl of Manchester and the Lord Fairfax, Against the Forces Commanded by Prince Rupert and the Earl of Newcastle, on Hesham-Moore, on Tuesday July 2 1644*, B.M., T.T. E54 (11).

Cholmley: Cholmley, Sir Hugh, 'Memorials Touching the Battle of York', *English Historical Review*, V, 1890, p. 347.

Clarke to Bartlett: 'Letter from Captain Robert Clarke to Captain Bartlett', *Transactions of the Royal Historical Society*, New Series, Vol. XII, 1898, pp. 76–78.

Cocket Island: *A True Relation of the Taking of Cocket Island*, reproduced in *Richardson's Reprints*.

CSPD 1644: *Calendar of State Papers, Domestic, 1644.*

De Gomme: Sir Bernard de Gomme, *Order of His Majties Armee*, York Minster Library.

Douglas: Douglas, Robert, 'Diary of Robert Douglas', in Terry, C.S., *Life and Campaigns of Alexander Leslie*, 1899, pp. 281–282.

Eminent Person: *Newes from the Siege Before Yorke, Being a Letter from an Eminent Person Out of the Leaguer There, Dated the 16 of June 1644*, York City Library, Y942.062.

Exact Newes from York: *Exact and Certaine Newes from the Siege at Yorke, and of Many Remarkable Passages of Our Armys in Those Parts, Extracted Out of Diverse Letters Which Were Sent by This Last Post from Hull, to a Gentle-Man of Grayes-Inne*, B.M., T.T. E53 (12).

Exact Relation of the Scottish Army: *An Exact Relation of the Last Newes from the Quarters of His Excellency the Lord Generall of the Scottish Army, Dated from Sunderland March 12 1643*, reproduced in *Richardson's Reprints*.

Extract of Letters: *Extract of Letters, Dated at Edenburgh the 14, 16, and 17 of April 1644*, B.M., T.T. E44 (10).

Fairfax Correspondence: Bell, R., *Memorials of the Civil War, Comprising the Correspondence of the Fairfax Family with the Most Distinguished Personages Engaged in That Memorable Contest*, 1849, Vol. I.

Faithful Relation of Scots Army: *A Faithfull Relation of the Late Occurrences and Proceedings of the Scottish Army: Dated from His Excellencies Lord Generall Leslie's Quarters Before Newcastle, 21 February 1644*, reproduced in *Richardson's Reprints*.

Fuller: Fuller, Thomas, *The History of the Worthies of England*, 1662.

Glemham to Argyle: *Sir Thomas Glemham's Letter in Answer to the Marquesse of Argyl's and Sir William Armyne's*, reproduced in *Richardson's Reprints*.

Goring to Musgrave: *Letter from Colonel Goring to Sir Philip Musgrave*, Cumbria Record Office (Carlisle), D Mus correspondence (Civil War), bundle 1, number 29.

Hodgson: Hodgson, Captain John, *Autobiography of Captain John Hodgson*, Brighouse, 1887.

Hulls Managing: *Hulls Managing of the Kingdoms Cause: or, a Brief Historicall Relation of the Severall Plots and Attempts Against Kingston Upon Hull, from the Beginning of These Unhappy Differences to This Day, and the Means Whereby through God's Blessing It Hath Been Preserved, and the Kingdom in It*, B.M., T.T. E51 (11).

Late Proceedings of Scots Army: *The Late Proceedings of the Scotish Army, Certifying Their Passing over Tyne, with the Particulars, Together with Their Possession of Sunderland, and Their Advance After the Enemy, Who Is Fled to Durham, Sent by an Expresse, from His Excellency the Lord General Leslie His Quarters, and Dated at Sunderland, March 12, Number 4*, reproduced in *Richardson's Reprints*.

Lilly: Lilly, William, *History of His Life and Times*, London, 1822.

Lord Fairfax to CBK: *A Letter Sent from the Right Honourable, the Lord Fairfax, to the Committee of Both Kingdoms: Concerning the Great Victory Lately Obtained (by God's Blessing) at Selby in Yorkshire*, reproduced in Wenham, P., The *Siege of York 1644*, York, 1994.

Lord Fairfax to Hull: *A Copy of a Letter Sent from the Lo: Fairfax to the Major of Hull, and by Him Sent to the Committee of Both Kingdoms: Concerning the Great Victory Obtained Against Prince Rupert About the Raising the Siege at York*, York City Library, Y942.062.

Ludlow's Memoirs: Firth, C.H., ed, *The Memoirs of Edmund Ludlow, Lieutenant-General of the Horse in the Army of the Commowealth of England, 1625–1672*, Oxford, 1894, pp. 98–100.

Lumsden: *Letter to Lord Loudon and Allied Battle Plan*, York Minster Library.

Massacre at Bolton: *An Exact Relation of the Bloody and Barbarous Massacre at Bolton in the Moors in Lancashire, May 28*, Bolton Library, B901.043PB EXA.

Monckton: 'Sir Philip Monckton's Narrative', *Transactions of the Royal Historical Society*, New Series, Vol. XII, London, 1898, pp. 52–53.

Newcastle's Memoirs: Firth, C.H. (ed), *Memoirs of the Duke of Newcastle*, 1886.

Ogden: 'Mr Ogden's Narrative', *Transactions of the Royal Historical Society*, New Series, Vol. XII, London, 1898, pp. 71–72.

Prince Rupert's Diary: *Prince Rupert's Diary*, Manuscript Held in Wiltshire County Record Office, Trowbridge, f. 33.

Prince Rupert's Marches: *The Journal of Prince Rupert's Marches, 5 Sept 1642 to 4 July 1646*, Clarendon MSS. xxviii, 129.

Proceedings of His Majesty's Army: 'Proceedings of His Majesty's Army in England under the Command of His Highness Prince Rupert', *Transactions of the Royal Historical Society*, New Series, Vol. XII, 1898, pp. 69–71.

Rupert to Musgrave: *Letter from Prince Rupert to Sir Philip Musgrave*, Cumbria Record Office (Carlisle), D Mus correspondence (Civil War), bundle 4, number 11.

Rushworth: Rushworth, J., *Historical Collections*, Vol. V, London, 1692.

Scots Army Advanced: *The Scots Army Advanced into England Certified in a Letter, Dated from Addarston, the 24 of January: from His Excellencies the Lord Generall Leslie's Quarters, with the Summoning of the County of Northumberland: Expressed in a Letter by the Commissioners and Committees of Both Kingdoms, to Sir Thomas Glemham Governor of Newcastle, and to the Colonells, Officers and Gentlemen of the Forenamed County: with Sir Tho: Glemham's Answer Thereunto*, reproduced in *Richardson's Reprints*.

Short Memoriall: 'A Short Memoriall of the Northern Actions During Ye War There, from Ye Yeare 1642 Till 1644', *Yorkshire Archaeological Journal*, Vol. 8, 1884.

Slingsby: Parsons, D. (ed.), *The Diary of Sir Henry Slingsby*, 1836.

Somerville: Somerville, Lord James, *Memorie of the Somervilles*, Vol. II, pp. 345–352, Edinburgh, 1815.

Somerville at Wetherby: *Letter Written by John Somerville from Wetherby*, reproduced in *Richardson's Reprints*.

Stewart: *A Full Relation of the Victory Obtained (through God's Providence) by the Forces under the Command of General Leslie, the Lord Fairfax, and the Earl of Manchester, Being About Twenty Seven Thousand Horse and Foot, Against His Majesties Forces under the Command of Prince Rupert and the Earl of Newcastle, Being Much About the Same Number, Fought on Marstam-Moor, Within 5 Miles of York on the Second of July 1644*, B.M., T.T. E54 (19).

Stockdale: *Letter from Thomas Stockdale to John Rushworth*, B.M., Harleian MSS. 166.87.

Trevor: Carte, T. (ed.), *A Collection of Original Letters and Papers Found Among the Duke of Ormonde's Papers*, 1739, Vol. I, pp. 55–58.

True Relation of Scots Army: *A True Relation of the Late Proceedings of the Scottish Army, Sent from His Excellency the Lord Generall Leslie's Quarters Before Newcastle the 8th of February 1643*, reproduced in *Richardson's Reprints*.

True Relation of Scottish Army: 'A True Relation of the Proceedings of the Scottish Army from the 12 of March Instant to the 25', *Archaeologia Aeliana*, 1899.

True Relation of Selby: *A True Relation of the Great Victory It Hath Pleased God to Give the Lord Fairfax and Sir Thomas Fairfax His Son, &c., over the Remnant of Newcastle's Forces in Yorkshire, Upon Thursday, the 11th of April, 1644*, reproduced in Morrell, W.W., *The History and Antiquities of Selby*, London, 1867.

Tunstall to Radcliffe: 'Letter from William Tunstall to Sir Edward Radcliffe', *Archaeologia Aeliana*, 1899.

Turner: Turner, Sir James, *Memoirs of his own Life and Times*, Edinburgh, 1829.

Vicars: Vicars, J., *Parliamentarian Chronicles, 1644*, Vol. II.

Warburton: Warburton, Eliot, *Memoirs and Correspondence of Prince Rupert and the Cavaliers*, 1849.

Watson: *A More Exact Relation of the Late Battell Neer York, Fought by the English and Scotch Forces, Against Prince Rupert and the Marquess of Newcastle*, B.M., T.T. E100 (12).

White: *A True Relation of the Late Fight Between the Parliament Forces and Prince Rupert, Within Four Miles of Yorke with the Names of Divers Commanders That Were Slain and Wounded*, York City Library, Y942.062.

Notes and Sources

Chapter 1

1 *Scots Army Advanced.*
2 Ibid.
3 Turner.
4 Rushworth, Vol. V, pp. 604–605.

Chapter 2

1 *Scots Army Advanced*:

Gentlemen,

Although wee justly presume that the solemne mutuall Covenant entred into by both Kingdoms, hath long since come to your Hands, and likewise that you have had notice of the raising of the Army desired by the Parliament of England for the prosecution of those ends therein expressed; viz. The preservation and reformation of Religion, the true honour and happinesse of the King, and the publick peace and liberty of his Dominions. Yet that it may appeare both to you and all the world how unwilling we are to make a forcible use of these armes which we have beene constrained by the disappointment of all other means of safety to take up, We the Commissioners and Committees of both Kingdoms have thought fit, besides that Declaration (a copy whereof we herewith send) lately emitted in the name of the Kingdom of Scotland, for the satisfaction of the people concerning the entrance of this their Army, to take more particular notice of you the chiefe Gentlemen and Commanders, hopeing likewise, that things of so great and considerable consequence will finde with you such entertainment as may answer the weight and importance of them. We will not so much wrong the cause we have undertaken, as to goe about after so many evident Demonstrations of the necessity of our present posture, to dispute it with you, but rather in stead of arguments we think it reasonable to acquaint you with our well weighed resolutions, which are, through the assistance of that God in whose cause we are engaged, and whose strength wee trust in, with our utmost industry and hazard to endeavour the prevention of that imminent danger not only of corruption but of ruine, which we see evidently intended to the true Protestant Religion by the Popish and Prelatical faction, who never wanted will, but now thinks they want not strength and opportunity to accomplish it; as also the rescuing of his Majesties person and honour so deeply and unhappily entangled in the counsels and practices of them, whose actions speak their ends to be little better then Popery and Tyranny, and the redeeming the peace and liberty of his Majesties dominions, in which the Irish Rebellion, and the sad and unnatural divisions in England have made so great a breach; To the accomplishment of these so just and honourable designs, wee have reason to expect the concurrence of all men who either are or pretend a due love to their Religion, King, and Countrey; and shall be very sorry to want yours: but if mis-information or any other unhappy grounds shall so far prevail with you as to reckon us in the number of your enemies, (which certainly we are not if you be friends to those ends mentioned in our Covenant) and if in stead of that concurrence with us which we wish and hope to deserve, we finde from you opposition and acts of hostility, the Law of nature and your owne reason will tell you what you are to expect; we only adde that though it will not a little trouble us to see men withstanding not only us but their owne good and happinesse, yet it doth in good measure satisfie us that wee have not neglected this or any other meanes to the best of our power or understanding, to prevent these inconveniences and mischiefes that may arise from those acts of force which we shall be necessitated unto.

Subscribed at Berwick, 20 Ianuarii 1644 by the warrant and in the name of the Committee of both Kingdoms, by us your friends

Argyle

W. Armyne.

Postscript.

One of these direct to Sir Thomas Glemham, and the rest of the Commanders with him at Alnwick or elsewhere.

2 Anderson to Glemham:

Sir,

The Last night I had notice that Weltons [Weldon's] Regiment was quartered in Warke Barony at Preston, Leermouth, Wark, and Mindrum, it was twelve of the Clock at night before the intelligence came to me, whereupon I immediately caused the guards to be strengthened and doubled, my Scoutes attending untill this morning for more perfect information, that I might advertise you of it; it is now confirmed by one that was this morning amongst them, that there is six Colours of Horse, which were drawing out, and the Drums beating for the calling out of some Companies of Foot, which also are come over, but the certain number of foot, I cannot as yet learne, but suppose them to be a part of Lord Maltlands Regiment, which lay at Calstreame. I shall endeavour to keep my Quarters hereabouts, untill I receive farther orders from you. I am now drawing my whole Regiment into Wooller, having heard for certain as I was now writing, that a great body of the Enemies Foot, and very many Troopes of Horse advanced over Barwick Bridge yesterday, and were as farre as Haggeston; it is conceived they will forthwith march towards Bellforde, for they are Quartered on the English side; you will please to take these things into a present consideration, and afford a present answer to Sir Wooller.

Your very humble servant,

FRANCIS ANDERSON.

20 Ian [Jan.] 1643.

3 *Scots Army Advanced*:

My Lord.

I Have received by your Trumpeter a Letter from your Lordship and Sir William Armyne; it is long and of great concernment; and the other directed to Colonell Gray, who for the reason before-mentioned, and for that here are none but Officers, he cannot return you an Answer so suddenly by your Trumpeter: But I will send presently to the Gentlemen of the County to come hither, and then you shall receive my Answer with the Officers, and theirs by themselves, by a Trumpeter of my own. So I rest

Your Servant,

Tho. Glenham

Alnwick 20 January 1644.

4 Ibid.

5 Glemham to Argyle:

My Lord,

I have this day received yours, together with one to the Gentlemen of the Countrey, and having communicated with them, we returne you this Answer. That without the sight of that Letter we could not have bin induced by any flying rumours to beleeve, that the Scottish Nation, or the prevailing party for the present in that Nation, would have attempted an Invasion of England: so contrary to the Lawes of God, of Nations, of both Kingdoms, and especially to the late Act of Pacification: so opposite to their Allegiance and gratitude to His Majesty, to that neighbourly love which they pretend, to that discreet care which they should have of their own safety. We could not otherwise have imagined that they who by His Majesties goodnesse enjoy a settlement of their Church and State, according to their own desires, should needlesly and ingratefully imbroyle themselves in a business that concernes them not, forfeit their Rights, disoblige His Majesty, and hazard the losse of their present happinesse.

No Order of any Committee or Committees whatsoever of Men or Angells, can give them power to March into the Bowels of another Kingdome, to make offensive Warre against their naturall Soveraigne, upon the empty pretence of Evill Councellors, who could never yet be named. And for the English agents, we cannot believe them to be any Commissioners Lawfully authorized, either by the Parliament, or by the two Houses, or yet by the House of Commons, whence so many of the Members are expelled by partiall Votes, so many banished by seditious tumults, so many voluntarily absent themselves out of Conscience, where desperation or want of opportunity to depart, or feare of certain Plunder, are the chiefest Bonds which hold the little remnant together from dissipation, where the venerable name of Parliament is made a stale to Countenance the pernitious Counsailes and Acts of a Close Committee.

For Subjects to make forraigne Confederacies without their Soveraignes assent, to invade the territories of their undoubted King, to goe about by force to change the Lawes and Religion established, is grosse Treason without all contradiction; And in this case it Argues strongly, who have been the contrivers and fomentors of all our troubles. No Covenent whatsoever, or with whomsoever, can justify such proceedings, or oblige a Subject to runne such disloyall courses. If any man out of Ignorance, or Feare, or Credulity, have entred into such a Covenant, it bindes him not, except it be to repentance. Neither is there any such necessity, as is pretended, of your present posture, your selves cannot alleadge that you are any way provoked by us, neither are we Conscious to our selves of the least intention to molest you.

Those ends which you propose are plausible indeed to them who doe not understand them, the blackest designes did never want the same pretences; if by the Protestant Religion, you intend our Articles, which are the publique Confession of our Church, and our Book of Common Prayer established by Act of Parliament, you need not trouble your selves, we are ready to defend them with our Bloud: If it be otherwise, it is plain to all the World, that it is not the Preservation, but the Innovation of Religion which you seek, how ever by you stiled Reformation. And what calling have you to reforme us by the sword. We do not remember that ever the like indignity was offered by one Nation to another, by a lesser to a greater, That those men who have heretofore pleaded so vehemently for Liberty of Conscience, against all Oathes and Subscriptions, should now assume a power to themselves by Armes to impose a Law upon the Conscience of their fellow Subjects. A vanquished Nation would scarce endure such Tearmes from their Conquerors. But this We are sure of, that this is the way to make the Protestant Religion odious to all Monarchs, Christian or Pagan.

Your other two ends, that is the Honour and happinesse of the King, and the publique Peace and Liberty of His Dominions, are so manifestly contrary to your practice, that We need no other motives to withdraw you from such a Course, as tends so directly to make His Majesty Contemptible at home and abroad, and to fill all His Dominions with Rapine and Blood.

In an Army all have not the same intentions, Wee have seen the Articles agreed upon, and those vast Sums and Conditions, contained in them, as if our Countreymen thought that England was indeed a Well that could never be drawn dry, and whatsoever the intentions be, We know right well what will be the consequents: if it were otherwise, no intention or consequent whatsoever can justify an unlawfull Action. And therefore you do wisely to decline all disputation about it, it as an easy thing to pretend the Cause of God, as the Iewes did the Temple of the Lord, but this is farre from those evident demonstrations, which you often mention, never make. Consider that there must be an Account given to God for all the blood which shall be shed in this quarrell. The way to prevent it, is not by such insinuations, but to retire before the Sword be unsheathed, or the breach be made too wide; you cannot think that we are grown such tame Creatures, to desert our Religion, our Lawes, our Liberties, our Estates, upon command of Forreigners, and to suffer our selves and our Posterity, to be made Beggers and Slaves without opposition. If any of ours shall joyne with you in this Action, we cannot look upon them otherwise then as Traitors to their King, Vipers to their native Country, and as such as have been Plotters or Fomentors of this designe from the beginning. But if misinformation or Feare, hath drawn any of yours ignorantly or unwillingly into this Cause, We desire them to withdraw themselves at last, and not to make themselves accessaries to that deluge of Mischiefe which this second voyage is like to bring upon both Kingdoms.

6   *True Relation of the Scots Army.*
7   *Scots Army Advanced.*
8   *True Relation of the Scots Army.*
9   *Cocket Island.*
10   *True Relation of the Scots.*
11   Warburton, p. 368:

May it Please Your Highness,
I know they tell you, sir, that I have great force; truly I cannot march five thousand foot, and the horse not well armed. The Scots advanced as far as Morpeth, and they are fourteen thousand as the report goes. Since I must have no help, I shall do the best I can with these, and ever acknowledge myself infinitely bound to your Highness for your many favours. God preserve your Highness. Your Highness's most faithfull, obliged servant,
W. Newcastle
York, 28th January 1644

12   Ibid, p. 370.
13   *Newcastle's Memoirs*, p. 199.

14 *True Relation of the Scots Army*:

Right Worshipful and Loving Friends,
Our Appearance here in this Posture, through Mis-informations and Mis-understandings, may occasion strange thoughts in you. If we had opportunity of speaking together (which hereby we offer and desire) it is not impossible, that as we held forth the same Ends, viz., The Preservation of Religion, the King's true Honour and Happiness, the publick Peace and Liberty of his Dominions, so we might agree upon the same way to promote them: If you yield to this Motion, you shall find us ready to do Our parts therein; but if worse Counsel take place with you, and all Parley be rejected, altho' thereby you will be unjust to your selves, yet we have reason to expect ye should be so just to Us, as to acquit us of the Guilt of those manifold Inconveniences and Calamities that may be the fruit of those forcible ways you will thereby Constrain us to. We desire your present Answer.
Subscribed the 3d of February, 1643/4 by the Warrant, and in the Name of the Committees and Commissioners of both Kingdoms, by Us,
Your Friends,
Argyle,
W. Armyne.

15 *Faithfull Relation of the Scots Army*:

That upon Saturday the third of this instant, we came before the Town of Newcastle without any opposition, till we came before the Town, where the enemy had made up a Fort against us; for gaining whereof, my Lord Generall sent forth a party of Muskettiers to storm the East side of it, and another party to storm the West: they went on with as much courage and resolution as ever any did to so great an attempt, discharging their Muskets very couragiously in the midst of the greatest disadvantage that could be, being in the open fields, almost fully in the view of their enemy; the enemy being sheltred with Fortifications, and answering our Musket-shots with shots of Canon and Muskets. In which posture they continued till twelve of the clock at night, with the losse onely of Patric English, Captain-Lieutenant to the Lord Lindsey and 9 common Souldiers.

True Relation of the Scots Army:

Some of our men, were drawn up to a stone-Bridge a quarter of a mile from the town, at the entrance into the Shieldfield, to beat out some men of theirs out of a little Sconce that lay near it, and did it presently without losse; but they retired to a sharper work near the Windmill, where the controversie was more hot, and our arguments not strong enough; the great peeces being not come in regard of the uncertainty of the Sea by which they were to come: And lest some terrible report of a great losse come to your hands, the certainty is, that in six houres assault or thereabouts wee lost only fourteen men. The enemy having lost about seven or eight, fled to the Town, and we possessed the Fort, which is within halfe musket shot of the walls: After that they sent forth eight Troopes of horse which the Generall-Major of the Horse charged with five, though they could not charge above three in breast together in respect of the Coale-Pits; notwithstanding which, the charge was so hard upon the enemy, that they presently retired into the Town, there was none killed on either side, only we took two prisoners, whereof one was Lievtenant, who cursed and railed for halfe an houre together, so that we could learn nothing of him, but afterwards being in cold blood, hee informed us the my Lord of Newcastle, was there himselfe, Generall King, and the Lord Widdrington, that they had three Regiments of foot, and about sixteen or seventeen Troopes of Horse, besides the people of the Town: They discharged many great Pieces from the Town towards night, but to little purpose.

Slingsby, p. 102:

The first attempt ye Scots made, was upon a sconce yt lay on ye North Side of ye Town; but was gallantly defend'd by Sr. Charles Slingsby who gave ym such a repulse, yt they forbore after to make any more attempts, but lay at a defensive guarde.

Newcastle's Memoirs, pp. 33–34:

They marched up towards the town with such confidence, as if the gates had been opened for their reception; and the General of their Army seemed to take no notice of my Lord's being in it, for which afterwards he excused himself. But as they drew near, they found not such entertainment as they expected; for though they assaulted a work that was not finished, yet they were beaten off with much loss.

16 *True Relation of the Scots Army*:

My Lord,
We have received a Letter of such a Nature from you, that we cannot give you any Answer to it more then this, that his Majesties General being at this Instant in the Town, we conceive all the Power of Government to be in him. And were he not here, you cannot sure conceive Us so ill read in these Proceedings of yours, as to Treat with you for your satisfaction in these particulars you write of, nor by any Treaty to Betray a Trust reposed in Us, or forfeit Our Allegiance to his Majesty, for whose Honour and Preservation, together with the Religion and Laws of this Kingdom, we intend to hazard our Lives and Fortunes: And so we rest,
Your Servants,
John Marlay, Major.
Nicholas Cole.
Subscribed by Us, the 3d. of February, 1643/4, in the Names of the Common Council and the rest of the Inhabitants of the Town of New-Castle.

17 *Cocket Island*.
18 *Faithfull Relation of the Scots Army*.
19 *Newcastle's Memoirs*, p. 200:

Thomas Riddell sent about 50 musketeers from Tynmouth Castle to destroy some corn in the enemy's quarters, from whence they were drawn out as he was informed. But it seems his intelligence betrayed them to the enemy, and about 45 of them were taken prisoners, who being carried to Leslie he sent them to me as a token, and I returned him thanks for his civility with this answer, that I hoped very shortly to repay that debt with interest: which I did within a few days.

Faithfull Relation of the Scots Army:

The enemy burn and spoyl what they can reach on this side Tyne, especially corn; at which work, a Squadron of our Horse, about 15 men, with whom other 10 accidentally joyned, fell upon 100 Muskettiers of the enemy sent from Tinmouth for that service, killed 14 or 15 of them, and took prisoners 50; whereof the Generall kept onely 2, and sent 48 into Newcastle; and the Marquesse sent back 7 or 8 of ours who were catched stragling.

The Gentleman who gave this Defeat is the Earl of Eglentons Major, his name is Montgomery.

20 *Cocket Island.*
21 *Newcastle's Memoirs*, p. 199.
22 Turner.
23 Warburton, pp. 381–2.
24 *Faithfull Relation of the Scots Army*:

Monday morning early, the 19 of this instant, 2 Regiments of horse of the Scottish Army, in which were 15 Troups, under the command of the Lord Balgoney the Generalls son, and the Lord Kirkudbright lying at Corbridge 2 miles from Hexam, had an Alarme given them by 25 Troups of the Enemy, who under the command of Sir Marmaduke Langdale and Colonel Fenwick, who had also waiting on them, three or 400 Musquettiers, which the other Troups wanted: Both partees drew up betwixt Corbridge and Hexham; and Ballentyne the Lievtenant Colonell to the Generalls Regiment, charged the enemy and made them give way with losse, and so the second time, and had taken above 100 prisoners, but not satisfied with that, gave a third charge, which drove them to their Musquettiers which were placed behind them, and being thus engaged with horse and foot, our Troups were disordered and had a very strait retreat through a gap, where some men were lost, but the enemy pursued not far, for they were, as I suppose, loath to engage beyond their foot notwithstanding their advantage. Our men wheeling in that disorder, were met by Colonell Robert Brandling, with ten Troups more, who crossed the water below Corbridge, and was to have fallen upon the Reere of our men, but it fell out to be the Front in their returne. Brandling forwardly rode out before his Troupes to exchange a Pistoll, and one Lievtenant Ellot rode up to him, and they had discharged each at other, and wheeling about to draw their swords, Brandlings horse stumbled, and the Lievtenant was so neere him as to pull him of his horse, which when his men perceived they retreated, which gave courage to our men to fall on, which they did, and drove them over the River againe, killed some, and forced others through the water so hastily, that they were some of them drowned, and thus was the day divided: We cannot yet perfectly understand the losse on each side, but the numbers were something equall of the slaine, there were about 60 men killed upon the place. We have lost Maj. Agnew, Cap. Forbes, a Cornet, and I heare of no other Officers, tis not certaine whether they are killed or taken: We have taken Colonell Brandling, one Lievtenant, none else of note.

Newcastle's Memoirs, p. 200:

The 19th of February 1643 [1644] Sir Marmaduke Langdale fell upon their quarters at Corbridge in Northumberland, but the enemy having timely notice of his coming were drawn into the field. He thereupon sent some troops to second those that first entered the towns, who charged the enemy, but the enemy with their lancers forced them to retreat. He sent more, but the enemy charged them gallantly, but durst not pursue them because of our reserve. At last he rallied his forces and took about 200 foot with him and forced the enemy to retreat. He routed them totally and followed the chase 3 miles, killed above 200, took above 150 prisoners, besides divers officers slain, whereof one named Captain Haddon. The prisoners Major Agnew, major to the Lord Kirkcudbright, dangerously hurt, Archibald Magee his Quartermaster, Haddon's Cornet Carr, grandchild to the Lord Roxburgh. There was 15 of their troops of horse, whereof Leslie's life-guard was one, and

3 troops of dragooners, and that Leslie's son was their general, who is shot through the shoulder. There is 2 horse colours and a dragoon colour taken. The same morning Colonel Dudley from his quarters about Prudhoe marched over the river with some horse and dragoons and fell into a quarter of the enemy's in Northumberland and slew and took all that was in it, which was 55 prisoners, and gave such an alarm to four of their quarters that they quit the same with disorder and some loss; in which neither had we suffered any loss at all had not Colonel Brandling been taken prisoner by the unfortunate fall of his horse; and Colonel Dudley, perceiving a greater force preparing to assault him, retreated, and in his retreat took eight of the Scots prisoners, both horse and men, but they took four of his dragoons, whose horse were so weak they could not pass the river.

Slingsby, p. 102:

Yet Sr. Marmaduke Langdale met wth ym at Corbridge, where he fell upon Kilcowbrie [Kircudbright] & took 200 prisoners, besides wt was killed, & all of ym sent to York.

Newcastle's Memoirs, p. 34:

However, though it failed in the enemy's foot-quarters, which lay nearest the town, yet it took good effect in their horse-quarters, which were more remote; for my Lord's horse, commanded by a very gallant and worthy gentleman [Sir Marmaduke Langdale], falling upon them, gave them such an alarm, that all they could do was to draw into the field, where my Lord's forces charged them, and in a little time routed them totally, and killed and took many prisoner, to the number of 1500.

25 Ibid, pp. 200–1.

Chapter 3

1 *Late Proceedings of the Scots Army*.
2 Ibid:

The Lords providence was very observable, in vouchsafeing two fair days upon us in our march; the day preceding our march being very Snowie, and a terrible storm of Drift and Snow ensuing the day after.

3 Ibid.
4 Ibid.
5 *Exact Relation of Scottish Army*:

We remained in our Quarters on Munday and Tuesday, taking what care wee could for supply of Provisions in this Enemies Countrey, for so we finde it, not receiving any intelligence or willing supply from them. But it is no wonder wee finde not many friends, when there are so few men, the whole Countrey being in Armes, either willingly or forcedly: so great a power hath the Cathedrall here.

6 Ibid.
7 *Newcastle's Memoirs*, p. 201.
8 *Exact Relation of the Scots Army*:

On Wednesday the sixth of March the Enemy having united their Forces, and received an accession of strength by Sir Charles Lucas, who brought 21 Troopes from York-shire, and by 1500 Foote, from Cumberland, they drew their Forces to a place about 2 or 3 Miles to the West of Sunderland, and shewed themselves upon the top of Worme-Hill: This Army was accordingly drawne forth; and both lay at about half a mile distance, on Wednesday night in the fields.

Late Proceedings of the Scots Army:

Upon Wednesday, the enemies Forces of Durham and Newcastle being joyned, and likewise strengthned by the accession of 12 Troops of Horse from York-shire, under the command of Sir Charles Lucas, being supposed to be about 14,000 Horse and Foot, did shew themselves upon the top of a hill about 3 miles distant from Sunderland. Such of our Army as could be presently advertised were drawn up within half a mile of them, and continued all that night (though it were very cold and snowing) in the fields.

Newcastle's Memoirs, p. 201:

Upon Wednesday the 6th of this instant March, at one o'clock afternoon, our first troops passed Newbridge and within a while after the enemy appeared with some horse; when they advanced towards us with more than they first discovered, after some bullets had been exchanged and they appeared again with a greater force, we backed our party with my Lord Henry's regiment, Lieutenant-Colonel Scrimsher commanding them – being part of Colonel Dudley's brigade, with which he drew up after them – with whom also we sent some musketeers; which caused the enemy that day to look upon us at a further distance, we judged they were about 500 horse when they appeared most, yet they continued most of that day in our sight, which satisfied us extremely in hopes the rest were not far off, yet far from troubling us except it were sometimes to make use of our perspectives.

9 Ibid, p. 201.

10 *Late Proceedings of the Scots Army*:

Upon Thursday the 7, the enemy drew up their Forces upon a hight about 2 short miles from us; but the snow fell in such aboundance, that nothing could be done till the middle of the day, that it was fair; at which time we advanced towards them, and they marched Northwards, as is conceived to gain the winde. Both Armies were drawn up in Battell, the enemy having the advantage of the ground; but we could not without very great disadvantage engage our Armie, in regard of the unpassable ditches and hedges betwixt us. Both Armies faced each other till the setting of the Sun, at which time the enemy retreated, and we kept the ground till the next morning in a very cold night.

Exact Relation of the Scots Army:

On thursday morning they were againe drawne up something nearer, the Enemy still keeping to the advantage of his ground upon the Hill, so that notwithstanding the nearnesse of some part of both Armies, being not above a quarter of a Mile distant, we could not without very great disadvantage engage this Army, in regard of the impassable Hedges and Ditches betwixt us, so that likewise after the Armies had faced each other that day, they remained in the fields that night also.

11 *Late Proceedings of the Scots Army*:

Upon Friday the 8 in the morning, there was some little skirmishing betwixt some small parties of Horse, wherein the advantage that was, fell upon our side: three or four were killed on either side; we took divers prisoners, by whom we understood that many of theirs were wounded. Our commanded Muskettiers and Horse advanced, and gained the ground where the enemy stood the day preceding; The enemy still retired, and, as appeared, with a purpose to retire altogether; for they fired the nearest villages, and retired under the smoke thereof: Our commanded men advanced neerer the hight, the enemy giving ground all the time: We had resolved to fall upon their rere; but there came suddenly a great storm of Snow, which continued for an hour, so that we could not see the enemy: and before we could discover them again, it began to snow again, and continued snowing till night: Which opportunity the enemy made use of, and marched away in great haste to Durham.

Exact Relation of the Scots Army:

On Friday morning some little Skirmishes there was, betwixt some small parties of Horse, wherein that little advantage that was, fell to us, taking some few prisoners, by whom wee understood, that they had on Thursday night drawne off their Canon, and withdrawne their Foote, and left a full body of Horse which faced us in the morning till about tenne of the Clocke, and then taking the advantage of a very thicke storme of Snow, which lasted two or three houres, (and in as sore a manner sure as ever was seene) marched away, and this Army, through the ilnesse of the weather and wayes, rendred uncapable of pursuing, they also having so great a strength of horse in the Reare, and we not supplied with Provisions to march: whereupon on Friday night this Army returned to their Quarters.

Newcastle's Memoirs, pp. 202–3:

The next morning both armies drew up again into batalia, when with the continual snow that fell all that day, and by reason of the great fatigation of the horse it being the third day they had received little or no sustenance, it was thought by the consent of all the general officers not expedient that the Army should suffer such extremity or for that time seek any further occasion to engage an enemy whom we found so hard to be provoked, who found from us I believe, contrary to their expectations, so much forwardness as they might plainly perceive we endeavoured what we could to fight with them, and were confident enough of our own strength could we have come unto them upon any indifferent terms of equality. And truly the forwardness of the soldiers was such as we would have been contented to have given them some advantages to boot rather than to have deferred it. But upon such disadvantages we had no manner of reason, being the ground would not permit us to draw up the fourth part of the Army, by which we had been defeated of the advantage we had over them with our horse, and besides we should have been forced to have fought for that ground which afterwards we should have stood upon. We being now resolved to march off, and they having been so niggardly to afford us occasion to try what mettle each other was made of, in some measure to satisfy the great forwardness we found in our people, and also to give the enemy warning that they should not be too bold upon our retreat. For these reasons we sent off 120 horses to entertain them near their own leaguer, Sir Charles Lucas his major commanding them, where meeting with 200 of the enemy's, the first that charged them not passing 60 of this one regiment, notwithstanding the enemy was so placed before a hedge, where they had some dragooners as it seems, they were confident ours would not have come up unto them; but when they saw that their muskets could not prevent the courage of our men, they turned their backs and leaped over their dragooners, affording our men the execution of them to a great body of theirs, in which chase our men killed some 40 of them, and had taken near 100 men, but they advanced so suddenly that we could bring off but 20 of them, of whom there were three English – one of them were handed (was hanged) immediately, having formerly served in our Army: their lancers did seem to follow eagerly upon our men in their retreat in great numbers, but we had not passing six men hurt, whereof one died, and not any of the rest miscarried or are missing. In the meantime, we were drawing back our Army, and the enemy, when they saw the greatest of our number to be marching, made a show as if they would have followed us: they therefore sent down about 600 horse and as many musketeers to try, as I suppose, our behaviour in our retreat, as also to requite us if they could, sending three bodies of horse into the field next the moor, by the side of which we passed, but still under the favour of their musketeers, which lined the hedges; but we, being content to play with them at their own game, whilst we amused them by presenting some horse before them, our musketeers, which in the meantime stole down upon their flank towards their passage, gave them such a peal, that it made the passage which they retired over seem I believe a great deal straiter, and the time much longer than at their coming over, after which they were a great deal better satisfied with our retreat, and this was all we could do with the enemy. I must confess we brought our horse home very weary, which did us more harm then the enemy could have done, until they be again refreshed, which we make no doubt will be in a very short time.

12 *Late Proceedings of the Scots Army*.
13 *Exact Relation of the Scots Army*.
14 *Late Proceedings of the Scots Army*.
15 *Exact Relation of the Scots Army*.
16 *Extract of Letters*:

Upon Saturday the 16 of March, some commanded men in the morning, about the spring of day, were to have assaulted the Fort at south Shields upon Tine, but fearing too much the danger and difficulty, they returned without doing any thing.

True Relation of the Scottish Army:

On the 16 at night, a party was commanded out to assault the Fort upon the South side Tine over against Tinemouth Castle, which they did, but with no successe, though with little losse.

17 Tunstall to Radcliffe.
18 *Extract of Letters*:

Upon Tuesday the 19 wee kept a solemne Fast through the Army, and it pleased God the next morning to shew us a token of his favour: a party not so strong as the former, was sent to storme the Fort, there being no other way of taking it; Col. Stewart, Col. Lyell, Leutenant Col. Bruce, and Lieutenant Col. Ionston, with some inferior Officers, led on the party, the Fort was very strong, the Graffe without being esteemed 12 foot broad, and 11 deep, the work above ground 3 yards high, and within it five iron peece of Ordnance, some 9-pound ball, some more, an hundred souldiers, seventy Musquetiers, and thirty Pike-men: It was situated with great advantage, being defended on the one side by the Ordnance of Tinemouth Castle, and on the other by a Dunkirk Frigot with ten peece of Ordnance; notwithstanding 140 of our souldiers, without any other Armes but their swords, carried bundles of straw and sticks, wherewith they filled the ditch, set up the scaling ladders (whereof some did not reach the top of the Fort, the ditch not being well filled) and with their swords gave the first assault, then a party of Musquetiers, and after them a party of Pikes, all marching up till they entred the ditch, where they disputed the matter abouve an houre, in which time the Enemy discharged upon them 28 shot of Canon, some with Musquet ball, others with cut lead and iron, beside many Musquet shot: Our souldiers did resolutely scale the ladders, and some entred at the gunports; the Defendants behaved themselves gallantly till it came to stroke of sword, and then they fled away by water in boates: sixteen of them were killed, a Lieutenant and five souldiers who stood out to the last, were taken, and so we gained the Fort, with the peeces, and some barrels of powder, and their colours. The providence of God wonderfully preserved our men, for only seven of them were killed, some few hurt with stones and cut iron, but none deadly, no Officer at all killed.

True Relation of the Scottish Army:

After we had considered of this repulse two or three dayes, and fasted on the nineteenth, the Fort was again assaulted by another party; for the encouragement of which the Generall went with them in person, and on the 20, being Wednesday in the morning, we tooke it with the losse of nine men, the hurt of more: In it wee found five Peeces of Iron Ordnance, seven Barrels of Powder, seventy Muskets; the men escaped in the dark to the water-side, where boats received them, only the Lievtenant and foure or five more were taken Prisoners; This Fort was commanded by one Captaine Chapman, an inhabitant of the South-Shields. I went that day to see the Fort, my own judgement in such cases is nothing worth, but others thought it a difficult peece, and I confesse I wondered much to see it taken on that manner.

Tunstall to Radcliffe:

Soe for the last Weddensdaye they set upon it againe, and gained the fort and five eyron peece of ordenance in it, our men fleying doune to a penisse in which it was reported that Sir John Pennington was in, but the penisse dischargeing sume ordenance at the Scotes they retreated; and it is said they lost 3 houndred men at the takeing of it, and we losing but five men.

19 *Extract of Letters.*
20 Rushworth, Vol. V, p. 615:

Understanding there was a troop of the Marquess's Horse Quartered at Chester-on-the-Street, came with a Party into the Town a private way, and wholly surprized them, and took the Guards last, and brought away 40 Horse with their Arms.

Extract of Letters:

Upon the same day Lieutenant Col. Ballantine fell upon a party of the Enemies horse at Chester, killed ten of them, and took two Captains of Foot, and twenty horsemen, of ours none killed or hurt.

21 *True Relation of the Scottish Army:*

On the 23 of this instant, the Enemy drew up their Army from Durham and thereabout towards Chester, and on the 24, being the Lords day, drew up on the north side of Ware, at a place called Hilton, 2 miles and a halfe from Sunderland, the same distance as when they faced us before, only this is on the north side Ware, the other on the south; we accordingly drew up on a hill east from them towards the sea.

    Our Cannon, were at Sunderland, our head quarter, but by the help of the Sea-men lying in the haven, wee conveyed one great peece over the water, who themselves drew itt up to the field where it was to be planted, the tide failed for carrying the rest at that time. Some small field peeces wee had. After the Armies had faced each other most part of that day, toward five aclock the Cannon began to play, which they bestowed freely though to little purpose, and withall the commanded Foot fell to it to drive one another from their hedges, and continued shooting till eleven at night, in which time we gained some ground, some barrels of gun-powder, and ball and match; wee lost few men, had more hurt and wounded, among whom no Officer of note hurt with danger but the Lievenant Colonell of the Lord Lothians Regiment; what their losse was is yet uncertain to us, but we know they had more slaine, as wee finde being masters of their ground.

The words given out on both parts were these, On ours, The Lord of Hosts is with us. On theirs, Now or Never.

This morning, being the 25, they are faceing each other, but the ground they possesse inaccessible by us without great disadvantages in regard of the many hedges and ditches betwixt; what the event of this meeting will be I do not know, nor will not guesse, hitherto hath the Lord helped us: our men are chearfull, our hopes good.

Extract of Letters:

Upon the 24, being the Lords day, the Enemy marched toward our Quarters intending to have set upon us in Sermon time, and being a foggie day to have surprised us; their approach being discovered, a great part of the Army was presently drawn together: The Enemy sent down from Bouden Hill where they were drawne up, some commanded Musquetiers to line the hedges betwixt them and us, and wee did the like, for the Armies could not joyn, the Field between us being so full of hedges and ditches, our Dragoones beganne the play, and then the Musqueteers in the hedges upon both sides, our bodies of foot advancing at all Quarters to the hedges, the Enemies Cannon discharging upon them an houre and a halfe with very small hurt: This service continued very hot, till after twelve of the clock at night: Many Officers, who have been old Souldiers did affirm they had never seen so long and hot service in the night time; there was divers killed on both sides, but the number of their slaine did very farre exceed ours, as wee understood by the dead bodies wee found the next day upon their ground, beside the seven Waggons draught of dead, and hurt men not able to walk, that the Constable of Bouden affirmed he saw carried away. The Enemy quit their ground, where they left much of their powder, match, and armes behinde them; and retired to the Hill where the Body of the Army lay.

The next day the Enemy began to retire, but laboured to conceale it from us, causing their men to march about the hill, and casting up two brest-works to plant Canon: In the afternoone, when we understood the certainty of their retreat, we followed them, and their horsemen who had stayed on the hill while their Foot marched away, retired more swiftly then an ordinary march, our Horse and Dragoons marched up the hill, charged them, and routed all that were not passed the ditches; divers of them were killed, and some men of note whom we know not, save one Rutmaster Harrison, and Sir Marmaduke Langdales Capt. Lieut. Divers taken, amongst whom was Sir Richard Gladill, Lieut. Col. and Sir Francis Steward; there was also a Cornet taken, bearing a Crown above and a hand and a sword beneath, with this Motto, what Law cannot, the Sword must maintain. The night hindred us from doing any further execution upon them. The day following, the enemy (who the day proceeding thought it a point of honour to retire in the day, and not in the night) did not appear, having stollen away in the night time.

Newcastle's Memoirs, pp. 203–4:

It being extremely certified from the noble Marquis of Newcastle that on Sunday last (March 24) he got the Scots out to West Bedwick near Hilton Castle in the Bishopric of Durham, where they sat fast upon Bedwick Hill: my Lord Marquis had often invited them to fight, with overtures of many advantageous opportunities, but could not possibly draw them out: on this hill four regiments of his Excellency's foot fell to work with six regiments of the rebels. The fight began about three in the afternoon (March 24) and continued from that time till night, and continued more or less till next morning, the rebels all this while being upon their own Mickle Midding, and there they lay all night; next morning (being Monday) the Lord Marquis followed them till afternoon, and then they vanished instantly into their trenches and retirements in Sunderland. Then his Excellency (seeing no hope of getting them out) drew off towards his quarters, and they being sensible of so many provocations, came on his rear (which was 500 horse) with all the horse they had (for as yet they never looked the Lord Marquis in the face), but the rear (with the loss of some thirty men killed and taken) presently faced about, being seconded by that valiant knight, Sir Charles Lucas, with his brigade of horse, who fell on so gallantly that he forced all their horse (which is about 3,000) to hasten up the hill to their cannon, all the way doing sharp execution upon them so as their Lancers lay plentifully upon the ground (many others being taken and brought away prisoners) their cannon all that while playing upon the Lord Marquis his horse with so little success as is not easily imagined. In both these fights (on Sunday and Monday) they that speak least reckon a full 1000 Scots killed and taken which cost the Lord Marquis 240 of his common soldiers, scarce an officer being either killed or taken, though many of their leaders are certainly cut off. Their foot ran twice, and would not stand longer than their officers forced them on with the sword; the Lord Marquis hath taken many of their arms, especially of their Scottish pistols. Next morning (Tuesday) his Excellency drew towards them again, faced them a long while, but they had too much of the two days before, and would by no means be entreated to show themselves.

22 Warburton, p. 397.
23 Ibid, p. 400.
24 Somerville at Wetherby.
25 Ibid.
26 *Newcastle's Memoirs*, p. 36.

Chapter 4

1 *Newcastle's Memoirs*, p. 33.
2 Belasyse, p. 383:

This second winter my Lord was again commanded northwards, where a considerable employment attended him, the government of York and Lieutenant-General (under the Marquis of Newcastle) of Yorkshire during his absence against the Scots' Army who entered England to the assistance of the Parliament, their fellow Rebels and Covenanters.

3 Leeds City Archives, Vyner MSS., VR 5809 T/32/50.
4 Belasyse, p. 383.
5 *Newcastle's Memoirs*, p. 33.

6 Warburton, p. 371:

> The necessity of leaving these parts so bare, with the ill neighbourhood of Gainsborough, makes it to suspect that the free intercourse between Newark and the more northern parts might be cut off if the enemies should possess themselves of Doncaster; to prevent which we are fortifying the place, I being left here with two thousand horse for the security of what is left behind. This has caused my longer stay here, and has hindered my Lord's intent to send for me for the present, and especially my own great desire to be an actor in that service which cannot be more eagerly bent upon anything.

7 Belasyse, p. 384.

8 Warburton, p. 381.

9 Slingsby, pp. 103–4:

> Now was Sr. Wm. Constable crept out of Hull wth their Horse, making their Carrocols upon ye woulds, & was heard of as far as Pickering. Against him Collonell Bellasyse sends all our horse, & some foot, together wth Sr. Charles Lucas, to fource him to keep wthin Hull, or else to fight him. They march & Quarter about Colham: they send about for intelligence where he lay: but [he] could not be heard of: wn yt night, they little fearing of him, he comes & beats up their quarters, takes many prisoners, & so returns to Hull. The Regiments he fell upon were Sr. Walter Vavasors, Sr John Keys, & my brother Tho. Slingsby's whose major was taken prisoner.

10 Vicars, II, p. 160.

11 *Hulls Managing*.

12 Vicars, II, p. 160.

13 *Fairfax Correspondence*, Vol. I, p. 95.

14 CSPD 1644, p. 26:

> The Committee of Both Kingdoms to Ferdinando Lord Fairfax. By reason of the continual uncertainty and often crossness of the winds we cannot keep, by sea, so constant and frequent intercourse and intelligence between us in this place and the Scottish Army in the north, as is necessary for the most advantageous managing of those affairs, and for that the way from hence to you is perfectly cleared by land, whereby we may constantly and securely make our despatches to you, we desire that you will endeavour to settle a course of conveyance from thence to the Scottish Army, whereby by the way of the east of Yorkshire (for there is also care taken for intelligence hither by the way of Lancashire) that so intelligence may be held as the exigency of affairs shall require. Enclosed is a cipher by which you may hereafter advise matters of importance and secrecy unto this Committee. Our messengers shall call upon you weekly for the Scottish letters, and your dispatches on Friday night. Signed by the Earl of Northumberland and John Lord Maitland.

15 *Short Memoriall*, pp. 218–9.

16 Hodgson, p. 26.

17 Newman, P.R., 'The Defeat of John Belasyse: Civil War in Yorkshire, January–April 1644', *The Yorkshire Archaeological Journal*, Vol. 52, 1980.

18 Hodgson, pp. 26–7:

> We found the enemy in Bradford, but they over-run the kirk. Our horse had some pickering with them up to the lane head, and was put to flight; but our foot gave them such a salute with shot, as made them run for it.

Slingsby, pp. 102–3:

> Sr. Charles Lucas at this time was sent out of ye south wth a 1000 horse & Dragoons, to do us cervise in ye North, & now sent for by his Excellence; but Collonell Bellasyse yt commanded all ye Yorkshire forces, desir'd an assistance before he went, thinking yt wth their joynt forces, they should be able to beat out of ye town [Bradford] some few forces of Collonell Lamberts yt lay in it; but ye success prov'd not; they assault'd ye town but was beaten from it wth loss, having some prisoners taken, & some kill'd. Strange fortune we have had at this Town, for untill his excellency took it after ye battle upon Allerton [Adwalton] Moor, we never attempt'd any thing upon it but receiv'd an affront, once by Sr. Tho. Glemham, once by my Ld Goring, & now by Coll. Bellasyse.

19 *Fairfax Correspondence*, Vol. I, p. 94:

> Sir,
> The last night I sent out a party of horse and foot, commanded by Captain Asquith, to fall upon the enemy's quarters at Hunslett, which accordingly was done, through God's assistance, with good success. We took some prisoners; Major Vavasour, Captain Hughes, Captain Cardhouse, Captain Laine, Captain Labourne, and Captain Talbot; three lieutenants, four gentlemen, about 200 common soldiers, besides some slain: and I bless God, without any loss on our part at all. Divers others of better quality very narrowly escaping. We all, in these parts, exceedingly long for and desire your appearance here, which I am confident, were enough to clear these parts, if the opportunity be not slipped. General King is certainly at Durham, but I cannot tell with what force, but I fear lest his intentions may be for this country.
> Sir, I desire you not to think my following lines tedious unto you, which are in the behalf of my chirurgeon, who, having spent all his chest at Nantwich, desires that you will be pleased to afford him some recruit. Sir, I beseech you pardon his tedious petition, who rests, Sir,
> Your most faithful and humble servant,
> Jo. Lambert.
> Bradford, March 6th, 1643, [N.S. 1644.]

20 *Exact Relation of the Scottish Army*:

> On Wednesday the sixth of March the Enemy having united their Forces, and received an accession of strength by Sir Charles Lucas, who brought 21 Troopes from York-shire.

Late Proceedings of the Scots Army:

> Upon Wednesday, the enemies Forces of Durham and Newcastle being joyned, and likewise strengthned by the accession of 12 Troops of Horse from Yorkshire, under the command of Sir Charles Lucas.

Newcastle's Memoirs, p. 202:

> For these reasons we sent off 120 horses to entertain them near their own leaguer, Sir Charles Lucas his major commanding them.

21 Belasyse, p. 384:

> He formed several bodies of horse into three general head-quarters, at Leeds for the west, at Malton for the east, and York for the North Ridings, and he settled considerable

garrisons of foot at Halifax, Doncaster, Leeds, Stamford Bridge and other places, and at all the castles and forts which he found possessed with good garrisons.

22 *Fairfax Correspondence*, Vol. I, p. 95.
23 Belasyse, p. 384.
24 *Newcastle's Memoirs*, pp. 35–6.
25 CSPD 1644, p. 35:

> The Committee of Both Kingdoms to Ferdinando Lord Fairfax. We have considered the opportunity that is now offered for reducing and assuring of Yorkshire whilst the Marquis of Newcastle has drawn the greatest part of his forces towards the north to oppose the Scots, and how necessary it is to hinder all further levies there to increase his Army, which the better to effect, we have written to Sir Thomas Fairfax to forthwith march into the West Riding, with all his horse, and take with him two regiments of foot out of Lancashire. We desire that you will also take the field with as great a force of horse and foot as you can, and joining with Sir Thomas Fairfax make the best advantage you can of the present opportunity and of those forces for effecting the ends aforesaid. We also desire that you will hold a continual intelligence with the Scottish Army, and by drawing near to the Tees or otherwise to give them the best accommodation you shall be able, and that you will continually advertise us all your occurrencies and affairs.

26 Ibid, pp. 39–40.
27 Ibid, p. 40.
28 Ibid, p. 39:

> We have desired my Lord General to give directions to the Earl of Denbigh to relieve the besieged in Wem and the distressed people in Shropshire, and those parts from the enemy. How much this is conducing to their safety and the good affairs of the whole kingdom, you, who have done so exceeding good service, well know. We have desired my Lord General to direct you to appoint six troops of horse and two regiments of foot of Lancashire to meet at such a rendezvous as the Earl of Denbigh, who is to command them in chief, shall appoint. We desire you and do assure ourselves that you will show them that their own safety will most consist in the good success of those their neighbours, and that no way will be so much to their own ruin as the enemies taking them. There are appointed other very considerable forces of horse and foot to meet them. We inclose some letters which we desire you to subscribe with the names of such Colonels or other officers as are most fit for this service.

29 Ibid, p. 62.
30 Ibid, p. 62.
31 Belasyse, p. 384.
32 Tibbutt, H.G. (ed.), *The Letter Books 1644–45 of Sir Samuel Luke*, 1963, p. 637.
33 Newman, P.R., 'The Defeat of John Belasyse: Civil War in Yorkshire, January–April 1644', *The Yorkshire Archaeological Journal*, Vol. 52, 1980.
34 Belasyse, p. 384:

> At Selby he made a bridge of boats over the river Ouse to communicate with the East Riding; from hence he marched 1,000 foot and 500 horse to join in a design with Sir George [Gervase] Lucas, who brought 1,000 horse more to attack Lambert at Bradford, where he fell on with the foot, and had certainly taken both the place and him but for a gallant sally Lambert made through our horse, commanded on that side of the town by

Colonel George Porter, and escaped to Halifax, so as the pursuit of him engaged us so late at night as, our ammunition being spent, we drew back to Leeds.

Rushworth, Vol. V, p. 617:

In the mean time Colonel Bellasis, Governour of York for the King, was not idle; but understanding Colonel Lambert with his Regiment was quartered at Bradford, marched thither to surprize them: but Lambert having notice of their Approach, sallied out to meet them, till perceiving how numerous their Party was, he thought it not safe to adventure beyond his Work, which they briskly assaulted, and he as well defended, forcing them to retreat; and then falling on the Rear took Colonel Bagshaw [Bradshaw], several Captains, one hundred and fifty Horse, and sixty foot, Prisoners.

35 Vicars, II, pp. 168–9.
36 CSPD 1644, pp. 87–8.
37 *Short Memoriall*, pp. 218–20.
38 Lord Fairfax to CBK.
39 *Short Memoriall*, p. 220.
40 Lord Fairfax to CBK:

Upon Wednesday, our Forlorn-Hope of Horse beat in a partee of the Enemies Horse, and followed them into the Town, taking divers of them prisoners, and the day being far spent, I quartered the Army within a mile of Selby that night.

41 Slingsby, p. 105:

Whereupon Collonell Bellasyse resolves to hold ym out at Selby. They send in their summons; he sends ym word back again he would not deliver it up to a rebell; this answer insens'd my Ld Fairfax; they prepare to storm; Coll. Bellasyse to defend himself; Coll. Strickland offers, that give him but 200 men, & he would undertake to make good yt part of ye town wch should be judg'd ye weakest, & falls a working yt night.

42 Lord Fairfax to CBK:

and drew them out again early the next morning, and then with the Foot in three divisions, one led by my self, a second by Sir John Meldrum, and a third by Lieutenant Colonell Needham, fell upon the Town, to storm it in three places altogether.

43 Ibid:

where the Enemy received us with much courage, and made strong resistance for two hours or thereabouts; but in conclusion, my own Foot Regiment forced a passage by the River side, and my son with his Regiment of Horse rushed into the Town, where he was incountred by Colonell Belasyse, and the Enemies Horse; but they being beaten back, and Master Belasyse himself wounded, and taken prisoner, and our Foot entred on all sides the Town, the Enemy was wholly routed, and as many as could saved themselves by flight, some towards Cawood, some towards Pontefract, and the rest towards York, over the River by a Bridge of Boats laid by themselves; We pursued them every way, and took in the Town and chase, the Prisoners, Ordnance, Arms, Ammunitions, and Colours mentioned in the List inclosed.

Slingsby, pp. 105–6:

The next morning my Ld Fairfax falls on & in a short time enters ye town both wth horse & foot: such as could get over the bridge (for a bridge they had made of boats) made speed to York, some to Cawood: taken & list'd as prisoners to ye number of 80 officers besides Comon soulgiers.

Short Memoriall, p. 220:

The enemy wthin, defended ymselves stoutly, a good while; or men, at length, beat ym from ye Line, but could not advance furthur, bec: of ye Horse wthin. I getting a Barricado open, wch let us in betweene ye Houses and the river, we had an Encounter wth their Horse. After one charge they fled over a bridge of boats, to Yorke. Other Horse came up and charged us agn, where my horse was overthrowne, being single, a little before my men, who prsently releived me, & forced ye enemy back, who retreated also to Yorke. In this charge we tooke Coll: Bellases, Governor of Yorke; By this time ye Foot had entered ye Towne, and also tooke many prisoners.

Belasyse, p. 384:

By break of day he defended the place gallantly for the space of eight or ten hours, and at the last by the treachery or cowardice of one Captain Wilson, afterwards condemned to death by a council of war, at his post, Sir Thomas Fairfax's horse entered; whereupon my Lord charged him in person at the head of his horse. But they (the officers only excepted) not advancing, but taking occasion to fly over the aforesaid bridge of boats, he found himself engaged in the midst of Sir Thomas Fairfax' troops, who killed his horse under him and discharged some pistols and blows with swords at him: so as he had certainly beene slaine but for the goodness of his arms, and thereby received but two wounds; one in his arm, the other in his head; both with swords: so as (tho' he asked it not), yet they gave him quarter, and carried him to the Lord Fairfax, their General and my Lord's near kinsman, who treated him civilly and sent his chirurgeon to dress his wounds, and ordered his going down the river, together with Sir John Ramsden, Sir Thomas Strickland and other prisoners taken to Hull.

True Relation of Selby:

They fell on the enemy in three severall places at once. The first was led on by my Lo: Fairfax himself, the next by that valiant commander, Sir Jo: Meldrum, and the third by Col: Bright, brother in law to that valiant gentleman, Colonel Lambert. Sir Thomas Fairfax led on the Horse, the matter was a long time disputed with equality on both sides, till the Horse forced a passage into the Towne.

Hulls Managing:

The next morning early his Lordship set upon the Town, which after three houres very sore fight, and some repulses they gained, took the Governour with some Knights and Gentlemen of great note, and above 100 Officers besides, and more then 2000 common Souldiers, our horse pursued them toward Yorke and Pomphret, killing many in their flight, and taking many prisoners, in summe, they tooke more prisoners within the Town, then they had foot that stormed it, and this was done with very small losse.

44 Lord Fairfax to CBK.
45 *True Relation of Selby*.
46 Slingsby, p. 106.
47 *Hulls Managing*.
48 Lord Fairfax to CBK.
49 Somerville at Wetherby.

Chapter 5

1 Slingsby, p. 107.
2 *Hulls Managing.*
3 Slingsby, p. 108.
4 *Hulls Managing.*
5 *Newcastle's Memoirs*, p. 36.
6 Rushworth, Vol. V, p. 620.
7 Cooke, D., *Adwalton Moor, The Forgotten Battle*, Battlefield Press, 1996.
8 Ash, No. 2:

> Afterwards wee speedily endeavoured to make a bridge of Boats neer Gainsborough, that
> we might have constant converse with the Scottish Army, and appointed two Regiments of
> foot, with Canon to guard that Work: This bridge being made, neer. 3000 horse were
> dispatched unto Bantre, Ralford and Tuxford; and there joyned with 2000 horse sent from
> the Scots, and the Lord Fairfax, But before this body of horse was conjoyned, our own
> horse, commanded by Lieutenant Generall Cromwell, advancing into Notinghamshire
> towards the enemy, the enemy, (who had above 90 Colours, which wee esteemed 4000 and
> themselves accounted 6000 horse) was so affrighted, that they did swim over the Trent,
> within 2 or 3 miles of Newark, where three men and one woman were drowned, besides
> the prejudice otherwayes received by the waters, into which many of them were forced, by
> the swords of their own Commanders. There were also before this flight of the enemies,
> divers small skirmishes, wherein they always were put to the worse; but because they were
> not of any great consequence, therefore we forbear to particularize them.

 9 CSPD 1644, p.171.
10 Ibid, p. 174.
11 Ibid, p. 188.
12 Ibid, pp. 190–1.
13 Ibid. p.191.
14 Ibid. p. 206.
15 *Prince Rupert's Marches.*
16 Ash, No. 2.
17 CSPD 1644, p. 191.
18 Ibid, p. 176.
19 *Exact Newes from Yorke.*
20 Ash, No. 3.
21 *Hulls Managing.*
22 Ash, No. 3.
23 *Newcastle's Memoirs*, p. 37.
24 Slingsby, p. 108.
25 Ash, No. 3.
26 Slingsby, p. 108.
27 CSPD 1644, pp. 206–7.
28 Ash, No. 3.
29 Ibid:

> About midnight, a commanded Company of the couragious Scots, assaulted fiercely and
> bravely the three Forts on the west side of the City, and after a very hot service, for the

space of two houres (whereof many of us, with deepe affections were eye witnesses at a distance) they became possessors of two of them. The one of the Forts (which was the nearest to the Towne) was strengthened with a double ditch, wherein there were 120 souldiers, above 60 were slaine, and all the rest taken prisoners. The other Fort taken, had only 50 men to maintaine it, who were all either killed, or taken prisoners desiring quarter. And the 3d Fort had been possessed by the Scots also, if that a strong party both of Horse and Foot, had not come out of the Towne for the reliefe thereof. In this brave and bold service, the Scots lost 3 Captaines and some others (whether 6, 7, or some few more as yet is not manifested) were killed, one Lieftenant-Colonell and 2 Captaines deadly wounded, with many others wounded, but (as its hoped) not in danger of death.

Slingsby, p. 110:

Some redoubts they took by storm, as one in Bishopfeilds, & another on a windmill hill towards Bishopthorp. But this was no great loss more yn ye killing of ye men; for but one they kept, ye other they slight'd, & we still send [to] ye feilds to keep our cows and horses.

30 Ash, No. 4.
31 Slingsby, p. 110.
32 CSPD 1644, pp. 216–7.
33 Ash, No. 4.
34 Ibid.
35 Ibid.
36 CSPD 1644, p. 224.
37 Ibid.
38 Ash, No. 4.
39 Ibid.
40 Ibid.
41 *Eminent Person.*
42 Ibid.
43 Ash, No. 4.
44 Ibid.
45 Ibid.
46 *Eminent Person*:

The last night the enemy made fires on the top of the Minster, and Cliffords Towers, and were answered by the like from Pomfret Castle, which is a signall of succours comming towards them.

Slingsby, p. 110:

We made fires upon ye minster wch ansuer'd us again from Pomphret.

47 CSPD 1644, p. 241.
48 Ash, No. 4:

Upon the sixteenth day, the Earle of Manchesters men (having by many dayes labour undermined a Tower belonging to the Mannour neere Bootham Barre) were compelled to spring the Mine, for that worke could not be longer delayed, in regard of waters which increased upon them, in the chamber of the Mine. The Tower being blown up, the bold Souldiers adventured too farre through inconsideratenesse, and hope of plunder, many of them having scaled two or three inner walles, possessed themselves of the Mare. But the enemy comming from all parts of the City suddenly and unexpectedly surrounded them, yea they blocked up the breach, the only way to retreat. Hereupon they having spent all their powder and shott, and fresh assistance not getting over the walles to their reliefe soone enough, we receved some losse, both of men and arms. As it is supposed betwixt 12 and 20 men were slain and 200 taken prisoners, whom we expect to have restored unto us again ere long. Some who were in the service, say that many more of the enemies then of our souldiers were killed in the skirmish, but they are too wily to suffer us to know what loss they in the City received by our assaults.

Ash, No. 5:

The last intelligence from hence gave only a generall touch upon those passages which then appeared, when the Tower at Bootham Barre was blown up by the Earle of Manchesters Souldiers, whose quarters are on that side the Citie: Now you shall have the true report of some particulars concerning that businesse, which since have been discovered.

In the fall of the Tower many were slain, and found dead on the ground, the most of them were Townsmen and women. While the skirmish was betwixt our Souldiers and the enemy, some barrels of Gun-powder were fiered in the Town, whereby many were slain and wounded.

About 15 of our men were slain within the Citie, and 20 at the most without the walls; well nigh 40 were wounded without the Town, and about 60 (as we heare) within, who together with an hundred more taken prisoners. We cannot get a full account of the loss sustained in the Citie by that dayes skirmish; but this we are assured of, that 4 Colonels, one Major, were slain, with divers Captains, and other commanders. Some who are come since out of the Towne, tell us, that their loss was greater then ours, and that they rather lament then glory in the successe of that dayes service.

Slingsby, pp. 108–109:

Likewise Manchester, who had his Quaters about Clifton & Huworth, was not less active, but makes his approaches, works his mines under St. Mary's Tower wthout Botham barr, & rais'd a battery against ye mannor Wall yt ly'd to ye orchard; he begins to play wth his Cannon & throws down peice of ye Wall. We fall to works & make it up wth earth & sods; this happn'd in ye morning: at noon they spring ye mine under St. Mary's Tower, & blows up one parts of it, wch falling outwards made ye access more easy; Then some at ye breach, some wth Ladders, getts up & enters, near 500.

Sr. Philip Biron yt had ye guard at yt place, leading some men was unfortunately kill'd as he open'd ye doors into ye bowling green whither ye enemy was gotten; but ye difficulty was not much, we soon beat ym out again, having taken 200 prisoners & kill'd many of ym, as might be seen in ye bowling green, Orchard & Garden.

Eminent Person:

After I had concluded this letter, word was brought mee that the Earle of Manchesters men never acquainting our other Forces with their intention, sprung a myne this afternoon, which did good execution, making a large breach in the wals into the mannour, by which those forces entred and possessed themselves of the Mannour, the enemies guards laying down their armes: But the enemie drawing all their forces that way, beate our men againe, with the losse of 200 of our partee, and the other armies could not come to their succour, having no notice of it.

CSPD 1644, p. 246:

> Yesterday within my quarters I sprang a mine, which did great execution upon the enemy, blowing up a tower which joined to the Manor-yard, and this mine taking so great effect my Major-General commanded 600 men to storm the Manor-house, who beat the enemy and took 100 prisoners, but, being over confident, 2,000 of the enemy's best men fell upon them and beat them back. I lost near 300 men, but still maintain the breaches and the enemy dare not make any sally out; we are now so near them that we are very ill neighbours one to another.

Newcastle's Memoirs, p. 37:

> At last, the General of the Associate Army of the enemy, having closely beleaguered the north side of the town, sprung a mine under the wall of the Manor Yard, and blew part of it up; and having beaten back the town forces (although they behaved themselves very gallantly), entered the Manor House with a great number of their men, which as soon as my Lord perceived, he went away in all haste – even to the amazement of all that were by, not knowing what he intended to do – and drew 80 of his own regiment of foot, called the Whitecoats, all stout and valiant men, to that post, who fought the enemy with that courage, that within a little time they killed and took 1,500 of them; and my Lord gave present order to make up the breach which they had made in the wall.

Short Memoriall, pp. 220–1:

> Till, in my Ld Manchesters Quarters, Approaches were made to St Mary's Tower; & soone came to myne it; wch Coll: Crawford, a Scotchman, who commanded yt Quarter, (being Ambitious to have the honor, alone, of springing ye myne) undertooke, wthout acquainting ye other Generalls wth it, for their advice and concurrance, wch proved very prjudiciall; for having engaged his party agt ye whole strength of ye Towne, wthout more force to second him, he was repulsed wth ye losse of 300 men; for wch he had surely beene called to Acct, but yt he scaped better by reason of ye Triumvirall Government.

49 Ash, No. 4.
50 Slingsby, p. 109.
51 *Short Memoriall*.
52 Ash, No. 4.
53 Ash, No. 5.
54 Ibid.
55 CSPD 1644, p. 246.
56 Ash, No. 5.
57 *Exact Newes from Yorke*.
58 Slingsby, pp. 111–2.

Chapter 6

1 Warburton, pp. 382–4.
2 *Short Memoriall*, p. 220.
3 Warburton, pp. 384–5.
4 Ibid, p. 397.
5 Ibid, pp. 400–1.

6 Ibid, p. 397:

> For all the affairs in the North, I refer your Highness to this bearer, Sir John Mayne, who
> can tell your Highness every particular.

Ibid, pp. 384–5:

> This is all I am commanded at present to write unto your Highness, or have occasion to
> do, since by Will Legge, within a day or two, I shall give your Highness an account at large
> of all his Majesty's affairs.

7 *Prince Rupert's Marches.*
8 *Proceedings of his Majesty's Army.*
9 Ibid:

> Prince Rupert advanced with his Army towards Lancashire consistinge of 2,000 hors, and
> 6,000 foote, or above (as is supposed), drawne out of the Countyes of Herreford, Woster,
> Stafford, Salop, Chester.

Hulls Managing:

> Prince Rupert is in Lancashire with his uncertain numbers, our best Intelligence sayes
> 8000, plundering and Arraying the Country.

10 *Prince Rupert's Marches.*
11 *Proceedings of his Majesty's Army*:

> After 10 dayes march by reason of the Roughness of the wayes, and the weather wee came
> to Stopford, a large village in the confines of Lancashire Mannour with the Enemy without
> fortifications, saveing a ryver with high bancks and a bridge devideing Cheshire from
> Lancashire, there the Prince intended to quarter that night, which after a little dispute from
> hedges and ditches, uppon an universall assaulte was abandoned by the Enemy, who fled
> towards Manchester some 6 myles distant, and by reason the sunn was downe, the night
> made way to theyr escape, though they were pursued a great way, and as was beleived noe
> man lost of eyther syde; the goods of the towne was the souldiers reward.

Prince Rupert's Diary:

> From Shrewsbury ye P drew [together] all ye forces he could, and beat their way over ye
> Passe of Stopford. And upon that ye Enemy went from ye Siege of Latham, and went to
> Bolton.

Rushworth, Vol. V, p. 623:

> After this his Highness marched towards Lancashire, designing to relieve the Countess of
> Derby, who for the space of eighteen Weeks was besieged in Latham-House, and made a
> gallant Defence; but in his way on May the 25th came before Stopworth, a Town in
> Cheshire, but seated on the Bank of the River Mersey, which divideth that County from
> Lancashire, where the Parliament had a strong Garison, who marched out to meet him,
> and lined the Hedges where he was to pass with Musqueteers; but they were beat from
> thence by Colonel Washington and a Party of Dragoons, who forced them into the Town
> in such disorder, that the Prince with his Horse followed then at the heels, and entred pell
> mell with them, and so took the Town, with all their Cannon, most of their Arms and
> Ammunition, and some Hundreds of them Prisoners.

From thence he sent Forces to relieve the beforementioned Countess; but the Besiegers hearing of the Prince's Advance, and his Success at Stopworth, had raised the Siege of their own accord, and marched away with Bag and Baggage.

CSPD 1644, p. 193:

That Prince Rupert has taken Stopford, which is upon the edge of Cheshire next Lancashire, and a pass into that country where there were 3,000 of the country people, but were in disorder at his coming and so left it to him.

Ibid, p. 206:

About 14 days since, when we first heard of Prince Rupert's bending his course towards Lancashire, the forces of that country, estimated at least twelve troops of horse and 7,000 foot, were ordered to be drawn together on the frontier of the county towards Cheshire, where there are only two passages, the one by Stopfort, and the other by Warrington, which those forces might easily have made good against Prince Rupert's Army, not then exceeding 8,000 men, part horse and part foot; yet to give the more encouragement to the country, we sent Sir John Meldrum with two regiments of foot and two troops of horse from hence, who arrived not at Manchester until the Lancashire forces had deserted Stopfort, and left the passage open for the enemy, who instantly overran the country, and being assisted by the Earl of Derby, and the Popish gentry of Lancashire, have already doubled their strength.

12 *Proceedings of his Majesty's Army.*
13 CSPD 1644, p. 173.
14 *Prince Rupert's Marches.*
15 Rushworth, pp. 623–4:

And Colonel Rigby with part of those Forces, went to Bolton in Lancashire, where before there was little Ammunition, few Men, or other means of Defence. But with this Accession there were in all about two thousand Soldiers, and five hundred Club-men, which yet proved insufficient.

For on Tuesday, May 28th, Prince Rupert bringing thither his whole Army, consisting of ten thousand or upwards, appeared about two of the Clock in the Afternoon before the Town, approaching on the Moor, on the South-West part of it; but presently cast themselves into several Bodies, and sent out Scouts to discover where they might advantageously enter. Those in the Town prepared for their Defence, and gave the Assailants half an hours sharp Entertainment, and repulsed them; but in the second Attack, which was performed with all imaginable Fury, a Party of Horse broke into the Town, at a place called The private Akers, (it being suspected that a certain Townsman for a Reward had been their Guide that way, as the most feasible Passage) and they being once got in, every one endeavoured to shift for himself; and the Prince's Forces rushed in on all quarters of the Town, and put great Numbers to the Sword, pursuing their Victory not only in the Town, but for some Miles round, in Out-houses, Fields, High-ways and Woods, killing, destroying, and spoiling almost all they met with; and (as the Towns-People alledged afterwards) denying Quarter and using other Violences, besides totally plundering the Town, and slaying four Ministers. It was acknowledged by the Prince's own Party, that they there put to the Sword about twelve hundred; but for this severity alledged, That the Prince sending an Officer to summon the Town, they not only refused, but in defiance caused one of the Prince's Captains whom they had taken not long before, to be hanged in his sight. But as I find not this Captain's Name any where mentioned, so the other Party wholly denied that part of the Story. On the Parliament's side two Captain's were slain, but Colonel Rigby, a Counsellor at Law, and Member of the House of Commons, who commanded here in chief, escaped with some scattered Forces to Bradford in Yorkshire.

Proceedings of his Majesty's Army:

Upon the 28th of May the Army marched towards Bolton, a large Country towne in Lancashire, some 16 myles from Stopford as wee marched, mann'd lykewise with 4,000 men (as was informed, there the Prince intended to quarter that night, onely gates and highwayes fortifyed lightly, the rayne was soe immoderate that it cost an howre or two dispute, being impetuously stormed it was taken with the fall of 1,000 menn of the Enemy in the streetes and feilds, above 20 cullours, 600 prisoners, 50 officers, 20 barrells of powder, match and armes a great quantity; the towne [was the] souldiers reward.)

Ash, No. 3:

On Tuesday the day before the publike Fast, he stormed Bolton, the next Garrison Towne to us, 8 miles from us, the next Towne for Religion to Manchester in all the Countie, unto which many of Gods deare servants were fled, in an houres space he tooke it, denying quarter to any, whether souldiers or men in the houses, till the sword drunke with bloud was sheathed, 1500 two daies after buried, 500 taken prisoners, not a man left in the Towne, the rich in the Towne asking bread, and none to be had.

CSPD 1644, p. 206:

And being assisted by the Earl of Derby, and the Popish gentry of Lancashire, have already doubled their strength and have taken Bolton by assault, being defended by Col. Rigby with 2,000 armed men and 1,500 clubmen and they made a great slaughter of the defenders as the vulgar reports tell us; though Col. Rigby himself says that he conceives he lost not 200 men, nor 500 arms, the rest saving themselves by flight.

Prince Rupert's Diary:

Who found ye Enemy there before him, getting into qrs in disorders, Of wch sending ye P word he marched wth the whole Army Imediately thither. A River [the Mersey] runs through ye Town, and ye Enemy having drawen a good line round the Town with four or five thousand men in it and a Troop of horse under ye Comand of one Shuttleworth. The P. attaqued ye Place, with Col: Ellises, Tillslyes and Warren's Regts which were all beaten off and of ye Ps Regt L:C: John Russell hurt, his Major a Prisoner, & 300 men lost. So that there was but Col. Robert Broughton's Regt, who being comanded on by ye P enterd ye Town and took it. 700 got into ye Church, and ye P gave them quarter.

Which two latter [Warren's and Rupert's] were beaten off and ye 2 former [Ellis' and Tyldesley's] after entering ye town were beaten out again.

During ye time of ye Attaque they took a prisonr (an Irishman) and hung him up as an Irish papist. And after defended ye Town to ye Last with great obstanacy, so that a great slaughter was made ye Enemy.

After ye taking of ye Town they fir'd out of their Cellars at ye Ps troop of Horse drawn up in ye markett place; and yet ye P was pleased to give them Quarter.

Massacre at Bolton (quoted in full in Appendix III).

16 Ibid.
17 CSPD 1644, p. 206.
18 Ash, No. 3.
19 *Massacre at Bolton*.
20 Ibid.
21 *Prince Rupert's Diary*.
22 Ibid.
23 Rushworth, Vol. V, p. 624.
24 Seacome, J., *Memoirs of the House of Stanley*, 1741, p. 108.
25 Ash, No. 3.
26 *Massacre at Bolton*.
27 CSPD 1644, p. 206.
28 Ash, No. 3.
29 Pendlebury, G., *Aspects of the English Civil War in Bolton and its Neighbourhood 1640–1660*, Manchester, 1983.
30 *Prince Rupert's Marches*.
31 CSPD 1644, p. 188.
32 Ibid, pp. 191–2.
33 Ibid, 193.
34 *Proceedings of his Majesty's Army*:

Wee pitched before Liverpoole with our whole Army, haveing beleaguered it with our horss the day before; it has mudd walls with barrs and gates, 14 peeces of ordinance, 1,000 souldiers (as was supposed); the matter was disputed very hotly untill the tenth day of June with muskett and great shott without measure out of the towne and from the shipps, uppon which day our line approached within a coites cast of the gate where our great shott had almost filled the ditch with the ruines of the sod wall, and about noone a furious assaulte was made by our men where a terrible fight was on both sydes above the space of an houre uppon the workes, the Enemy resolute, ours not seconded retreated with some loss. The Enemy whether dispayreing of relief, or of theyr owne strength against soe great power at Midnight they shipped themselves the chiefe of theyr menn and goods and left 12 collours on the workes, hoysted sayles, and road within halfe a league of the towne. Which Colonell Tilyer perceivinge haveinge the Guarde next the Sea, supposeing the Enemy to bee gone, entred the towne with little or noe resistance, found about 400 of the meaner sorte of menn, whereof most were kill'd some had quarter, 14 peeces of ordinance, left uppon theyr carriadges att theyr batterys whatsoever was desiderable was the souldiers right for theyr hard service, 26 smale vessells without tacklings were left in the harbour.

Rushworth, Vol. V, p. 624:

In the next place his Highness advanced to Leverpool, an Haven-Town of Lancashire, on the Edge of Cheshire, where Colonel More was Governor for the Parliament, to whose relief forty English and Scots (of the Party sent off from York into those Parts) were lately come from Manchester to Warrington, and so by Water to Leverpool: But notwithstanding their Assistance, and the stout resistance made by them and the rest of the Garison, the Prince made himself Master of the Town, but of no great Booty besides: For the Governor finding it not tenable against so great a Force, privately drew off his best Ordnance, Arms and Ammunition, and afterwards most part of his Soldiers, and richest Goods in the Town, and safely convey'd them on board the Ships in the Pool; and then the Assailants with little Opposition entered the Town, where finding themselves disappointed of Plunder, the Common Soldiers were much incensed, and reveng'd themselves on the Inhabitants, and those Soldiers they found left behind, and would scarce allow them Quarter.

Prince Rupert's Diary:

After ye taking of Leverpool his H saw great numbers of Ratts coming from the ships at low water, bein layd dry; in troops into ye Town for Provisions, and so back again toward floud.

The town quitted and ye P took possession of it; the P desiring to prserve it from Plunder ... it was Sr Robt Byron being left Governr.

Mercurius Britannicus, No. 39, June 17, 1644:

The brave repulse which Colonel More, Governor of Liverpoole, gave twice to Rupert (who assaulted that place with greate fury) is worthy of your notice. The seamen were very active in that Service, and all are resolute to defend that place against Rupert, the Viper who devours his nourisher. 400 English and Scots are sent from Manchester to Warrington, and from thence by water to Liverpoole, for their better assistance, and the Ships in the Harbour are well fitted to defend and make good a part of that town ... Rupert hath at length with the number of his souldiers and continual assaults stormed the towne of Liverpoole, but the prudent Governor, with the losse of not above sixty men, kild him fifteen hundred, and finding that he could not hold the place any longer, he privately drew off his Ordnance, Armes, and Ammunition, and afterwards his goods in the Towne, and safely conveyed them on board the Ships riding in the Poole, and disappointed Rupert's hopes therein, but he cares for nothing so much, as that he hath got that nest, for his Uncle's loyal subjects the Irish Rebels to come over and build in, and help setle the Protestant Religion.

CSPD 1644, p. 231:

Col. Moore is in it with about 600 of his own men and 300 newly sent to him from Warrington.

Ibid, p. 241:

Liverpool we hear is quitted by the garrison after great loss to the enemy in his attempts upon it.

35　Seacome, J., *Memoirs of the House of Stanley*, 1741, p. 110.
36　CSPD 1644, p. 230.
37　Ibid, p. 231.
38　Warburton, pp. 437–9.
39　Goring to Musgrave.
40　*Prince Rupert's Diary*.
41　Ibid.

Chapter 7

1　Stockdale.
2　CSPD, pp. 265–6.

3 Stockdale.

4 White.

5 *Short Memoriall.*

6 Fuller, p. 224.

7 Slingsby, p. 112:

> The prince now was come wthin 3 or 4 miles of York, upon ye forest side, & sends in to my Ld of Newcastle, to meet him wth those forces he had in York.

Ogden, p. 71:

> The Prince marching towards Yorke Munday July the 1st, the Enemy raysed theire seige and went away: the Prince having intelligence wh way they went, marched towards them, haveing left order wth the Marq. of Newcastle to meete him next morning with his foote.

Cholmley, p. 347:

> That evening the Prince sent General Goring to the Marquess to desire he might the next morning by four a clock have all his forces drawn out of the city to join with his, for which the Marquess presently gave order.

8 Newcastle's Memoirs, p. 38.

9 Ibid, pp. 38–9.

10 Watson.

11 *Short Memoriall*, p. 221.

12 Ash, No. 5.

13 Cholmley, p. 347.

14 Stockdale.

15 Watson.

16 Stockdale.

17 Stewart.

18 Cholmley, pp. 347–8.

19 Ibid.

20 Watson.

21 Stockdale.

22 Cholmley, pp. 347–8.

23 Ordnance Survey 1:10,000 Sheet SE 45 SE.

24 *Short Memoriall*, p. 221.

25 Watson.

26 Ash, No. 5.

27 Stewart.

28 Stockdale.

29 Watson.

30 Ash, No. 5.

31 Slingsby, p. 113.

32 Watson.

33 Stewart.

34 Ash, No. 5.

35 Stewart.

36 Newman, P.R., *The Battle of Marston Moor 1644*, Antony Bird, Chichester, 1981.

37 *Short Memoriall.*
38 See: Newman, P.R., *The Battle of Marston Moor 1644*, Antony Bird, Chichester, 1981. Peter Newman has done some sterling work on the geography of the battlefield. Although I do not agree with some of his conclusions as to the course of the battle, his work on the layout of the field in 1644 is beyond reproach.
39 Watson.
40 Ibid.
41 Stockdale:

> and part of them drawne up within shot of our Ordinance which about 2 a clock begann to play upon the Brigade of horse that were nearest and did some execution upon them which forced the enemye to leave that ground and remove to a greater distance.

Capt. W.H.:

> We began about two of the clock in the afternoon with our great guns, which continued till between 7 and 8 with equall success.

42 Slingsby, p. 112.
43 Carlyle, T. (ed.), *Oliver Cromwell's Letters and Speeches*, 1902, Vol. I, p. 188.
44 Ash, No. 6.
45 Slingsby, p. 112.
46 Cholmley, p. 348.
47 *Newcastle's Memoirs*, p. 39.
48 Trevor.
49 Cholmley, p. 348.
50 *Ludlow's Memoirs*, pp. 98–100.
51 Several contemporary authors give a start time of between seven and seven thirty for the Allied attack: Watson, Stockdale, Ash No 5, Capt W.H.
52 Ash, No. 5.

Chapter 8

1 For a detailed discussion of the tactics and equipment of the Civil War soldier see: Firth, C.H., *Cromwell's Army*, Greenhill Books, 1992; Roberts, K., and McBride, A., *Soldiers of the English Civil War: 1 Infantry*, Osprey, 1989; Tincey, J., and McBride, A., *Soldiers of the English Civil War: 2 Cavalry*, Osprey, 1990.
2 Articles of Surrender.
3 Young, P., *Marston Moor*, 1970, p. 31.
4 De Gomme.
5 For a detailed discussion of the Marquis of Newcastle's army see: Evans, D., *The Battle of Marston Moor 1644*, Stuart Press, 1994.
6 Ibid, pp. 29–30.
7 Evans, D., *The Battle of Marston Moor 1644*, Stuart Press, 1994, pp. 28–9.
8 Monckton.
9 Douglas.
10 Lumsden.
11 Watson.
12 Stockdale.
13 Stewart.

14 White.

15 Ash, No. 5.

16 Lumsden.

17 Evans, D., *The Battle of Marston Moor 1644*, Stuart Press, 1994.

18 Monckton.

19 Stewart.

20 Slingsby.

21 Watson:

> Our front divisions of Horse charged their front, Lieutenant General Cromwels division of three hundred Horse, in which himselfe was in person, charged the first division of Prince Rupert's.

22 As you will see in due course I subscribe to the 'Fairfax in the centre' school. The evidence for both schools will be discussed in this chapter and Chapter Nine. Hopefully, a convincing argument will be put forward for the centre theory.

23 Firth, C.H., 'Marston Moor', *Transactions of the Royal Historical Society*, New Series, Vol. XII.

24 Young, P., *Marston Moor*, 1970.

25 Newman, P.R., *The Battle of Marston Moor 1644*, Antony Bird, Chichester, 1981.

26 Evans, D., *The Battle of Marston Moor 1644*, Stuart Press, 1994.

27 Stewart.

28 Capt. W.H.

29 Stockdale.

30 Ash, No. 5.

31 Douglas.

32 Young, P., *Marston Moor*, 1970, map between pp. 136–7.

33 Ibid.

34 Slingsby, pp. 112–3.

35 White.

36 Evans, D., *The Battle of Marston Moor 1644*, Stuart Press, 1994, pp. 21–2.

Chapter 9

1 Watson.

2 Capt. W.H.

3 Lumsden.

4 Stewart.

5 *Short Memoriall*, p. 77.

6 Clarke to Bartlett.

7 Stewart.

8 Newman, P.R., *Marston Moor, 2 July 1644: The Sources and the Site*, Borthwick Papers No. 53, 1978, p. 37. Newman, P.R. and Roberts, P.R., *Marston Moor 1644: the Battle of the Five Armies*, Blackthorn Press, 2003.

9 *Short Memoriall*, p. 221.

10 Stewart.

11 *Short Memoriall*, p. 222.

12 Ibid, p. 221.

13 Ash, No. 5:

> Our signal was a white Paper, or handkerchiffe in our hats; our word was God with us. The enemies signal was to bee without bands and skarfes. Their word was God and the King.

14 Ibid.
15 Monckton.
16 Douglas.
17 *Newcastle's Memoirs*, p. 40.
18 Stewart.
19 Lumsden.
20 *Short Memoriall*, pp. 221–2.
21 De Gomme.
22 Watson.
23 Ibid.
24 Stewart.
25 Ash, No. 5.
26 Fuller, p. 225.
27 Ash, No. 5.
28 Ibid.
29 De Gomme.
30 Stewart.
31 Stockdale.
32 Ash, No. 5.
33 Douglas.
34 Stewart.
35 Douglas.
36 *Newcastle's Memoirs*, p. 40.
37 Ash, No. 5.
38 Lumsden.
39 Trevor.
40 Stockdale.
41 Lumsden.
42 Stewart.
43 Lumsden.
44 Somerville.
45 Douglas.
46 Stewart.
47 Fuller, p. 225.
48 Slingsby, p. 113.
49 Carlyle, T. (ed.), *Oliver Cromwell's Letters and Speeches*, 1902, Vol. I, p. 188.
50 Watson.
51 Douglas.
52 Stockdale.
53 *Newcastle's Memoirs*, pp. 39–40.
54 Stewart.
55 Cholmley, p. 348.

56 Fuller, p. 225.
57 Ogden.
58 Somerville.
59 Cholmley, p. 348.
60 Carlyle, T. (ed.), *Oliver Cromwell's Letters and Speeches*, 1902, Vol. I, p. 188.
61 Watson.
62 Newman, P.R. and Roberts, P.R., *Marston Moor 1644: the Battle of the Five Armies*, Blackthorn Press, 2003.
63 Somerville.
64 *Newcastle's Memoirs*, pp. 40–1.
65 Slingsby, pp. 113–4.
66 Lilly, pp. 178–80.
67 Fuller, p. 225.
68 Ash, No. 5.
69 Watson.
70 Capt. W.H.
71 Monckton.
72 Lord Fairfax to Hull.
73 Watson.
74 Stockdale.
75 Ash, No. 5.
76 Stewart.
77 Ash, No. 5.

Chapter 10

1 Slingsby, p. 114.
2 *Newcastle's Memoirs*, p. 41.
3 Stewart:

> We heare that there have been some differences betweene the Prince and the Earle of Newcastle, which appeare to be more reall that they have parted since; the Earle of Newcastle, Generall King, and the Lord Widrington are gone to Scarsborough, and as wee understand since, are shipped for Holland, and Prince Rupert towards the North.

Prince Rupert's Diary:

> And then m ye E of Newcastle and drew up or men. Sayes Genll Kig wt will you do. Sayes ye P I will rally my men. Sayes Genll Kg now you wt Ld Newcastle will do? Sayes Ld Newcastle I will go in to Holland (looking upon all as lost).
>
> The P: would have him endeavour to recruit his forces. No (sayes he) I will not endure ye laughter of ye Court and King sayd hee would go with him; and so they did and left ye Governr of York wth wt force he had to defend himself. Then ye P. march'd away into Shropshire, according to ye methode he had before layd for his retreat taking wth him all ye Northern Horse which ye E of Newcastle left to his H and brought them into his Qters in Wales. And there endeavoured to recruit wt he could.
>
> The P offer'd to stay with ye E. of Newcastle and to try to recruite in ye West Riding and form an Army; but he would not hear out.

Ash, No. 5:

Wee heare that there were warme words passed betwixt Prince Rupert and the Marquesse Newcastle in Yorks, after their Rout; they charging each other with the cause thereof. The Prince told the Marquess, That hee made not good his promise in his assistance; but the Marquesse replyed in such a manner as moved much passion. It is reported that they parted in great discontent.

Newcastle's Memoirs, p. 41:

That night my Lord remained in York; and having nothing left in his power to do his Majesty any further service in that kind; for he had neither ammunition, nor money to raise more forces, to keep either York, or any other towns that were yet in his Majesty's devotion, well knowing that those which were left could not hold out long, and being also loath to have aspersions cast upon him, that he did sell them to the enemy, in case he could not keep them, he took a resolution and that justly and honourably, to forsake the kingdom; and to that end, went the next morning to the Prince, and acquainted him with his design, desiring his Highness would be pleased to give this true and just report of him to his Majesty, that he behaved himself like an honest man, a gentleman, and a loyal subject. Which request the Prince having granted, my Lord took his leave.

Cholmley:

The Prince after two days rest having rallied together about 4,000 horse and some few foot, marcheth towards Westmorland, he and the Marquess having once agreed that the Marquess should go to Newcastle, whither the Prince would return as soon as he could recruit his foot; which if it had accordingly been pursued had been of great advantage to the King's affairs, for had the Marquess remained in those parts surely a great number of the broken foot would have been rallied together, and it would have given encouragement to the King's friends and party there, whereas upon his departure almost everyone (especially such as had particular relation or affection to his person) quitt the Kings service and went to their own homes; but as is said General King considering the King's affairs absolutely destroyed by loss of this battle persuaded the Marquess (against all the power of his other friends) to quit the kingdome so that the Marquess leaving Sir Thomas Glemman in York to gain as good terms for the city as he could.

4 Cholmley.
5 *Newcastle's Memoirs*, p. 41.
6 Cholmley.
7 Ibid.
8 Ibid.
9 Warburton, pp. 477–8.
10 Stewart:

and Prince Rupert toward the North; his Rendezvous was 12 miles on the North side of Yorke, where appeared about fifteene or sixteene hundred horse, and eight hundred foot.

Cholmley:

The Prince after two days rest having rallied together about 4,000 horse and some few foot, marcheth towards Westmorland.

11 *Prince Rupert's Marches*:

> 3. Wednesday, wee retreated to Thrusk. By the waye, Sir Robert Clavering came to us with 1,300.

Stewart:

> While I was about to close my Letter we received information that the Lord Clavering with about 2000 foote and horse are joyned with the Prince, and that he is gone to Lancashire.

12 Rupert to Musgrave.
13 *Prince Rupert's Marches*.
14 Ash, No. 5.
15 Stockdale:

> After the Battell our men pursued the enemy neare Yorke, and then settled upon the ground where the battell was fought, and there continued all Wednesday and most part of yesterday, untill the Cheshire and Lancashire forces came up to them, and then they marched together towards Yorke againe, and are set down yesternight in their old quarters, from whence I hope they will not bee forced to rise againe untill the Citty be surendred.

16 Ogden.
17 Stewart.
18 Ash, No. 5.
19 CSPD 1644, pp. 375–376.
20 Slingsby, p. 114.
21 Ibid, p. 115.
22 Ibid.
23 Ash, No. 6.
24 Ibid.
25 Ibid.
26 Ibid.
27 Ibid.
28 Slingsby, p. 116.
29 Ash, No. 6.
30 CSPD 1644, pp. 385.
31 Ash, No. 6.

Bibliography

Primary Sources

Articles of the Surrender of the City of Yorke to the Earle of Leven on Tuesday July 16, 1644. Together with an Explanation of Some Part of the Articles, B.M., T.T. E3 (5).

Calendar of State Papers, Domestic, 1644.

Continuation of True Intelligence from the Armies in the North, from the 10 Day, to the 27 of This Instant July, 1644. Wherein Is Given a Full and Particular Accompt of the Surrender of York, and of the Removes of the Armies Since (Number 6), B.M., T.T. E4 (6).

Continuation of True Intelligence from the English and Scottish Forces, in the North, for the Service of King and Parliament, and Now Beleaguring York, from the Eighth of This Instant June to the 17th Thereof (Number 4), B.M., T.T. E51.

Continuation of True Intelligence from the English and Scottish Forces, in the North, for the Service of King and Parliament, and Now Beleaguring York, from the 16th of June, to Wednesday the 10th of July, 1644 (Number 5), B.M., T.T. E2 (1).

Continuation of True Intelligence from the Right Honourable the Earl of Manchester's Army, Since the Taking of Lincolne; May 6th Until the First Day of This Instant Iune, 1644 (Number 2), B.M., T.T. E5 (33).

Copy of a Letter Sent from the Lo: Fairfax to the Major of Hull; and by Him Sent to the Committee of Both Kingdoms: Concerning the Great Victory Obtained Against Prince Rupert About the Raising the Siege at York, York City Library, Y942.062.

Exact and Certaine Newes from the Siege at Yorke. and of Many Remarkable Passages of Our Armys in Those Parts, Extracted Out of Diverse Letters Which Were Sent by This Last Post from Hull, to a Gentle-Man of Grayes-Inne, B.M., T.T. E53 (12).

Exact Relation of the Bloody and Barbarous Massacre at Bolton in the Moors in Lancashire, May 28, Bolton Library, B901.043PB EXA.

Exact Relation of the Last Newes from the Quarters of His Excellency the Lord Generall of the Scottish Army. Dated from Sunderland March 12 1643, reproduced in *Richardson's Reprints*.

Extract of Letters, Dated at Edenburgh the 14, 16, and 17 of April, 1644, B.M. T.T. E44 (10).

Faithfull Relation of the Late Occurrences and Proceedings of the Scottish Army: Dated from His Excellencies Lord Generall Leslie's Quarters Before Newcastle, 21 February 1644, reproduced in *Richardson's Reprints*.

Full Relation of the Victory Obtained (through God's Providence) by the Forces under the Command of General Leslie, the Lord Fairfax, and the Earl of Manchester; Being About Twenty Seven Thousand Horse and Foot Against His Majesties Forces under the Command of Prince Rupert and the Earl of Newcastle, Being Much About the Same Number. Fought on Marstam-Moor, Within 5 Miles of York on the Second of July, 1644, B.M., T.T. E54 (19).

Historical Relation of the Life of Mr Joseph Lister, Late of the Society at Kippin Containing an Authentic Account of the Siege of Bradford, Etc., Bradford, 1821.

Hulls Managing of the Kingdoms Cause: or, a Brief Historicall Relation of the Severall Plots and Attempts Against Kingston Upon Hull, from the Beginning of These Unhappy Differences to This

Day; and the Means Whereby through Gods Blessing It Hath Been Preserved, and the Kingdom in It, B.M., T.T. E51 (11).

Journal of Prince Rupert's Marches, 5 Sept. 1642 to 4 July 1646, Clarendon MSS xxviii. 129.

Late Proceedings of the Scotish Army, Certifying Their Passing over Tyne; with the Particulars. Together with Their Possession of Sunderland, and Their Advance After the Enemy, Who Is Fled to Durham. Sent by an Expresse, from His Excellency the Lord General Leslie His Quarters, and Dated at Sunderland, March 12, reproduced in *Richardson's Reprints*.

'Letter from Captain Robert Clarke to Captain Bartlett', *Transactions of the Royal Historical Society*, New Series, Vol. XII, 1898, pp. 76–8.

Letter from Colonell Francis Anderson to Sir Thomas Glemham, reproduced in *Richardson's Reprints*.

Letter from Colonel Goring to Sir Philip Musgrave, Cumbria Record Office (Carlisle), D Mus correspondence (Civil War), bundle 1, Number 29.

Letter from Prince Rupert to Sir Philip Musgrave, Cumbria Record Office (Carlisle), D Mus correspondence (Civil War), bundle 4, Number 11.

Letter from Thomas Stockdale to John Rushworth, B.M., Harleian MSS, 166.87.

Letter from Thomas Stockdale to William Lenthall, Portland MSS, Volume I, p. 717.

'Letter from William Tunstall to Sir Edward Radcliffe', *Archaeologia Aeliana*, 1899.

Letter Sent from the Right Honourable, the Lord Fairfax, to the Committee of Both Kingdoms: Concerning the Great Victory Lately Obtained (by God's Blessing) at Selby in Yorkshire, reproduced in Wenham, P., *The Siege of York 1644*, York, 1994.

Letter to Lord Loudon and Allied Battle Plan, York Minster Library.

Letter Written by John Somerville from Wetherby, reproduced in *Richardson's Reprints*.

Mercurius Britannicus, No. 39, June 17, 1644.

Miraculous Victory Obtained by the Right Honorable Ferdinando Lord Fairfax, against the Army under the Command of the Earl of Newcastle, at Wakefield in Yorkshire, Wakefield Library, 942.815 Wak. W.

More Exact Relation of the Late Battell Neer York; Fought by the English and Scotch Forces, Against Prince Rupert and the Marquess of Newcastle, B.M., T.T. E100 (12).

'Mr Ogden's Narrative', *Transactions of the Royal Historical Society*, New Series, Vol. XII, London. 1898, pp. 71–2.

Newes from the Siege Before Yorke. Being a Letter from an Eminent Person Out of the Leaguer There; Dated the 16 of June. 1644, York City Library, Y942.062.

Particular Relation of the Most Remarkable Occurrences from the United Forces in the North, under the Command of Those Three Approved and Faithfull Friends Both unto the Church and Common-Wealth, Generall Lesly, the Lord Fairefax and the Earle of Manchester. from Saturday the 1 Untill Munday the 10th of This Instant Iune (Number 3), B.M., T.T. E51 (3).

Prince Rupert's Diary, manuscript held in Wiltshire County Record Office, Trowbridge, f. 33.

'Proceedings of His Majesty's Army in England under the Command of His Highness Prince Rupert', *Transactions of the Royal Historical Society*, New Series, Vol. XII, 1898, pp. 69–71.

Relation of the Good Successe of the Parliaments Forces under the Command of General Leslie, the Earl of Manchester and the Lord Fairfax Against the Forces Commanded by Prince Rupert and the Earl of Newcastle on Hesham-Moore, on Tuesday July 2 1644, B.M., T.T E54 (11).

Scots Army Advanced into England Certified in a Letter, Dated from Addarston, the 24 of January: from His Excellencies the Lord Generall Leslie's Quarters. with the Summoning of the County of Northumberland: Expressed in a Letter by the Commissioners and Committees of Both Kingdoms, to Sir Thomas Glemham Governor of Newcastle, and to the Colonells, Officers and Gentlemen of the

Forenamed County: with Sir Tho: Glemhams Answer Thereunto, reproduced in *Richardson's Reprints*.

'Short Memoriall of the Northern Actions During Ye War There, from Ye Yeare 1642 Till 1644', *Yorkshire Archaeological Journal*, Vol. 8, 1884.

Sir Thomas Glemham's Letter in Answer to the Marquesse of Argyl's and Sir William Armyne's, reproduced in *Richardson's Reprints*.

'Sir Philip Monckton's Narrative', *Transactions of the Royal Historical Society*, New Series, Vol. XII, London, 1898, pp. 52–3.

True Relation of the Great Victory It Hath Pleased God to Give the Lord Fairfax and Sir Thomas Fairfax His Son, &C., over the Remnant of Newcastle's Forces in Yorkshire, Upon Thursday, the 11th of April, 1644, reproduced in Morrell, W.W., *The History and Antiquities of Selby*, London, 1867.

True Relation of the Late Fight Between the Parliament Forces and Prince Rupert, Within Four Miles of Yorke with the Names of Divers Commanders That Were Slain and Wounded, York City Library, Y942.062.

True Relation of the Late Proceedings of the Scottish Army, Sent from His Excellency the Lord Generall Leslie's Quarters Before Newcastle the 8th of February 1643, reproduced in *Richardson's Reprints*.

'True Relation of the Proceedings of the Scottish Army from the 12 of March Instant to the 25', *Archaeologia Aeliana*, 1899.

True Relation of the Taking of Cocket Island, reproduced in *Richardson's Reprints*.

Contemporary Sources

Bell, R., *Memorials of the Civil War, Comprising the Correspondence of the Fairfax Family with the Most Distinguished Personages Engaged in That Memorable Contest*, 1849, Vol. I.

Carte, T. (ed.), *A Collection of Original Letters and Papers Found Among the Duke of Ormonde's Papers*, 1739, Vol. I, pp. 55–8.

Cholmley, Sir Hugh, *Memorials Touching the Battle of York*, English Historical Review, V, 1890, p. 347.

De Gomme, Sir Bernard, *Order of His Majties Armee*, York Minster Library.

Douglas, Robert, *Diary of Robert Douglas*, reproduced in Terry, C.S., *Life and Campaigns of Alexander Leslie*, 1899, pp. 281–2.

Firth, C.H. (ed.), *Memoirs of the Duke of Newcastle*, 1886.

Firth, C.H. (ed.), *The Memoirs of Edmund Ludlow, Lieutenant-General of the Horse in the Army of the Commowealth of England, 1625–1672*, Oxford, 1894, pp. 98–100.

Fuller, Thomas, *The History of the Worthies of England*, 1662.

Hodgson, Captain John, *Autobiography of Captain John Hodgson*, Brighouse, 1887.

Lilly, William, *History of His Life and Times*, London, 1822.

Moone, J.A., *A Brief Relation of the Life and Memoirs of John Lord Belasyse*, HMC Ormonde MSS, New Series, 1903, Vol. II.

Parsons, D. (ed.), *The Diary of Sir Henry Slingsby*, 1836.

Richardson's Reprints of Rare Tracts, Vol. II.

Rushworth, J., *Historical Collections*, Vol. V, London, 1692.

Seacome, J., *Memoirs of the House of Stanley*, 1741.

Somerville, Lord James, *Memorie of the Somervilles*, Edinburgh, 1815, Vol. II, pp. 345–52.

Tibbutt, H.G. (ed.), *The Letter Books 1644–45 of Sir Samuel Luke*, 1963.

Turner, Sir James, *Memoirs of His Own Life and Times*, Edinburgh, 1829.
Vicars, J., *Parliamentarian Chronicles*, 1644, Vol. II.
Warburton, Eliot, *Memoirs and Correspondence of Prince Rupert and the Cavaliers*, 1849.

Modern Accounts

Barratt, J., *The Siege of Liverpool and the Lancashire Campaign 1644*, Stuart Press, 1993.
Carlyle, T. (ed.), *Oliver Cromwell's Letters and Speeches*, 1902, Vol. I, p.188.
Cooke, D., *Adwalton Moor, the Forgotten Battle*, Battlefield Press, 1996.
Cooke, D., *Northern Thunder, the Battle of Marston Moor, 2nd July 1644*, Battlefield Press, 1997.
Cooke, David, *The Civil War in Yorkshire – Fairfax Versus Newcastle*, Pen and Sword, 2004.
Evans, D., *The Battle of Marston Moor 1644*, Stuart Press, 1994.
Firth, C.H., *Cromwell's Army*, Greenhill Books, 1992.
Firth, C.H., 'Marston Moor', *Transactions of the Royal Historical Society*, New Series, Vol. XII, 1898.
Johnson, David, *Adwalton Moor 1643 – the Battle That Changed a War*, Blackthorn Press, 2003.
Leadman, A.D.H., *Battles Fought in Yorkshire*, 1891.
Morrell, W.W., *The History and Antiquities of Selby*, London, 1867.
Newman, P.R., *Marston Moor, 2 July 1644: The Sources and the Site*, Borthwick Papers No. 53, 1978.
Newman, P.R., 'The Defeat of John Belasyse: Civil War in Yorkshire, January–April 1644', *The Yorkshire Archaeological Journal*, Vol. 52, 1980.
Newman, P.R., *The Battle of Marston Moor 1644*, Antony Bird, Chichester, 1981.
Newman, P.R. and Roberts, P.R., *Marston Moor 1644: the Battle of the Five Armies*, Blackthorn Press, 2003.
Pendlebury, G., *Aspects of the English Civil War in Bolton and Its Neighbourhood 1640–1660*, Manchester, 1983.
Roberts, K. and McBride, A., *Soldiers of the English Civil War: 1 Infantry*, Osprey Elite Series No. 25, 1989.
Terry, C.S., *Life and Campaigns of Alexander Leslie*, 1899.
Tincey, J. and McBride, A., *Soldiers of the English Civil War: 2 Cavalry*, Osprey Elite Series No. 27, 1990.
Wenham, P., *The Great and Close Siege of York, 1644*, York 1994 (reissue).
Young, P., *Marston Moor*, 1970.

Index